The "Tar Baby" Option
American Policy Toward Southern Rhodesia

The "Tar Baby" Option

American Policy Toward Southern Rhodesia

ANTHONY LAKE

Œ A Study from the Carnegie Endowment
for International Peace

New York **Columbia University Press** *1976*

Library of Congress Cataloging in Publication Data

Lake, Anthony.
  The "tar baby" option.

  Bibliography: p.
  Includes index.
  1. United States—Foreign relations—Rhodesia,
Southern. 2. Rhodesia, Southern—Foreign relations—
United States. 3. United States—Foreign economic rela-
tions—Rhodesia, Southern. 4. Rhodesia, Southern—
Foreign economic relations—United States. 5. Rhodesia,
Southern—Politics and government—1966– I. Title.
E183.8.R5L34   327.73'0689'1   76-2455
ISBN 0-231-04066-0
ISBN 0-231-04067-9 pbk.

Columbia University Press
New York   Guildford, Surrey

Copyright © 1973, 1976 by the Carnegie Endowment for International Peace
Printed in the United States of America

Contents

E
183.8
.R5
.L34

AUG 30 1976

407079

402029

Foreword

Perhaps it is true that the United States has never really had an Africa policy. But it is also true that if you have seen one Africa policy, you have not seen them all. As Anthony Lake makes clear in his book, however uninspiring or humdrum our Africa policy may have been before 1969, at least it was not conspicuously wrongheaded, immoral, or illegal. How we went about squandering our limited assets and achieving all three of these latter reputations in recent years in our handling of Southern Rhodesia issues is the subject of this insightful account.

President Nixon's decision to choose the "Tar Baby" option was explicitly based on the now obvious miscalculation that when it came to control of the brittle societies of southern Africa the "whites are here to stay." That assumption underlay the White House's decision to stay on too, out in front, with the decrepit Portuguese colonial regime right through the last week of Portugal's 500-year plan for Africa. Only after the old regime in Lisbon was exiled, and Portuguese withdrawal from Mozambique and Angola was underway, did Washington go through its ineffectual last-minute motions to accuse Congress of "losing" Angola by cutting off disparate, small-scale, covert funding. Meanwhile America's new Africa policy was already further discredited by appearing to be publicly guilty by association with a white South African military adventure inside Angola.

The recent miserable Angolan side of the Tar Baby story was a sequel to a longer, sadder, but equally tawdry account of how Washington turned away from its moderate Rhodesian policy of the 1960s. The latter, which had uneasily but not disgracefully combined both the pro-African and pro-British wings of an anti-Salisbury posture, was cast aside in favor of deliberate moves toward "communication" with the white rebel regime. This was consistent with expanded contacts with white governments, relaxed arms sales policies toward Lisbon and Pretoria, benign neglect at the UN, the authorized violation of sanctions, and the temptations toward "business as usual" with the white regimes.

The Tar Baby tilt was recommended by the Nixon NSC staff, approved by Dr. Kissinger, and secretly adopted by the President in the winter of 1969–70. As described by Anthony Lake, it resulted over the next five years in a striking display of four kinds of interacting politics on Southern Rhodesian issues: (1) regular private meetings between the NSC Africa staffer and the Washington representative of the racist Rhodesian regime; (2) unremitting bureaucratic politics inside the Executive Branch, usually pitting a skeptical State Department against an assertive White House; (3) persistent congressional politics against a divided Executive Branch which allowed the pro-Byrd Amendment pressures to succeed in officially positioning the United States before the world in violation of UN sanctions and international law; and (4) a dramatic hands-across-the-sea vignette of international partisan politics as the then-leader of the British Opposition attempted to lobby against the British government inside the White House on the symbolic issue of withdrawing the American consulate in Southern Rhodesia in the spring of 1970.

All of these elements, and more, are detailed by Anthony Lake in this fascinating study of America's recent Southern Rhodesian policy. The book contains much new material. In the chapters on sanctions, Lake's account shows how the United States Executive and Congress alike succumbed to short-sighted lobbying. In the process we moved from one of the two best records on the enforcement of sanctions against

Southern Rhodesia to become one of only three members of the United Nations (along with Portugal and South Africa) which, as a matter of official policy, allowed the import of Rhodesian goods in violation of international law.

The decision to violate sanctions was, at first glance, limited to a relatively small country of little importance to the United States. But the decision has far-reaching implications. The most dire and immeasurable effect is the possibility that United States actions may have contributed to the continued suppression of the 95 percent by the 5 percent—of five million African blacks by 250,000 whites. That prospect does not bode well for U.S. relations with a future black Rhodesian government. It has right along been a major source of friction between the United States and independent African countries.

But beyond that, the United States action has important implications for the remainder of southern Africa. During 1975, even South Africa recognized that failure to resolve the Rhodesian problem peacefully at an early date reduced the chances of a peaceful solution to black/white confrontations over Namibia and South Africa. Finally, there is the adverse effect on the development and strength of the United Nations and of respect for international law. For the United States, respect for both was obviously secondary when it came to sanctions, but Washington thereby may well have contributed to the further weakening of institutions which it may find useful if not essential in the future.

How the United States decides and acts when faced with a choice between narrow short-term business and other pressures and broader considerations of the national interest has been a major issue in the debate about what is wrong with American foreign policy and, indeed, about what ails the United States in its 200th year. A number of Endowment publications from our Humanitarian Studies Program have also examined these policy questions with the objective of contributing to a better understanding of the issues involved. The issues themselves are seldom seen in better focus than in this

account from our Special Rhodesia Project about the combined White House–congressional willingness to tilt toward
this pariah state in southern Africa.

Anthony Lake directed the Special Rhodesia Project for
the Endowment during 1972–74. A Foreign Service Officer
from 1962 to 1970, he served in Vietnam, in the Department
of State, and, in 1969–70, as Special Assistant to the Assistant
to the President for National Security Affairs. Currently,
Anthony Lake is Executive Director of International Voluntary Services, a private multinational development organization.

Here, as always in Carnegie publications, the views expressed are those of the author.

THOMAS L. HUGHES, *President*
Carnegie Endowment for International Peace

THE CARNEGIE ENDOWMENT FOR INTERNATIONAL PEACE

The Carnegie Endowment for International Peace was established in 1910
in Washington, D.C. with a gift of $10 million from Andrew Carnegie, for the
purpose of promoting international peace and understanding. In 1929 the
Endowment was incorporated in New York.

As an operating (not a grant-making) foundation, the Endowment
conducts its own programs of research, investigation, discussion, publication,
education, and training in such international affairs fields as arms control,
humanitarian policy, the Middle East, pre-crisis fact-finding, and international
law and organization. The Endowment is engaged in several co-located joint
ventures with other tax-exempt organizations to reinvigorate and extend the
domestic and foreign dialogue on world affairs issues. The Endowment is
associated with the publication of the quarterly *Foreign Policy.*

The Endowment's work is conducted from its centers in New York and
Washington, and by its representative in Geneva, Switzerland.

Preface

No area of the world has been viewed by Americans with greater moral disapproval and yet less attention than southern Africa. We would do well to look at the area more closely. The coup in Lisbon in 1974 speeded along the course of southern African history, and the Portuguese empire in Africa has finally become a thing of the past. As a result, the white regime in Southern Rhodesia is under greatly increased pressure. The course of the struggle between black and white for control of Southern Rhodesia is therefore of particular concern both to the white government of South Africa and to black African states throughout the continent, as well as to the United Nations, which imposed sanctions against Southern Rhodesia in the late 1960s.

There is also much to be learned from an examination of the process that produced the American response to the Rhodesian problem. It lacks the drama of political battles and episodic public furor which one finds in accounts of the American approach to war in Vietnam or Soviet missiles in Cuba. The stakes, as well as the events, are less dramatic. Decisions on U.S. policy toward southern Africa have not borne great consequences for the people either of the United States or of that region, when compared with the dangers of false steps in a missile crisis, in Indochina or in the Middle East.

But the subject's relative lack of drama does not mean it lacks interest, for the story of how U.S. relations with southern Africa are shaped by American society demonstrates the way in which this nation approaches its relations with most nations of the world. It illustrates how most American foreign policies are made—the day to day non-crisis problems to be resolved in U.S. relations with Chad, Burma, Uruguay, or any of the many other nations not considered vital by American global strategists.

The Rhodesian problem presents Americans with a series of conflicting choices: between immediate economic interests and the claims of international law; between American opposition to racial injustice abroad and the impulse to seek smooth relations with foreign powers-that-be, especially if they are "anti-Communist"; between calculations of short-term national interest and a longer view of what is good for us as well as for others. Analysis of our government's reaction to these choices on Southern Rhodesia and to the pressure groups that represent them, illuminates the priorities that shape our foreign policies.

This account of American policy and the bureaucratic and congressional politics behind it includes, especially in the third, fourth and sixth chapters, information that was not previously on the public record. There are descriptions of strong disagreements within the Executive branch since 1965, as well as references to private messages between London and Washington and to quiet meetings and communications between American officials and representatives of Rhodesia and South Africa. I should therefore add a personal note here: As a member of the American government during some of this period, I was peripherally involved from time to time in work on southern African issues. This study, however, is based solely on extensive interviews with participants in, and observers of, these events, both in and out of the American government. I am greatly in their debt for the time they took and the frankness with which they spoke to my colleagues and me.

In noting such debts of gratitude, I also recall with real pleasure my association with the Carnegie interns who assisted in the research and some of the writing of this study: Madeline Janover, Webster Moore, David Morrissey, Stephen Park, and Diane Polan. The project was theirs as well as mine and could not have been completed without them. Indeed, chapter 5 is an updated version of an interim report, "Business As Usual," written together with Stephen Park and published by the Carnegie Endowment in 1973. Similarly, chapter 7 is a revised version of another interim report released at the same time, "Irony in Chrome," of which Diane Polan was the primary author. The extensive interview reports and analyses provided by David Morrissey were especially useful in the writing of chapter 6.

Gloria Bozeman, John Semida, Christopher Hanson, and Beryl Wright made my work far easier through their skilled efforts as research assistants. And Millie Understein and Louise Platt deserve special thanks for their patient labors on the manuscripts.

Finally, I am indebted to the various readers who went over my drafts and to the Carnegie Endowment for International Peace and its president, Thomas Hughes, for suggesting I undertake this project and then supporting it.

Washington D.C.
March 1976   ANTHONY LAKE

The "Tar Baby" Option
American Policy Toward Southern Rhodesia

THE WONDERFUL TAR BABY STORY *

"Tar-Baby" was the name given by its State Department opponents to the southern Africa policy adopted in 1969 by the Nixon administration. The name, of course, refers to the famous Uncle Remus story.

Brer Fox, who was always trying to catch Brer Rabbit, took some tar one day and mixed it with some turpentine and made himself what he called a Tar Baby. He sat it down by the side of the road and hid in some bushes to see what would happen. Along came Brer Rabbit, who stopped short and greeted the Tar Baby. When the Tar Baby made no reply to his various friendly queries, Brer Rabbit, insulted, hit it with his fist and, of course, got stuck. Angered even more, he hit the Tar Baby with his other fist and again got stuck. He managed to get both his feet stuck the same way. Furious at the lack of any reaction from the Tar Baby, Brer Rabbit butted it with his head and now was totally stuck.

Then Brer Fox sauntered forth. "Good morning, Brer Rabbit," he said. "You look sort of occupied this morning. But I expect you'll take dinner with me tonight. I ain't going to take no excuses."

* Based on the story by Joel Chandler Harris in *Uncle Remus: His Songs and Sayings* (rev. ed.; New York: Appleton, 1925), ch. 2.

1
Southern Rhodesia
Two Nations in Search of a State

Defying its many enemies and perhaps its fate, the white minority regime which rules Southern Rhodesia has been attacked repeatedly by foreign spokesmen and editorials. Condemned by what is known as "world opinion," it is the object of a comprehensive, mandatory sanctions program ordered by the United Nations Security Council—the only case in which such sanctions have been imposed in the history of the world organization.

On November 11, 1965, Ian Smith and his white supporters in Southern Rhodesia unilaterally and illegally declared Rhodesia's independence of Great Britain. Since no provision was made to guarantee rule by the colony's 95 percent black majority in any foreseeable future, the Security Council, at Britain's request, imposed selective mandatory economic sanctions on the regime in December, 1966, and comprehensive mandatory sanctions in May, 1968.

Yet, despite these measures, the Smith regime is still alive and, according to some observers, well. Rich in a number of minerals and agricultural products, Southern Rhodesia still trades in the world market. The sanctions have made most trade surreptitious and have limited its scope in ways damaging to the Rhodesian economy. But one can still buy new European and Japanese goods in the shops of the capital, Salisbury, and foreign buyers quietly compete to buy Rhodesian chrome and other minerals. In addition, Americans have openly violated the U.N. sanctions since the Congress passed the so-called Byrd Amendment in late 1971 and blew a gaping hole in the American sanctions program. Under the terms of this legislation, the President cannot prevent the import into the United States of any "strategic and critical" material from a non-Communist nation if it is imported from any Communist nation. In the two years following its passage, importers in this country purchased more than $33 million worth of Rhodesian nickel, ferrochrome, chrome, and other commodities.

So, despite the active hostility of the world community, Southern Rhodesia remains a world problem. Its solution or evolution will have far-reaching consequences.

Southern Rhodesia occupies an area of only 150,333 square miles (roughly the size of the state of Montana), but it is strategically located in the white redoubt of southern Africa. Across the Zambezi River to the north lies Zambia, a country whose leaders have been among the most determined African foes of the Smith regime, but whose economy has had important ties to Southern Rhodesia. To the south is South Africa, with its powerful white regime. To the west is Botswana, like Zambia under African rule but geographically more exposed to pressures from South Africa. On the eastern border is Mozambique, where the Portuguese have moved at last to extricate themselves from what they finally perceived as an anachronism, a colonial war in a "post-colonial age."

Thus, the neighbors of Southern Rhodesia have differing hopes for and stakes in what happens within its borders. The future of Southern Rhodesia will help determine the course of their own foreign and domestic conflicts. Racial conflict in Southern Rhodesia can only complicate a difficult period of transition in Mozambique, while presenting the white government of South Africa with a dangerous choice between abandoning the Rhodesian whites or getting bogged down in a Rhodesian conflict. And such a conflict is threatening to Zambia, which has a strong interest in the fate of the African population living just across its southern border.

The issue that lies at the heart of the Rhodesian problem is one of world significance: race. As the Rhodesian drama unfolds, it will continue to touch domestic and international relationships far beyond its borders and beyond southern Africa. It has already provided the most divisive issue of recent years within the British Commonwealth and set British Members of Parliament to shouting unusually strong personal abuse at each other. The United States has been attacked repeatedly at the United Nations for its position on the Rhodesian question, and an Afro-Asian measure on Southern Rhodesia led to the first American veto ever cast at the United Nations.

Within the United States itself, there is a less easily observed but no less important consequence of the tragedy of southern Africa: the effect on the attitude of a black American toward his own government when it equivocates on, and acquiesces in, racial repression abroad. It is true, as one hears South African and Rhodesian supporters scornfully say, that organized public pressure by black groups in the United States on southern African issues is still modest in scope and effect. But this is hardly surprising; they face more immediate problems here at home. The point is that when compromises on foreign policy strengthen black cynicism about the ways of Washington, it makes resolution of domestic problems no easier. One should also consider the possible impact on our society if a racial conflict in southern Africa were to escalate dramatically, if televised reports of black and white bloodshed were to become even fractionally as familiar to American living rooms as the bloodletting in Indochina became in the 1960s. In short, the domestic divisiveness of the issue makes Southern Rhodesia all the more dangerous a problem for the United States.

In addition to its significance for the racial future of southern Africa and multiracial societies elsewhere, the outcome of the controversy over Southern Rhodesia is important to the future of the United Nations and international law. As many students of the organization have noted, a major inhibition on the United Nations' ability to resolve international political conflicts has been the veto power wielded by the Permanent Members of the Security Council. When one of these major powers has seen its own interests or those of its smaller allies or friends threatened by a proposed international peace-keeping action, it has been able to block it. However, U.N. action on Southern Rhodesia, limited though it has been, presents one of the rare cases in which ,none of the major powers stood in the way. In choosing to impose mandatory, comprehensive economic sanctions, the United Nations was picking up the strongest weapon it has at its disposal, short of force. (Whether the weapon has been wielded as effectively as possible is another question.)

Thus, if the sanctions program against Southern Rhodesia fails, it must damage the future credibility of action by the United Nations even when the major powers are in general agreement—especially considering the vulnerability of Southern Rhodesia and the very small number of its supporters. And to the extent that its members fail to meet their obligation under international law to support the sanctions program, the future of international law itself is flawed.

This is a study of the American approach to the Rhodesian question. It is a problem that presents for the United States a classic case of forced choice between narrowly conceived economic gain and our broader national interest in the observance of international treaty obligations and the promotion of international concern for human rights. More than a history of the substance of American policies, the study provides an example of how the American foreign machinery reacts to such choices. It describes how various American officials and private interest groups have combined and collided to produce the compromises and contradictions of American policy. Public indifference has left definition of policy to distracted senior officials seeking compromises among contending political, economic and bureaucratic forces and to a Congress which allowed itself to be swayed by the pleas of special interests. As the opposing camps have traded victories or neutralized each other, the policy has lurched back and forth between humanitarian rhetoric and quiet compromise, or evaded clear definition at all.

From the time of Rhodesia's Unilateral Declaration of Independence (commonly and hereafter referred to as UDI) in 1965 until late 1969, American policy was cautious but generally correct. The aim was a low posture on the issue; Washington would follow London's lead and try to hide behind British skirts in the face of African pressures for more forceful action against the Smith regime. Sanctions were quite faithfully observed. The policy lacked courage; it did not allow concerned American officials formally to express to the British their prescient fears that London's policies of compromise and caution could not resolve the problem. But the American position in this period at least avoided undercutting in any major way the efforts actually made by the British and the United Nations. And if the policy did not completely satisfy the Africans, at least it did not include unilateral acts that seriously damaged American relations with them.

Since late 1969, American policy has stumbled out from behind Britain's skirts, and on a number of occasions has gladdened the hearts of obdurate white Rhodesians while infuriating African leaders within the colony and elsewhere in the continent. Some of these actions were the result of decisions taken within the executive branch. The heaviest blow—the Byrd Amendment—was delivered by the Congress with an assist by the White House despite the opposition of the State Department.

Succeeding chapters describe the making of these Rhodesian policies from 1965 until 1974. The remainder of this chapter sets the stage by briefly describing the intractability of the Rhodesian problem itself. Readers familiar with the history and current situation of Rhodesia may wish to proceed directly to the following chapter or to chapter 3 if they are also conversant with the international politics of the issue.

If there were an easy solution to the problem, it would have been found by now. The international penalties and only partial successes of the sanctions program, the frustrations of what must be several man-years of bitter debate at the United Nations, and the tensions of life within Southern Rhodesia all argue for an end to the status quo. But neither the Africans

nor the Europeans in Southern Rhodesia have yet agreed to a
vision of the future which could resolve the others' fears. Britain and the international community cannot turn away from
the problem and abandon sanctions until agreement on such a
future is achieved—or until the issue is settled through the
agony of extended violence within the territory.

Peaceful resolution of their differences would take a tremendous act of will and faith by both races in Southern Rhodesia, for the psychological and historical gulf between them,
as well as the legal and economic distinctions that now separate them, inhibits any coming together. The divisions begin
with the name of the territory itself. The British and most
other governments, as well as the Security Council, call it
"Southern Rhodesia"—the name of the colony before its declaration of independence. Use of this name reflects acceptance
of the position that despite UDI, the territory is nonself-
governing and under the authority of Great Britain. According to the United Nations Charter, a colonial power has the
obligation "to develop self-government, to take due account of
the political aspirations of the peoples, and to assist them in
the progressive development of their free political institutions." Britain could hardly grant independence to the current
regime in the territory, under its current constitution, without
violating that obligation.

Smith and his supporters have used the name "Rhodesia"
since the early 1960s; the "Southern" has dropped away
together with their allegiance to the British government. Rhodesia is named, of course, after Cecil Rhodes, the extraordinary colonial entrepreneur responsible for bringing the territory under the British flag in the late nineteenth century.[1]

African nationalists generally refer to the territory as
"Zimbabwe," the name they intend to give it once majority
rule is established. Ruins of massive stone structures at Zimbabwe, a site in the southern part of the territory, indicate that

[1] The term "Southern Rhodesia" will generally be used in this study in
conformity with the United Nations' usage. "Rhodesia" will also occasionally
be used, for the sake of convenience.

it was the capital of a great African kingdom. Archaeological excavations suggest that the kingdom had traded with China, Persia, and India at least as early as the twelfth century, and probably earlier. Some have placed the flourishing of the kingdom in the period A.D. 800 to 1200 and its collapse sometime within the few centuries before 1800.

These distinctions in name symbolize the problem: Southern Rhodesia is in fact two "nations" or communities within one territory, a territory that is not, according to the United Nations, a state. To add to the complexity, the issue can be seen as a colonial problem at two levels. In addition to the international question of whether UDI was legal and Southern Rhodesia therefore no longer a colony, there is the essential fact that if it were recognized as independent before majority rule were achieved, the territory would still be caught up internally in persistent colonial relationships. This point becomes clear when one considers the circumstances and histories of both Rhodesian "nations."

RHODESIA'S WHITE "NATION"

The white "nation" within Southern Rhodesia includes about 265,000 Rhodesian Europeans (whites); they comprise less than 5 percent of a total population of more than 5.7 million people.[2] They live rather well, so well that Clive Kinsley, the managing director of the Rhodesian Printing and Publishing Company, called them, in January, 1973, "the luckiest people in the world." A few statistics support his point, at least in terms of material comfort. According to a survey presented by Mr. Kinsley, neither the United States nor South Africa has as high a percentage of car owners as white Rhodesia. Household servants are paid modest wages. By 1972, the number of hi-fi sets had risen to 65,000, from 24,000 in 1970. This amounts to better than one set of speakers for every four white Rhodesians, or about one hi-fi per family. Thirty-nine

[2] In June, 1972, a total population of 5,680,000 included 262,000 Europeans, 17,700 Coloureds and 9,600 Asians.

thousand swimming pools make white Rhodesia a Californian
dream; it is said to have the highest ratio of swimming pools to
population (white, of course) anywhere outside of Beverly
Hills.

Nor is there any real lack of consumer goods, although
occasional shortages of whiskey and some other luxury items
have been reported. While the sanctions program is taking its
toll on Rhodesian foreign exchange and limits access to the
heavy capital equipment the Rhodesians must purchase
abroad, the shops are not empty. According to a report from
Geoffrey Taylor in *The Guardian* on January 31, 1973, "there
is a far more ample range of consumer goods than is obtain-
able in, say, Prague or Budapest . . . and at much lower
prices." He also remarked upon the Toyotas, Datsuns,
Peugeots, and Mercedes to be seen.[3]

The Economy

But while the white Rhodesian consumer may not yet be
suffering under sanctions, his economy as a whole presents a
very mixed picture. (It is, in fact, *his* economy—managed by
white Rhodesians for the primary benefit of white Rhodesians.) Since some of its sectors are doing better than others,
there are sufficient statistical indicators (despite the regime's
restrictions on the publication of economic "intelligence") to
support the arguments of both sides of the debate about the
effectiveness of the sanctions. Yet even a brief, nonstatistical
review of some key sectors, the stronger with the weaker,
raises serious questions about the future.

Although Rhodesia continues to trade actively, sanctions
have increased the cost of the trade. As Smith himself has
said, "We buy at a premium and we sell at a discount." For example, South African middlemen who facilitate exports by

[3] A startling piece of evidence both of an illegal import into Southern
Rhodesia and of the high life there was reported in April 22–28, 1972, issue
of *Africa Diary*. In a Rhodesian court on March 24, 1972, Ian Smith's twenty-
two-year-old son, Alexander, was fined and given a suspended six-months'
jail sentence for possession of seven ounces of Malawi-grown marijuana.

providing false certificates of origin and bills of lading reportedly take a 10 to 15 percent cut.

The various sectors of the economy that depend on exports have been hit by the embargo with different degrees of
force. The mining sector has done relatively well, since mineral exports have found easy routes to international markets
through South Africa and Mozambique. Mining output has
increased since sanctions began; it is up more than 100 percent over the past decade. Tobacco, the main export commodity prior to sanctions, has been hard hit, however. Sugar
growers have also been hurt by the embargo.

Since exports have failed to generate sufficient foreign
exchange, the import picture is also mixed. Although the embargo on Southern Rhodesia's oil imports was a key part of
the sanctions strategy after UDI, it has failed to achieve its objective. The oil is more expensive than it would be in the absence of sanctions, but enough has been getting through to
meet Rhodesia's needs. Petrol rationing was abolished on May
13, 1971, and Rhodesians were even finding the energy crisis
of late 1973 to be less troublesome than it was to Americans.
Limited foreign exchange and the embargo have severely hin-
dered imports of expensive capital equipment, however. For
example, although three Boeing 720 jets were obtained in
mid-1973, Air Rhodesia is generally short of equipment. The
railways are operating poorly because of tired equipment.
These shortages are particularly serious because they interfere
with the movement of minerals for export. In 1970, import
allocations for other sectors reportedly had to be squeezed to
keep the railways going. Tractors have also been in short supply.

Thus, the sanctions have damaged those parts of the
economy most dependent on trade, with the most notable exception of the mining sector. Other sectors have been less
seriously affected. There were, for example, increases in agricultural production, particularly in cattle, cotton and wheat, in
1972. And the manufacturing sector may actually have prof-
ited from sanctions as the regime concentrated on import sub-

stitution. But the manufacturers' problem for the future is twofold: to fund imports of capital equipment and to expand production of exports as well as import substitutes. The commercial sector has not received as favorable attention as manufacturing in official planning, although a large proportion of the territory's excess liquidity has reportedly been devoted to it.

Despite the difficulties, in gross terms the Rhodesian economy showed some remarkable growth in the years after UDI. But the problems for the future remain awesome. Brian Blake, president of the Association of Rhodesian Industries, was reported in the *Rhodesia Herald* on April 7, 1973, to have gloomily stated: "It would seem that we have reached a situation where we need to increase our output on the home and export markets with less foreign currency while our imports are costing more and our plant and machinery is aging rapidly." Or, as the U.S. Department of State's *Background Notes on Southern Rhodesia* put it in August, 1970, "Rhodesia's economic future depends heavily on the expansion of export markets and the attraction of foreign investment capital. These are areas in which sanctions have had their most serious adverse impact." *The Economist* has suggested, in an article in April, 1972, that the key to the future is Rhodesia's ability to raise foreign loans at reasonable rates. If it cannot, "its rate of growth is doomed to decline or, at best, to stagnate" for want of foreign currency. Further problems for the future include a likely downward trend in tourism revenues and the loss of trade with Zambia since their common border was closed in early 1973. The loss to Rhodesia of foreign currency when this trade halted has been compounded by the loss of the revenue formerly paid by Zambia for use of the Rhodesia Railways. A further complication is the possible loss of access to Mozambican ports as Mozambique achieves complete independence, although this threat was partly balanced by the completion, in September, 1974, of Rhodesia's first direct rail link to South Africa.

In the long run, the most ominous economic problem facing the regime is growing unemployment. New employment opportunities are not keeping pace with a rapidly expanding African population. Although the number of Africans employed had increased between 1962 and 1972, the percentage of Africans employed dropped from 17 percent to about 14 percent in the same period. The social and political implications of this problem are clear. Whatever the statistics produced by the regime to show that "their" Africans have a higher per capita income or more years of schooling, on the average, than the populations of poorer African states, the fact will remain that growing unemployment must fuel African demands for greater economic benefits as well as social and political justice, and increase their determination to fight for both. For the economic, political and social strands of the relationship between the two Rhodesian races cannot be separated. White Rhodesia maintains its economic privileges through its political dominance, and it appears to believe that its hold on political power depends increasingly on social controls. A brief review of some of the restrictive legislation passed in recent years shows a disturbing trend.

Apartheid in Rhodesia

The basic pieces of discriminatory legislation are the Land Apportionment and Tenure Acts of 1930 and 1969. A stated purpose of the 1930 Act was to set aside areas for the Africans which could not be grabbed by white Rhodesians. It and the 1969 Act have "equally" divided the land between the races. This leaves, of course, the white 5 percent of the population with half of the land and the black 95 percent with the other half. Not surprisingly, the white lands contain the best agricultural areas.

The regime has declared a state of emergency and is able to arrest people arbitrarily, to hold them indefinitely and secretly, to outlaw African political organizations, and to censor newspapers as well as books and periodicals. (Among the

American authors whose books have been banned are Mary McCarthy, Gore Vidal, Norman Mailer, Erskine Caldwell, and Richard Brautigan.) Not only Africans, but also white moderates and white reporters have been victimized in recent years. The Official Secrets Act makes it an offense to "obtain, collect, publish or communicate to any other person information which is calculated to be, or which might be useful, directly or indirectly, to an enemy." This covers a rather broad sweep of information, since any unflattering report and any published fact on the Rhodesian military or economy, and especially its exports and imports, could be useful to Rhodesia's "enemies"—the United Nations and most of its members.

Late 1972 saw a wave of restrictive acts. Despite Smith's statement in September, 1972, that they "must not deliberately create conditions to make local Africans [their] enemies," pressure from the far right wing of Smith's ruling Rhodesian Front Party produced several new racial measures between September and mid-November. They included new pass laws, the segregation of swimming pools, closure of Salisbury's principal maternity home to patients of Asian or mixed blood, and restrictions on the hours during which blacks could visit bars in white areas—or whites could get a drink in black areas.

A rise in guerrilla activity in December led to another wave of punitive measures in early 1973. On January 19, the regime announced new state of emergency regulations. These allowed Provincial Commissioners to impose collective fines on African communities without court hearings if they were "satisfied" that any individual in such a community had been aiding the guerrillas or if the presence of guerrillas there had not been reported. The Rhodesians have apparently not learned that punishing groups for the actions of individuals is a form of brutality which probably does more to encourage a guerrilla movement than to suppress it.

In May, 1973, two new measures were reported. The Law and Order (Maintenance) Amendment Bill raised from five to twenty years the penalty for helping or harboring guerrillas. It is now also a crime with a prison sentence to reveal in print what anyone accused (under that law) of subversion was alleged to have said or done—unless the accused had been found innocent! And a new policy was adopted: the creation of "no-go" areas along the borders with Zambia and Mozambique. Local authorities were empowered to remove the African inhabitants of these areas and destroy anything left behind that might be of value to the guerrillas.

Despite these measures, racial restrictions in Rhodesia are not so harsh or pervasive as in South Africa. But the difference between the two societies is narrowing. There has been talk, for example, of a general approach to Rhodesia's future that recalls South Africa's policy of "separate development." "Provincialization," or decentralization, as described by the Rhodesian Minister of Internal Affairs in an interview published on July 13, 1972, would give limited executive power, in fields such as education but not defense or finance, to two provincial African parliaments. One provincial parliament would be created for Mashonaland South and another for Matabeleland North—Rhodesia's two largest provinces. Such a system could presage an eventual partition of the territory into African and white states. The problems in such a partition would be the same as those confronting "separate development" in South Africa: African objections to giving up any of what they consider to be their land, the inequitable distribution of the land if it were partitioned, and the fate of the Africans still living and working in the white areas.

These restrictive measures and policies reveal the same sort of colonial mentality that produced signs barring "Chinese and dogs" from British clubs in Shanghai or massacres of Indians by American settlers who, on arriving on these shores, "fell first on their knees and then on the aborigines." To be one of the privileged in a society divided along racial lines involves a psychological choice between active revulsion against racism and an unconscious decision to dehumanize the other race. Some choose the former. Most, in any such society, compromise by ignoring, deploring and dehumanizing at the same time. Others will not acknowledge the injustice around them and totally deny the worth of its victims. Injustice in Southern Rhodesia is apparently justified, in the minds of many of the white minority, by their belief that the African population is less "civilized" than they, by European standards. This is taken, ironically, as reason for uncivilized white behavior.

White History

The point extends to the history of white Rhodesia. To justify the present, it must dehumanize the Africans. The territory was "discovered," as if human beings were not previously there. A blank space on the map was filled; a European name was given to it. The colonizers who helped create a "nation" are seen as history's agents, since nations come to appear to be natural entities no matter how accidental or unnatural their boundaries. The military men who protected the colonizers from its original inhabitants are revered; the aboriginal warriors are the foils for their heroism. The subsequent political history of the territory is a story of constitutional crises, parliamentary deliberations, elections and international maneuvers. Racial problems are considered in the context of these "larger" issues.

White Americans who regret their lack of curiosity in school about Indian and black American history now recognize the injustice of Sitting Bull's role in American high-school history courses—to make General Custer a hero—just as Zulu warriors serve to prove the valor of the thin red line in British texts.

This is not to suggest that white Rhodesians do not know the history of their black neighbors, or that all of them wish to deny it. But the pressures are there to do so. The view of "Zimbabwe" is a case in point. Scholarly work describing this African kingdom has been savagely attacked in Salisbury. "Uncivilized" black Africans cannot have produced such a kingdom; if they had, they could rule themselves now. White Rhodesians prefer a white South African missionary's book, on sale in Salisbury bookstores, which shows that *Arabs* built Zimbabwe.

The white history of Rhodesia naturally begins with Cecil Rhodes, the hero of subsequent generations of white Rhodesian schoolboys. Anthony Harrigan, a conservative American columnist, has well captured their view of the empire builder: "Rhodes was only 47 when he died. But in his short lifespan he pushed Western civilization deep into Africa. He was responsible for the establishment of Rhodesia, sending a pioneer column across the veld and laying a railroad line that linked the landlocked country with the seacoast. He built the foundations of an advanced society in a land that had been wilderness since the end of Zimbabwean civilization created by pre-Islamic Arabs in the 7th Century A.D." [4]

Rhodes was an extraordinary figure. At the age of seventeen, leaving England for Africa, he made a fortune in South African gold and diamonds, was responsible for the chartered company which created and ruled Rhodesia, and became Prime Minister of the Cape Colony. None of these accomplishments was an end in itself; each was a part of Rhodes's work toward his larger dream, British control of a route from the Cape to Cairo that would help the Anglo-Saxon race dominate all of Africa. [5]

In 1888, Rhodes's agents negotiated concessions and trad-

---

[4] *Rhodesian Minerals and Industry: A Report,* United States Industrial Council, International Business Report Series. A less charitable American view of Rhodes was once expressed by Mark Twain: "Whether Cecil Rhodes is the lofty patriot multitudes believe him to be, or Satan come again, when he stands at the Cape his shadow falls to the Zambezi. He robs and slays, and enslaves the Matabele, and gets Charter-Christian applause for it."

[5] Nor did his dream, in its most grandiose form, stop there. At the age of twenty-five, Rhodes wrote a will that left his fortune to the British Colonial Secretary, who was to establish a secret society to work for "the extension of British rule throughout the world." This would include occupation by British settlers of all Africa and South America, much of the Near East and the Pacific, "and the ultimate recovery of the United States." Rhodes later changed the terms of this will but would still refer approvingly to its vision.

ing rights from local African leaders, and Rhodes himself deftly obtained from London a charter for the British South African Company to rule over a large area of Central Africa including what is now Southern Rhodesia and Zambia (formerly Northern Rhodesia). Attracted by promises of high pay, gold claims and 3,000 acres of land each, a party of 184 white pioneers (and 300 nonwhite auxiliaries) set out for the territory from South Africa in June, 1890. It raised the British flag over Fort Salisbury in September. The march of the Pioneer Column is a legend for white Rhodesians that surpasses in force the legends of our West for modern young Americans. In announcing independence on November 11, 1965, Ian Smith struck a strong emotional note when he invoked this past. "The mantle of the pioneers," he said, "has fallen on our shoulders."

In 1891, the territories under the chartered company were placed under British protection, and the High Commissioner in Capetown was given power to administer justice and raise revenues. This was the origin of a problem that has hounded the British government to this day. For, in practice, these as well as other governmental powers were wielded by Rhodes and the chartered company, not by British representatives. Since the start, London has had formal but not real authority over the territory.

Two years later, white Rhodesia found its most important symbol: The Shangani Patrol. After a successful campaign against the Matabele people, the white settlers set to tracking down their leader, Lobengula—and the gold he was reported to have with him. On December 3, 1893, a patrol under the command of a Major Wilson who, like many heroes, had more courage than tactical skill, crossed the Shangani River and camped, against orders, for the night. The river flooded, and in the darkness the major and his men, cut off from help, fought bravely but were wiped out by Matabele warriors. A Rhodesian novel, *The White Men Sang,* expressed the emotion that surrounded the event. The white trader who buried them describes to Rhodes the soldiers' heroism: ". . . he went in to tell Cecil Rhodes, the Founder, how on the banks of the Shangani his country had suffered the agony of birth."

Another war with the Africans, in 1896, proved more bloody still, and Imperial troops had to be called in to win it. With the Africans thus subdued, the white settlers turned all their energies to building their nation. A legislature was formed in 1898. Railroads to outside markets were built. The charter was renewed in 1914, but the white settlers were chafing under the company's rule, and their power within the legislature was growing steadily at the expense of the company's representatives. The company clearly could not continue to manage the territory, and in 1922 a referendum was held. About 15,000 of the 34,000 European settlers in Southern Rhodesia were eligible to vote; they chose internal autonomy over incorporation in South Africa by 8,774 to 5,789 votes. (Nearly one million Africans living in the area were affected but not consulted.) On September 12, 1923, Southern Rhodesia became a "self-governing colony" of the United Kingdom.

Once again, the British retained more formal authority than they were willing to exercise. Under the terms of the 1923 constitution, the Rhodesians could manage their own affairs through their own legislature, but London reserved the power to reject laws "whereby Natives may be subjected or made liable to any disabilities or restrictions to which persons of European descent are not also subjected or made liable." These reserve powers were never exercised. The Land Apportionment Acts of 1930 and 1941 were not vetoed; nor was a series of repressive acts passed in 1959.

The British also did well by the white settlers in Southern Rhodesia in helping to arrange the birth, in 1953, of the Federation of the Rhodesias and Nyasaland. Amalgamation of Northern and Southern Rhodesia had been discussed for almost forty years, but the settlers of Northern Rhodesia had not wished to be dominated by the larger group of Europeans to the south, and in 1924 had chosen to have Northern Rhodesia become a British protectorate. They and the settlers of

Nyasaland (now Malawi) still balked at the creation of a single state in the early 1950s, but agreed that forming a federation made economic and political sense. The central government of the Federation had responsibility for defense, communications, and most economic matters. Each of the territories retained responsibility for local affairs, including African affairs—the key to the failure of the federalist effort. As Northern Rhodesia and Nyasaland moved toward majority rule, and Southern Rhodesia did not, it became evident that the three parts of the Federation could not have a single future. The fracture came in 1963, when London agreed that Nyasaland and Northern Rhodesia could secede from the Federation and gain independence under African governments. Southern Rhodesia would revert to its earlier status as a self-governing colony. (In an extraordinarily shortsighted concession, the British also agreed that the Royal Rhodesian Air Force, a parachute squadron, and a regular army of about 3,400 men would come under the control of the Southern Rhodesian government.) Malawi and Zambia became independent states in 1964.

Southern Rhodesia was not allowed independence because majority rule was not even on the horizon. In theory, under the 1923 constitution, individuals of all races were to be eligible to vote. In fact, qualifications based on property and education ruled out all but a small minority of Africans.

In 1957, the Legislature devised a neater scheme for including more African voters while ensuring that they remained a small minority. Two classes of voters were established, based on income and education. The less restrictive class permitted more Africans to join the rolls—but this class as a whole was limited to 20 percent of the size of the other, almost pure white class of voters.

A royal commission in 1960 recommended that the Federation be held together for economic reasons, providing that there were drastic changes in Southern Rhodesian racial policies. The next year, British and Rhodesian negotiators agreed on a new constitution for the territory. It was approved by a two-to-one margin in a referendum in July, 1961. (Few of the eligible Africans took part in the vote, in protest against the terms of the document. It was also opposed by the right wing of white opinion, since it did allow the theoretical possibility of eventual African rule.) Two voters' rolls were established. No mention of race was made, but the qualifications for the A-roll excluded all but a very small number of African voters. Indeed, only a small minority of Africans could qualify even for the less restrictive B-roll. And fifty of the sixty-five members of the Legislative Assembly would be elected by the A-roll, ensuring healthy European majorities. African influence would be increased marginally by allowing cross-over voting; voters on each roll could vote for candidates on the other, but with their votes discounted in value.

The new constitution dropped London's "reserve powers" with respect to safeguarding the rights of the Africans; a Declaration of Rights of limited force was substituted. But the British had not washed their hands of the problem. In March, 1963, the Rhodesians formally requested independence. The following two and one-half years witnessed repeated efforts by the Rhodesians to negotiate their independence, and British refusal to agree to their terms.

The British conditions for independence emerged in the form of the so-called "five principles":

1. The principles and intention of unimpeded progress to majority rule, at least as outlined in the 1961 Constitution, would have to be maintained and guaranteed.

2. There would also have to be guarantees against retrogressive amendment of the Constitution.

3. There would have to be immediate improvement in the political status of the African population.

4. There would have to be progress toward ending racial discrimination.

5. The British Government would need to be satisfied that any basis for independence was acceptable to the people of Southern Rhodesia as a whole.

In 1966, a sixth principle was added: It would be necessary to ensure that, regardless of race, there was no oppression of majority by minority, or of minority by majority.

These principles have remained a central part of the British position in the various negotiations with the Rhodesians since UDI. Their importance and interpretation has shifted at various stages, and they are in the background now, but they have never been explicitly repudiated. And the Rhodesian regime has never met these terms.

Political power within the white settler community of Southern Rhodesia was shifting steadily rightward in the years before UDI, as white opinion shifted ever further from the notion of "unimpeded progress to majority rule." In December, 1962, a relatively moderate Prime Minister, Sir Edgar Whitehead, and his United Federal Party were defeated by Winston Field and the recently formed Rhodesian Front Party. Although Whitehead, like Todd before him, had moved to the right during his term in office, he was still defeated by politicians and voters who feared any sort of real concession to the Africans. Field himself fell to a challenge from *his* right in 1964, resigning after a split with his own party over policy. His hard line successor, Ian Smith, represented the weight of opinion in the conservative Rhodesian Front. His hand strengthened by success in elections held in May, Smith was willing to do what Field was apparently so anxious to avoid: to announce in November, 1965, Rhodesia's unilateral break with Britain.

London reacted during the following six years with a series of unilateral economic measures, support for U.N. sanctions, and two unsuccessful efforts to settle the issue through diplomatic agreement with Smith. Tentative agreement was finally reached by the British Foreign Minister, Sir Alec Douglas-Home, and Ian Smith in November, 1971, but it foundered on the fifth of the British principles. A British commission headed by a distinguished jurist, Lord Pearce, arrived in Southern Rhodesia in January, 1972, to test African opinion. After numerous meetings with Africans throughout the territory—and witnessing or reading about a series of demonstrations by more militant black Rhodesians—it concluded that the majority there had the same view as the Organization of African Unity, the United Nations General Assembly, and many others, notably in the British press and Parliament: the terms of the settlement represented a sell-out of the Africans in Southern Rhodesia. They did not guarantee majority rule even in this century. The British government had no choice. It concluded that the deal with Smith could not be consummated; the status quo of sanctions and stalemate would not be altered.

In recent years, white opinion and white politics in Southern Rhodesia have, if anything, hardened in response to external pressures like the sanctions and events in Mozambique. In a referendum in 1969 the white electorate gave more than a two-to-one margin of support to a new constitution designed by the regime. Under its provisions, a multiracial House of Assembly is elected by two racially separated voter rolls. Fifty are elected by the white roll, sixteen by the African. In theory, increases in the number of African seats can take place as the proportion of the income tax paid by Africans rises. But in practical terms, it will be many years before this increase becomes meaningful, given the very small percentage of the income tax that is paid by Africans. And the Constitution denies majority rule for all time; the number of African seats can only equal, never surpass, the fifty reserved for whites. A referendum was held at the same time on Smith's plan to make Rhodesia a republic, thus severing the territory's last formal ties to the crown. This plan met with even more enthusiastic approval than the retrogressive Constitution, and in March, 1970, the Republic of Rhodesia was proclaimed. In the same year, parliamentary elections strengthened the hands of the hard-liners.

Right-wing reaction to the Pearce Commission exercise in 1972 (including the formation of the "United Front Against Surrender") must also have reminded Smith that his predecessors never satisfied the most militant whites. Continuing pressures from this quarter will probably make it very difficult for him to respond to the wishes of those white Rhodesian moderates, many of them industrialists, who hope for some sort of compromise arrangement that can put an end to sanctions. Nor does the white electorate seem in a mood to reward moderate political leaders. In elections at the end of July, 1974, white Rhodesians turned out in record numbers to give overwhelming support to the Rhodesian Front, smashing the hopes of white moderate candidates.

Thus, the white nation of Rhodesia remains, like the pioneers eighty years before, self-reliant and defiant in a largely hostile world. White Rhodesians have drawn strength from the symbols of their past and their ability to survive the sanctions of recent years. It is the future that must give them pause.

Dark Clouds on the White Horizon

Their concern should include more than the internal problems mentioned previously. The arrival of independence in Mozambique has severely threatened white Rhodesia in a number of ways.

The potential increase in guerrilla activity along the 700-mile border is a direct security problem. The placement of Rhodesia's lifeline through Mozambique to the sea in the hands of an African nationalist government is equally ominous.

These facts apparently led the South African government to conclude, in the autumn of 1974, that the position of the Rhodesian whites was practically hopeless, that a protracted losing struggle there would damage the interests of South Africa, and that pressure should therefore be placed on Smith to make the concessions necessary to achieve peace. These would, inevitably, include at least an agreement by the whites to majority rule within a few years.

After secret indirect contact with the Zambian government, reported by Charles Mohr of the *New York Times* (December 22, 1974), the South African government began to apply pressure on Smith while the governments of Zambia, Tanzania and Botswana tried to convince African nationalist leaders from Southern Rhodesia to be flexible.

In early December, 1974, there were signs of progress. A cease-fire was announced, as was the release of a number of black political prisoners from the Rhodesian jails. But by the end of December, the situation had soured. The cease-fire did not take hold; accusations of bad faith were made on both sides; and the public statements of both black and white Rhodesian leaders demonstrated a wide and growing gap in the terms of settlement, focusing particularly on the length of time before the blacks would assume control of the government. By March, 1975, Smith was reportedly back to affirming his opposition to majority rule in his lifetime, while black leaders were insisting more firmly than ever on its immediate achievement.

The prospect, then, was for increasing pressure on the Rhodesians from the South African government. No one could say how far the South Africans would go. The withdrawal of South African "police forces" serving in Rhodesia on the Zambian border, a symbol of growing South African concern, took place in 1975.

Nor were external pressures the only challenge to the white Rhodesians' position. In the long run, the darkest cloud on their horizon is more nebulous than the diplomatic pressures from Pretoria, but no less awesome: the future psychological effect on many white Rhodesians of a damaged, if still viable, economy and a deteriorating, if not yet critical, security situation.

The economy apparently cannot continue to expand at its past rate, with the limitations on purchases of new capital equipment, the railway problems, and the need for the manufacturing sector to turn from concentration on import substitution to the manufacture of export goods. As Ian Smith conceded at a press conference on June 14, 1972, "Regrettably, we may have to slow down, to a certain extent, some of the tremendous development and expansion which is taking place in Rhodesia." And at the same time that economic growth will probably be slowing, budget expenditures on security will probably continue to rise.

After a flurry of guerrilla activity during 1967–68, the security situation had seemed to stabilize. But in late 1972, the regime was confronted with a new upsurge of activity. The guerrillas were reportedly better armed and trained than ever before, and under a more coordinated command. Their routes of access into Rhodesia were also apparently more widespread than before and included new sections of the Mozambique border area. Perhaps of greatest concern to the regime was evidence that local Rhodesian villagers were being more cooperative with the guerrillas than in the past.

Smith's reaction to these events showed how seriously he regarded them. Police and army leaves were canceled over Christmas and territorial troops and police reserves were called up. National service was extended from nine to twelve months. In early January, 1973, he closed the Zambian border, and in the following weeks announced a series of draconian measures against any Africans aiding the guerrillas. Yet the guerrilla campaign continued and intensified, with a clear deterioration in the white security position in areas as close as thirty miles from Salisbury.

The costs thus imposed on the regime must greatly encourage African guerrilla leaders about the future. To support the Rhodesian army of some 4,000 men (plus a new battalion to be formed), an estimated 10,000 militia, 8,000 police and 35,000 police reservists, the fiscal year 1975–76 budget called for a $95 million expenditure, an increase of almost 25 percent, with an additional $21 million for barracks and road-building programs along the border. And, in addition to these fiscal costs, military service requirements have been strengthened.

In addition, the psychological as well as the physical consequences of related economic and military problems should concern the Rhodesian regime. A major threat to white Rhodesia is the current trend in population. The rate of growth for the African population in Rhodesia has averaged about 3.6 per annum, while the white growth rate has only been a little over 1 percent. The African population will probably have doubled to 10 million within eighteen years. Well aware of what this trend implies, the Rhodesians have tried hard to attract white immigrants to the country and to inhibit emigration. But, as sanctions and guerrilla activity make life more unpleasant for white Rhodesians, Rhodesia will become a less attractive place to live. It is not enough for the regime to demonstrate that white Rhodesia can survive; it must demonstrate that white Rhodesians can survive *comfortably* as well, or in the future an unfavorable balance between immigration and emigration could become disastrous.

Immigration into Rhodesia has dropped—from a net increase of 9,400 in 1971 to only 600 in 1974, and that was due largely to an influx of whites fleeing Mozambique. Even if the regime were able to attract increasing numbers of immigrants, back to the levels of the early 1970s, white emigration has been increasing (to over 9,000 in 1974) and will continue to pose a considerable threat both to the regime and to the hopes of those who believe in the possibility of a compromise solution to Rhodesia's racial conflict. For the immigrants into Rhodesia tend to be older than the emigrants, and in the long run, therefore less valuable to white Rhodesia. About one half of the white population of Rhodesia has lived in the territory for less than fifteen years; it is probable that their memories of an alternative life elsewhere would make them more likely than their Rhodesian-born neighbors to move to South Africa or elsewhere if life in Southern Rhodesia became very unpleasant. Of concern to those who believe in a peaceful solution to the problem is the fact that the white emigrants now include a disproportionate number of Rhodesian moderates and liberals who might have pushed for Rhodesia's moderating its current course.

A rational analysis of the future should lead white Rhodesians to the conclusion that compromise and a peaceful transition to majority rule in the near future is their best course. But the tragedy of Southern Rhodesia is that the white "nation" of Rhodesia seems no less trapped by its fears of, and contempt for, the Africans than the black nation of Rhodesia

is trapped by the discriminatory laws and customs of the territory. Raised in a tradition which views Africans as inherently
uncivilized, or attracted to the country by a high standard of
living based on racial discrimination, most white Rhodesians
seem unable to envisage a future in which their lives would be
affected by the decisions of a black government. The white
Rhodesian must fear that sooner or later he or his descendants may suffer for the injustices now inflicted on the black
population. But that distant fear seems overwhelmed by the
greater fear of meaningful compromise now. And there is
always the option of holding out as long as possible, and then
getting out. A survey of middle-level officials of the Rhodesian
Front by an American scholar, B. M. Schutz (reported in the
Star of Johannesburg on June 16, 1973), showed that 70 percent would leave the territory rather than live under majority—that is, black—rule. A private poll by Dr. Morris
Hirsch of Rhodesian whites of all persuasions found that none
favors majority rule; that 90 percent thought conditions for
whites would be intolerable under such rule; and that two-
thirds of those interviewed thought white control must be extended indefinitely because Africans are incapable of modern
government. Some of the statements by white Rhodesians reported in the American press in early 1972, while the Pearce
Commission was in the territory, reflected those views. White
Rhodesians seemed to have difficulty understanding why Africans would reject a settlement which provided them with some
economic benefits while offering them little or no hope of majority rule in their lifetime. "The Africans are having every-
thing handed to them on a gold plate," one white said. An Air
Rhodesia stewardess concluded that African rejection of the
agreement had to be the result of radical coercion: "It is all
those bloody agitators. Africans wouldn't turn down all those
schools we're offering them unless there was intimidation." [6]
One white, in a letter to the *Rhodesia Herald,* wrote: "Rhodesia
was a peaceful country with good race relations until the

[6] *Washington Post,* January 29, 1972, Jim Hoagland.

Pearce Commission came here and tried to elicit the political opinions of primitive people on matters beyond their comprehension. If Africans understood the settlement correctly, they would grasp it with both hands for they [the terms] are the most one-sided, Negrophilistic that could have been devised." [7]

RHODESIA'S BLACK "NATION"

The writer of that letter to the *Herald* was echoing a sentiment often expressed by Ian Smith: "Our Africans are the happiest in the continent." Yet a description of the black community of Rhodesia indicates that Africans living in the territory are not as happy as Smith and Rhodesian tourist brochures say they are. They have little reason to be so.

Some 80 percent of the African population in Southern Rhodesia are Mashona, descendants of the people of the kingdom of Zimbabwe. Toward the mid-1800s the Matabele, a roving Zulu clan which had split with the great Zulu kingdom of Tshaka and had then been driven from the Transvaal in South Africa by Boer settlers, arrived in the territory. Warlike and well organized under the skilled leadership of their chief, Mzilikazi, they defeated the peaceful and disorganized Mashona and established their authority throughout the territory. (The Matabele now comprise about 10 percent of the black population of Southern Rhodesia. The remaining 10 percent include some smaller indigenous African groups and immigrant laborers from Zambia, Malawi and Mozambique.)

The Portuguese had for some centuries been active to the east of the territory and from thence had come in contact with the Mashona people. But the first white settlement in what is now Southern Rhodesia was a mission station near Bulawayo, established in the 1850s. The greatest of the missionaries of Africa, David Livingstone had arrived in South Africa in 1841; his treks would take him throughout the continent's

[7] *New York Times*, February 14, 1973, Charles Mohr.

central region. As Patrick Keatley points out in his excellent history of the area,[8] Livingstone and his successors' legacy to the area differed greatly from that of Cecil Rhodes. Mission schools helped to educate young Africans who later were to become the nationalist leaders of Nyasaland, Northern and Southern Rhodesia, and other British colonies in the continent. These leaders played the essential role in the move to independence of the late 1950s and early 1960s.

The arrival of Rhodes's agents in the late 1880s must stir very different African memories. Under Lobengula, the son of Mzilikazi, Matabele warriors were engaged in extending their control to the east and the north, but white settlers from the south turned him and his tribe from conquerors to conquered in the short span of five years. On October 30, 1888, Lobengula signed the so-called Rudd Concession, assigning to an agent of Cecil Rhodes "complete and exclusive charge over all metals and minerals situated and contained in [his] kingdom." Lobengula soon discovered that his concession was the thin edge of a very large wedge, proving the prophetic quality of a statement he had made just before signing the paper Rudd had presented. Describing to a British missionary how a chameleon sneaks up on a fly, he said, "He darts his tongue and the fly disappears. England is the chameleon and I am the fly."

As Eshmael Mlambo, a Zimbabwean nationalist, points out in his history of the territory, Struggle for a Birthright, a charter which Rhodes quickly obtained from London gave to the British South African Company considerable administrative, legislative and judicial powers over the territory despite the fact that Lobengula had not relinquished them in the Rudd Concession. After the Pioneer Column arrived in Mashonaland in 1890, Lobengula disowned the Rudd Concession and wrote to the Queen that he had been tricked. He pro-

[8] Patrick Keatley, The Politics of Partnership: The Federation of Rhodesia and Nyasaland (Baltimore, Penguin Books, 1963), p. 121. As noted elsewhere, much of the historical material in this chapter is drawn from his detailed account.

posed to make a new agreement with another group. So
Rhodes sent an ally, E. A. Lippert, to portray himself to
Lobengula as one of Rhodes's bitter rivals. Lobengula conceded to him "the exclusive right for one hundred years . . .
to make grants of land to Europeans." Lippert then sold out,
at a fancy price, to Rhodes's chartered company. A former
missionary and friend of Lobengula, who by then was the
Crown's representative at the Royal Kraal, wrote to Rhodes: "I
look on the whole plan as detestable, in the light of policy or
morality. . . . When Lobengula finds it all out, what faith will
he have in you? I am thankful that my orders do not require
me to take part personally in this transaction; it is bad enough
to be cognizant of it."

In 1893, the Matabele were defeated by the white settlers
and Lobengula died in hiding. The settlers moved into Matabeleland as conquerors. After Lobengula's defeat Rhodes
said to his victorious white warriors, "You will be the first entitled to select land. . . . It is your right, for you have conquered the country. . . . The reason you came was that you
knew your property in Mashonaland was worthless unless the
Matabele were crushed." The crushing of the Mashona upris-
ing in 1896 completed the process, and white settlers ruled all
of the territory without challenge.

Black Rhodesian leaders today remember well that
Rhodes and the settlers took the territory by guile and gun-
fire. They are there by right of conquest, not by right of either
African or British law. Keatley quotes one white Rhodesian
farmer of the 1920s who showed his understanding of these
points: "We took the country from them by force, and when
they endeavored to regain it, we said they were rebels."
Today, white Rhodesian leaders look upon themselves as legitimate rebels against British authority. But they are unwilling
to admit the legitimacy of the African rebellion against their
own rule.

After the Matabele war, Africans soon discovered some of
the penalties of white rule. A hut tax and land apportionment
were formally instituted in 1894; a pass system was imposed in

1895. For several months each year, Africans were forced to work for white farmers and miners at pittance rates. The first British Resident Commissioner referred to this as "a system synonymous with slavery." Yet, while they were forced to work within the European economy, they were not allowed to learn skilled trades. This system of economic exploitation was strengthened by the African Labour Regulations Act of 1912, which provided jail terms for any African who, without lawful cause, left his place of employment. An uncooperative servant could be jailed. (In recent years, Africans have continued to be prosecuted under this act, which the United Nations Commission on Human Rights has called a clear manifestation of slavery.) And as Africans were thus forced to provide cheap labor for whites without the right either to form unions or to work to the fullest extent of their individual skills, they were denied a voice in decisions about the future of the territory.

As in other areas of Africa in which white settlers were taking the best, if not all the rest of the land that Africans still considered theirs, the land issue stimulated the growth of African organizations dedicated to the protection or recovery of African rights. The Rhodesian Native Association, whose primary roots were in the rural areas of the territory, was the leading black organization before World War II. As in other colonial territories around the world, the movement became increasingly political after World War II, as African nationalist leaders recognized the essential fact that without political power they could not prevent economic and social discrimination, much less work effectively for independence.

The African National Congress (ANC) was formed to demand the repeal of the worst of the discriminatory legislation and the exemption of educated Africans from the pass laws. It withered away in the early 1950s, however, and African nationalists increasingly turned to trade-union organizations as the vehicle for their protests. But the white authorities refused to recognize the legitimacy of an African labor movement, and active white opposition as well as black rivalries meant that by the mid-1950s the African trade unions had little power or authority to speak for the black Rhodesian majority. In 1957 the Southern Rhodesia Youth League, a youth organization which had evolved into a trade-union organization, decided to act politically; it organized a bus boycott in Harare, an African township, to protest a rise in bus fares. Its success led African nationalist leaders to the conclusion that the time was ripe to revive an explicitly political African National Congress. On September 12, 1957, a new ANC was formed by leaders of the Youth League and the old ANC. Joshua Nkomo was the compromise choice to be its leader.

The white authorities were clearly concerned that African nationalists were seeking to organize the African majority to political ends. Keatley quotes Sir Edgar Whitehead as saying, "I know my Africans and they are not interested in politics. They are interested only in things of immediate practical concern, schools for their children, the improvement of their land, raising their standard of living, and things of that kind." [9] Yet this smug paternalism did not blind Whitehead and his government to the danger that the ANC could be as successful as nationalist leaders had already been in newly independent Ghana and were on the way to being in many other African colonial territories. Urban rallies at the end of 1958 and the growth of rural African organizations in early 1959 led Whitehead's government to ban the ANC and round up its national and local leaders in "Operation Sunrise" on February 29, 1959. Nkomo was abroad and escaped the four years of subsequent detention suffered by most of the ANC's national leaders.

In January, 1960, the National Democratic Party was formed; Nkomo was elected its head in October. Three months later, he led the NDP delegation which attended the constitutional conference that would write Rhodesia's new constitution. After accepting and agreeing to its terms, Nkomo reversed course and renounced it, after being severely criticized by the other NDP leaders. In December, 1961, the NDP

[9] *Ibid.*, p. 219.

was banned and all its leaders within the country were de-
tained. Nkomo was again out of the country and escaped the
government's net.

Within weeks, Nkomo had formed a new party, the Zimbabwe African Peoples Union. ZAPU was banned in September, 1962. Whitehead hoped that the ban would win him
white votes in the December, 1962, elections; it did not, and
an African boycott of the elections cost him the votes of Africans who might have crossed over to vote (albeit with each
vote at a discounted value) for his European supporters, who
were opposed by the Rhodesian Front's hard-liners. Prevented
by recent legislation from forming a new party, Nkomo announced that ZAPU would carry on from new headquarters
established in Dar es Salaam. It would concentrate on taking
the case of the African majority to the United Nations as well
as on activities within Southern Rhodesia. ZAPU's chief representative abroad, Ndabaningi Sithole, soon broke with
Nkomo, and in July, 1963, formed with his supporters the
more militant Zimbabwe African National Union (ZANU).
Both ZAPU and ZANU soon began to struggle with each
other as well as against the white regime in Rhodesia. Their
struggle extended to black Rhodesian circles within Rhodesia
and abroad. As each came to depend more and more on
armed struggle and guerrilla incursions into the territory, they
drew their primary support in training and arms from different sources: ZAPU from the Soviet Union and ZANU from
the People's Republic of China.

In December, 1971, meanwhile, a new political organization operating within Southern Rhodesia had been formed.
The African National Council, under the chairmanship of
Methodist Bishop Abel Muzorewa, first proclaimed itself to be
a temporary body whose sole purpose was to lead African
opinion in opposition to the terms of the Home-Smith agreement of November, 1971. After leading the campaign against
the agreement—which resulted in the conclusion of the Pearce
Commission that African opinion was, in fact, opposed to the

deal—the ANC announced in March that it would continue as a permanent organization dedicated to achievement of "universal adult suffrage." Although he denied that the ANC was a "political party" and referred to it simply as an "organization," Muzorewa was clearly leading a new political movement. He has worked carefully to keep its activities within "reasonable" bounds; for example, he denied any links between the ANC and ZANU and ZAPU until late 1974, when Sithole and Nkomo were released by the white regime and their organizations came technically under the ANC umbrella for purposes of the discussions on Rhodesia's future. The white authorities have harassed the ANC by prohibiting it from receiving funds from outside Southern Rhodesia, by banning outdoor meetings, by arresting ANC officials, and by preventing it from selling membership cards. But by late 1975 at least, the authorities had not banned the organization.

The ANC has escaped banning, probably because of Muzorewa's caution and because Smith needs the ANC as an umbrella organization with which he can negotiate. The pressures on Smith to settle are enormous. But the barriers to agreement remain tragically high. In early 1975, the more militant voices on both sides, black and white, were gaining strength, as had happened repeatedly throughout Rhodesian history.

The essential barrier to a political agreement that can gain widespread African nationalist support is far broader than the specific differences between black and white negotiators as they might try to work out the technical arrangements that can provide some sharing of political power leading to majority rule. What is needed is a basic change in Rhodesian society that goes beyond adjustments with respect to voting rights. For the white "nation" is not likely to place its future in the hands of black politicians unless there is an extraordinary shift in essential white attitudes. Nor do African leaders have much reason to accept white assurances about some distant future, in view of the kind of life without equal rights, political or economic, that Africans are now forced to lead in Rhodesia. What is needed is trust on both sides, and there is little in the situation to engender it.

The more moderate leaders of the black Rhodesian "nation," like Bishop Muzorewa, are clearly concerned that if no solution is reached in the near future, then, in the Bishop's words, "other forces beyond their control could take over." Indeed, during mid-1975 the divisions among Muzorewa, Nkomo, and Sithole and the determination of Sithole's ZANU to force immediate majority rule blocked any peaceful compromise.

In the end, one cannot see how the whites in Rhodesia can hold on. But too much time may be lost, together with too many lives, before a solution is achieved. For both the black and white communities are trapped by a legacy of repression and suspicion, by conflicting symbols from the past and conflicting fears for the future. The Rhodesian problem will not be settled peacefully unless most white Rhodesians, prisoners of perverted principle, no longer see themselves as the defenders of white civilization in a sea of black barbarism, and come to accept the idea that they can survive under an African government—or leave altogether. Nor will it be settled peacefully unless black Rhodesian leaders find reason to believe that majority rule is imminent under some formula accepted by the whites. A continued spiral of violence and reaction seems all too likely, even if some interim agreement is reached. Unless South African pressure forces majority rule, the unhappy prognosis is that Rhodesia will continue to confront the conscience and test the determination of the United Nations and its members.

2

Dilemmas and Compromises
The International
Responses to UDI

The key to unraveling the motives behind most foreign policies, whether of superpowers or minipowers, is to define the dilemmas and conflicting pressures to which they respond. For the basic stuff of foreign policy is compromise: half measures designed to blunt the horns of international and domestic dilemmas, to postpone choices, to deflect external and domestic pressures. For every spectacular trip to China, there are thousands of cautious diplomatic efforts by governments attempting to avoid damage to any of their "national interests," no matter how inconsistent those interests may be. This has been the case with the world response to the Rhodesian problem. The sad fact is that in taking half measures—in voting mandatory United Nations sanctions against the Rhodesian regime, and yet refusing to do all they could to make those sanctions work—most U.N. members have helped undercut the effectiveness of the world organization. A major lesson of the Rhodesian sanctions program is that the United Nations should impose such measures only in the rare event that all the key member states have a fundamental interest in seeing the sanctions succeed—when their national policies on that issue are policies of determination rather than compromise.

The sanctions work well enough to offer hope for the future and cannot be abandoned, but they have not worked well enough to force Smith to terms acceptable to the Rhodesian majority.

BRITISH DILEMMAS

The key to the response of the international community to the Rhodesian rebellion has been the policy of the United Kingdom, a policy shaped by difficult political crossfires at home and abroad. The conflicting pressures which buffeted the British officials concerned with Southern Rhodesia fall into three categories: international pressures, domestic pressures, and pressures inherent in the situation within Southern Rhodesia.

Of the international pressures, perhaps the most serious to British policymakers have been the demands of many African governments, particularly the governments of Zambia, Tanzania, and Nigeria, for the strongest possible British efforts to put an end to the Rhodesian rebellion and for a British commitment to the principle of no independence before majority rule (often referred to as NIBMAR). Before the Unilateral Declaration of Independence (UDI), the Africans took the lead in moves to involve the United Nations in the Rhodesian questions. Immediately after UDI, most African governments called for British military action against the Smith regime, and spoke of action by African troops against Rhodesia that could have involved the British. Prime Minister Harold Wilson deflected these pressures by quickly sending an RAF squadron to neighboring Zambia, "purely for defensive purposes," and hinting at retaliation if the Rhodesians interfered with Zambia's power supply from the Kariba power station on the Rhodesian side of the Zambezi. While African rhetoric about the need for British military action against Smith and his supporters has continued, the Africans have been in no position to commit their own troops to action against the Rhodesians, and the British military hand has not been forced.

The British were also able to cool African anger somewhat by coupling a series of economic measures against the Smith regime with optimistic statements about their imminent effect. The halfloaf of such sanctions did not satisfy African spokesmen, but it tempered their irritation at the British refusal to use force.

In addition to calling on the British to take military action, and failing that, to move more quickly and firmly on the economic front, the Africans have tried to stiffen British backbones in the diplomatic dealings between the representatives of London and Salisbury. British efforts in 1966 (which culminated in talks between Wilson and Smith on a British warship, HMS *Tiger*), in 1968 (talks on the HMS *Fearless*) and in 1971 (with regard to the Home-Smith Agreement) were closely scrutinized by African leaders and attacked insofar as they implied or explicitly revealed a British willingness to accept independence before majority rule.

Perhaps of greater concern to the British than pressures from Africa have been the Afro-Asian attacks on British policy in the various Commonwealth meetings since 1965. They have touched a deep nerve. Beyond its practical diplomatic value to the United Kingdom, the Commonwealth is a reminder of empire, the child of an era of British glory. Although they have maneuvered skillfully to prevent fundamental splits within the Commonwealth while slipping away from flat commitments to the use of force or economic measures that would seriously jeopardize Britain's own economy, both Prime Minister Wilson and Prime Minister Edward Heath have been forced at Commonwealth meetings to concede more than they would have liked on the Rhodesian question. Prime Minister Wilson was driven into reluctant agreement to the idea of a new Rhodesian constitutional conference at a Commonwealth meeting in June, 1965. At the January, 1966, Commonwealth conference Wilson deflected pressures for stronger action by insisting on an extraordinary flight of optimistic fancy: His program of economic and financial measures, he said, "might well bring the rebellion to an end within a matter of weeks rather than months." Nine months later, at the Commonwealth conference of September, 1966, Wilson was forced to agree to accept the principle of no independence before majority rule (NIBMAR) and selective mandatory sanctions by the United Nations if he could not reach a satisfactory diplomatic settlement with Smith. (After the subsequent failure of the *Tiger* talks, the British went to the United Nations in December for the mandatory sanctions. Wilson backed off NIBMAR, however, in his 1968 negotiations with Smith.) At the August, 1973, Commonwealth conference at Ottawa, Heath was forced to agree to an ambiguous statement in the communiqué about "the need to give every possible assistance to all those engaged in the territories of southern Africa to achieve self-determination and independence." Although British officials then blandly stated that this did not require the United Kingdom to give assistance, even humanitarian, to the guerrillas, the communiqué also recognized "the legitimacy of the struggle to win full human rights and self-determination in southern Africa." Commonwealth opinion has also provided an implicit check on British diplomacy when it came to considering the concessions which might bring Smith to agreement. As J. D. F. Jones, the perceptive foreign editor of the *Financial Times* put it in 1969: "A British sellout would, I should think, be impossible to conceal from the rest of the world, and would surely mark the end of the Commonwealth as we know it now, not to speak of our relations with the rest of the developing world." [1]

Balancing the international pressures from African governments and other Commonwealth members, the British have been conscious of the stake in their relations with Portugal and, especially, the Republic of South Africa. British investments in, and trade with, South Africa dwarf their eco-

---

[1] *Financial Times,* London, June 23, 1969.

nomic relations with Portugal. As a result, while the British were willing in April, 1966, to defy the Portuguese and place an embargo on the shipment of oil to the port of Beira in Mozambique (from whence a pipeline could take it to a Rhodesian refinery at Umtali), British representatives at the United Nations have refused to allow the extension of sanctions to South Africa. And while cutting off oil from Beira, the British did not extend their embargo to the Mozambican port Lourenço Marques, since that would have interfered with South African oil imports. Thus, the Rhodesians were able to import sufficient quantities of oil from South Africa and Mozambique despite the embargo.

In addition, the British were loath to retaliate against the South Africans for their blatant violations of sanctions because, on the diplomatic front, London preferred to encourage the South Africans to use their influence with Smith in behalf of a settlement.

Thus, the British response to international pressures on Rhodesia was a contradictory compromise. Sanctions were a way to deflect pressures for the use of force. But they could not crush the Smith regime in weeks, months, or even many years, unless the South Africans and the Portuguese were prevented from supplying the Rhodesians with oil and other goods. At the same time, the British refused to enter into an economic war with the South Africans. Such a war might hurt South Africa more than the United Kingdom, but the spotty British economy had enough problems without adding the loss of the South African market.

British policy toward Rhodesia has also been shaped by the second category of conflicting pressures: divisions and debates within Britain itself. In late 1965 and early 1966, Wilson had a very thin majority in Parliament—not a strong base for adventures on a grand scale. He was anxious to avoid giving the Conservatives an issue which could be used against him. The more dramatic the action against Rhodesia, the greater the political risks of failure and embarrassment. Leaders of the Liberal party, which controlled a small but important

number of votes in the Parliament, joined Labour militants in
criticizing Wilson for reacting to the crisis too slowly and cautiously, while the Conservatives maintained a position which
was traditionally more favorable to the white Rhodesians. Wilson was in the middle. But the position had its advantages as
well as its penalties; Wilson could and did use his political difficulties to deflect international pressures. In January, 1966,
he asked President Kenneth Kaunda of Zambia to give him
more time in which to make sanctions work. Kaunda agreed,
and went so far as to persuade his own more aggressive cabinet members to avoid making statements which could hurt the
Labour party's prospects in the March, 1966, general elections. Yet even after Labour had gained a ninety-seven-vote
majority in Commons in these elections, Wilson remained
greatly influenced by buffetings within Parliament from right
and left. The Conservatives continued to press for a compromise settlement with Smith while more than one hundred Labour backbenchers pressed for British allegiance to NIBMAR.
It was impossible to satisfy both; Wilson could not achieve
what the Conservatives were asking if he agreed to the un-
compromising demands of these junior members of his own
party in Parliament. The venom of the parliamentary debate
over Rhodesia had been illustrated in an exchange between
Wilson and Heath on January 31, 1966. Heath stated that
there could be no honorable settlement in Rhodesia as long as
Wilson was Prime Minister. Wilson, in turn, answered that
"the only thing in Rhodesia standing in the way . . . of a dimi-
nution of the right-wing and semi-fascist resistance there . . .
was their [white Rhodesians'] belief that because of the arguments of the right honourable gentleman [Heath], delivered
with increasing heat every time he gets to his feet on the Rhodesian question, the Conservatives were taking a different
view from that of the Government in this country." [2]

The debate over Rhodesian policy which whipsawed Wilson was nearly as intense within his own government as in Par-

[2] Robert C. Good, *U.D.I.: The International Politics of the Rhodesian Rebellion*
(London: Faber & Faber, 1973), p. 154.

liament. The military and intelligence services were generally sympathetic to UDI, or extremely reluctant to consider active military or covert measures against the Smith regime. The Royal Air Force had once used Rhodesia as a training area, and there were strong personal ties between some RAF officers and former members of the RAF now living in Rhodesia. Smith himself was an RAF alumnus. On the other hand, a number of important officials in the Commonwealth and Foreign Offices favored much stronger action than Wilson was willing to take, and opposed any negotiated settlement that smacked of a sellout. In mid-1966, Sir Arthur Bottomley, Wilson's Commonwealth Secretary, was dropped from his position after expressing strong opposition to Wilson's first moves toward Smith. (Bottomley had pressed for a tobacco embargo very early in the game but had been thwarted by the Chancellor of the Exchequer on economic grounds.) And Lord Caradon, the British representative at the United Nations, was reportedly prepared to resign if there had been a settlement in late 1966 along the lines that Wilson was proposing.

In addition, there were conflicting pressures within British society, where Rhodesia is far more of an issue than in the United States. While the liberal press and anti-apartheid pressure groups called for stronger action, business interests were a powerful barrier to such policies. One British official who worked on the issue in those days recalls that Whitehall could not have ordered stronger sanctions because it would have meant "declaring war on the City."

The third category of pressures and problems for British policy, the situation within Southern Rhodesia itself, further complicated the problem. The Rhodesian problem simply would not go away; the growth of apartheid there has dramatized the issue in England and made it harder for the British government to wash its hands of the matter.

Just as American policymakers who feared the international and domestic political consequences of trying for an illusory "quick kill" in Vietnam relied on the hope that step-by-step escalation would unravel North Vietnamese will, so

Wilson tried to persuade his critics (as he seemed to have persuaded himself) that each new economic measure would produce significant political and psychological change in Salisbury. He apparently believed that there would be more internal opposition to the Rhodesian Front than there was; that Smith might be lured into formal agreement on a compromise settlement unacceptable to the Rhodesian Front, which he wasn't; and that limited economic measures would make an essential psychological difference and weaken white Rhodesian obduracy—which they didn't.

The persistence of political and military racial conflict in Rhodesia suggests a final dilemma for the British. For in addition to balancing short-term domestic and international pressures, the British government must make a close calculation between the immediate benefits of compromise (i.e., healthy trade with South Africa) and its long-term consequences. It is likely that as majority rule is achieved in Rhodesia and elsewhere in southern Africa, the new African governments will penalize in some fashion the foreign businessmen who had traded with their enemies.

The result of all these pressures, problems, and miscalculations was a series of British shifts, compromises, and half measures from 1965 to 1970 which confused friend and foe alike. By the time UDI was declared, the Wilson government had publicly ruled out the use of force, thus relieving Smith of one concern about the possible consequences of such an act. It has been variously argued that force was renounced because of Wilson's thin majority in Parliament; because of opposition from the British military who pointed to logistical problems and, in any case, simply didn't like the idea, since it would have required bombing Salisbury Airport and therefore meant civilian casualties (some of them the families of former members of the RAF); because of fears of getting bogged down in an inconclusive struggle if quick action proved fruitless; and because of potential public reaction to the spectacle of British bullets shedding the blood of white "kith and kin" in Rhodesia. In addition, some British officials who worked on the Rhodesian problem at the time of UDI believe that Wilson's public eschewal of the use of force was calculated to deflect backbench Labour pressures for military action: Once he had announced that force would not be used, it was harder for the more outspoken members of his party to urge Wilson to exercise it.

Nor, after UDI, did Wilson move quickly to bring all the economic pressure he could on the Rhodesian regime. Immediately after Smith's declaration, Britain only partially restricted its trade with the Rhodesians, banning British imports of Rhodesian tobacco and sugar and British exports of arms to Rhodesia. Aid was terminated, and financial penalties were imposed. Reversing the earlier British position that Rhodesia was a British problem beyond the competence of the United Nations, the British sponsored a Security Council resolution which condemned UDI, called upon all states not to recognize the "illegal racist minority regime," and asked them to refuse it any assistance. As it became clear that these initial economic measures would not create the local opposition to, and splits within, the regime which Wilson hoped for, further items were added to the embargo at the beginning of December; it now included 95 percent of Rhodesia's exports to the United Kingdom. These and further financial measures taken at the same time were followed on December 17 by a prohibition on imports of petroleum products into Rhodesia.

These piecemeal actions did not shake Smith's position, and in the first days of 1966 a new Wilson strategy, labeled the "quick kill," became apparent. Once the oil sanctions had crippled the Rhodesian economy, perhaps in a few months, Zambia would completely ban its imports from Rhodesia. The effect on the closely tied economies of both Southern Rhodesia and Zambia would be severe. Britain and others would assist the Zambian economy during the brief period before Smith fell. But the "quick kill" could not work. Zambia could not afford to agree to it, without more external assistance than it was able to obtain. In Robert Good's words, "It was a fanciful and irresponsible *scenario* for it assumed that Zambia should accept a level of risk which Britain itself had refused. Wilson also appeared to have placed a margin of hope on South Africa's willingness not to frustrate the oil embargo. It was another bad estimate. No one had more to lose than South Africa if sanctions had succeeded against Rhodesia." [3]

Despite Wilson's strengthened hand after Labour's success in the March 31, 1966, general election, the Prime Minister decided that if the tactics he had dared employ so far could not work, it was time to shift the goal. If Smith could not be shaken, perhaps a way could be found to reason with him. Just before the election, Wilson had ordered exploratory contacts with Rhodesian representatives to test the possibility of negotiations looking to a compromise settlement. By late April, 1966, they had agreed to pursue such talks. Richard Hall has described the shock with which this news came to Kenneth Kaunda.[4] When news of Labour's March electoral victory had reached Zambia, its president had jubilantly told his cabinet colleagues: "Now you will see. Harold will do the right thing." When Wilson revealed on April 27 that there would be informal talks with the Rhodesians to explore the basis for formal negotiations, Kaunda was in a remote area of Zambia. British diplomats were unable to reach him, and he first heard the news over the BBC. Zambian bitterness about what the British considered to be the "right thing" on Rhodesia has been evident ever since.

When the talks failed in December, 1966, the British took the lead in asking for mandatory sanctions imposed by the Security Council. But they blocked moves to extend the sanctions to South Africa or Portugal and did not support comprehensive sanctions against Rhodesia until the spring of 1968. And the British were careful to avoid at any point suggesting that the United Nations had primary responsibility for the Rhodesian problem; London maintained *de jure* sovereignty over Southern Rhodesia. Her Majesty's government found it

[3] *Ibid.*, p. 293.

[4] Richard Hall, *The High Price of Principles, Kaunda and the White South* (New York: Africana Publishing Corporation, 1969), ch. 10.

useful to use the United Nations in support of its own strategies and as a forum in which to anticipate and deflect Afro-
Asian pressures, but did not want to relinquish formal responsibility since it would not then have had the authority to negotiate a settlement with the Rhodesians.

Wilson thus turned over to Heath, when the latter became
Prime Minister in mid-1970, a Rhodesian policy which had
succeeded reasonably well in allowing the Labour Prime Minister to skirt major international and domestic political pitfalls.
The policy had not seriously damaged Wilson politically in England; British relations with African governments most concerned with the issue had been impaired but not irreparably
torn; the Commonwealth had survived; and British trade with
South Africa was thriving. But in terms of its effect on the
Rhodesian problem itself, the policy was a mess. The Rhodesians had learned how to survive sanctions; Smith's political
health was good; and the gulf between black and white had
widened further. In addition, the British had involved not
only their own diplomacy but the prestige and authority of the
United Nations as well and could not let go.

Prime Minister Heath had announced before the June,
1970, election that the Conservatives would make a new effort
to negotiate a solution. Responding to strong pressures from
within his own party, he made this effort. The result was the
Home-Smith agreement of November, 1971. But just as Wilson had grossly underestimated the determination of the
white Rhodesian community, so Heath's effort foundered on
the determination of Rhodesia's black community. The report
of the Pearce Commission did more than prevent the consum-
mation of the deal. It revealed also that African opinion in
Rhodesia is not likely to let the British off the sanctions hook
in the near future. The Commission found a strong prefer-
ence among Africans for the retention of sanctions, despite
the burden which they place on the African population. Ed-
dison Zvobgo, the Director of the External Commission of the
African National Congress (ANC), put it this way in Washington in February, 1973, at a Congressional hearing on the Rho-

desian problem. "It is not us who need sheets to sleep on or cars to come into the city, or spare parts to run the industries. We do not own the economy. Those comforts which have been siphoned off by sanctions are totally irrevelant to the African people.

"Over ninety percent of the African people live on the land. . . . They are fed by the very soil. So that to suggest that sanctions hurt the Africans and therefore in the interest of the African we ought to drop sanctions, is nonsense." [5]

AFRICAN CAUTION

It is likely that London will continue thus to muddle along on Rhodesia. Many Africans and many of those sympathetic to their cause quickly proclaim their indignation at Albion's perfidy over Rhodesia. But it should not seem so strange to most African leaders that another government should find compromise more satisfactory than heroism. Their own policies are the product of political and substantive compromise. The response of African nations to UDI has, of course, varied. Some, like Zambia and Tanzania, have made real sacrifices to oppose the Smith regime; others, notably Malawi, have chosen to avoid any kind of confrontation with the Rhodesians. In different degrees, all of the African governments have faced a similar dilemma. While almost all African leaders no doubt feel strong anguish and anger at racial injustice in Rhodesia, they have also found it increasingly difficult in the past decade to attract the economic assistance they require for desired levels of economic growth. Caught between principle and economic necessity, most have found it best to press at meetings of the Organization of African Unity (OAU) and at the United Nations for forceful action against Rhodesia by the British and the United Nations, but to avoid tearing their bilateral relationships with the British and other major powers over the

[5] Hearings before the Subcommittee on Africa and the Subcommittee on International Organizations and Movements of the House Foreign Affairs Committee, February 21, 22, and March 15, 1973, p. 52.

issue. This pattern became clear in the first months after UDI. The first reaction of leading African states was one of dramatic militancy. If the British would not crush the rebellion, the Africans would. President Kwame Nkrumah in Ghana mobilized his forces and called for an OAU military force which would act for the United Nations. Congo (Brazzaville) declared its willingness to contribute to the OAU force. Congo (Leopoldville) offered to assist the transit of OAU forces through its territory. The OAU Defense Committee met to discuss the crisis.[6]

The OAU itself met on December 3, 1965. The conference began with further calls for military action against Rhodesia, but when it came to specific proposals, the delegates preferred to turn to less desperate measures. Military posturing quickly gave way to discussions of diplomatic pressures. The organization called for an end to all communications and economic relations with Rhodesia, agreed to push for similar action by the United Nations, and decided to support and encourage the Rhodesian African nationalists. In addition, if the British had not crushed the rebellion by December 15, OAU members would sever diplomatic relations with the United Kingdom. But in the two weeks between the OAU meeting and the mid-December deadline, most OAU members reconsidered their position. Many seemed relieved when President Kaunda spread the word that Zambia could not sever all ties with London; it would then be at the mercy of the Rhodesians. After the diplomatic Armageddon arrived on December 15, only nine of the thirty-six members of the OAU broke with the British. The African members of the Commonwealth had the most to lose, of course, in severing their ties with the British. Of these, only two took that step—Ghana and Tanzania. (The price for Tanzania turned out to be approximately £7 million in British aid.) Thus, the distinction between multilat-

[6] Good quotes on page 21 of *U.D.I.* the less enthusiastic reaction of Dr. Hastings Banda, Prime Minister of Malawi: "Ten Rhodesian mercenaries will whip 5,000 so-called African soldiers; the Rhodesian army if Smith pushed could conquer the whole of East and Central Africa in one week."

eral and bilateral pressures was clear. African representatives walked out of the United Nations in mid-December, as Prime Minister Wilson spoke on Rhodesia; but the representatives of most members of the OAU remained at their embassies in London.

The coups in Nigeria and Ghana in early 1966 put an end to fantasies of an OAU military force to be used against the Rhodesian regime. The demand that the British use force against Rhodesia has remained a persistent theme of African statements at OAU meetings and the United Nations. But it must have been as clear to the Africans as it has been to the Rhodesians that this was simply not in the cards. The real questions confronting the Africans for the last seven years have been how to maximize the impact of economic measures against Rhodesia and how best to support the guerrillas operating against the Rhodesian regime. At the June, 1972, conference of the OAU, Tanzanian President Julius Nyerere suggested six ways in which African countries could bring increased pressure on Rhodesia: (1) they could actively enforce sanctions themselves and assist the neighbors of Rhodesia who were paying most heavily for sanctions (e.g., Zambia); (2) they could put strong pressure on other countries to observe sanctions faithfully; (3) they could discriminate against firms which broke sanctions; (4) they could press for stronger action by the United Nations in monitoring and enforcing sanctions; (5) they could seek to extend sanctions to communications and other areas; (6) and they could increase support for the liberation movements. It is interesting to note which of these six recommendations the Africans were already acting on or have since emphasized.

The African states have generally had a strong record with regard to the fourth and fifth of Nyerere's recommendations: it is they who have pressed most vigorously for stronger U.N. implementation of sanctions, and for extending their scope. They have also, through the OAU and in some cases individually, made important financial contributions to the guerrilla movements. Tanzania and Zambia have been particularly helpful to the movements, granting them the use of their territories. (Botswana, on the other hand, has not believed it could do so without suffering unacceptable economic and perhaps even political/military retaliation by South Africa; it has reportedly closed its borders to the guerrillas.) In a sense, however, African support for the liberation forces is the same sort of careful expression of concern that the sanctions program is for the British. It provides them with a vehicle for action which does not involve the severe penalties to themselves that action by their own military forces might.

It is Nyerere's first, second and third recommendations which could prove most costly to the Africans, if followed meticulously. With regard to the first, while many African countries have apparently observed sanctions, it is quite well known that many have not. One can reportedly find Rhodesian beef in Gabon and other Rhodesian products in Zaire. Rhodesian goods have passed through Dahomey, and Air Rhodesia regularly flies to Malawi. The OAU has apparently not tried to force its erring members to cease and desist.

The second and third of the Tanzanian President's recommendations have the most difficult implications of all for the Africans. Putting pressure on the major powers to observe sanctions and discriminating against important foreign firms could, of course, be very costly indeed. It is not surprising that African leaders have failed to cut their exports of raw materials to sanctions violators, or to nationalize existing investments and bar further foreign capital from each major power unless it agreed both to observe sanctions more faithfully and to vote as the Africans would wish at the United Nations. It may be that the successes of Arab oil diplomacy could encourage the Africans to move more in this direction. There are some signs that a few African nations are becoming more aggressive. Many believe that the British government would have made further efforts to compromise with Smith in 1973 if General Yakubu Gowon, the President of Nigeria, had not raised the Rhodesian issue with the British on a state visit to London in the middle of the year. About 8 percent of Britain's oil imports comes from Nigeria.

There is much evidence that Africans are thinking about

the leverage given them by their raw materials. It remains likely, however, that this leverage will be used primarily on economic issues, primarily to bargain for higher prices. The Arabs could afford to hold back oil (at a profit) on a political issue; the Africans probably cannot.

The African government which has faced the most excruciating dilemmas as a result of UDI is that of Southern Rhodesia's neighbor to the north, Zambia. No African nation has a greater stake in seeing majority rule in Southern Rhodesia. No African leader probably cares more deeply about the issue than Kaunda. But, at UDI, the economy of no African nation was more vulnerable to Rhodesian pressure than the Zambian economy.

As a result of a decade of federation and the intertwinings of their previous history, the economies of Southern Rhodesia and Zambia were as symbiotic as their governments were dissimilar. By the mid-1960s, Zambia's one rail link to foreign markets passed through Southern Rhodesia and thence across Mozambique to the ports of Beira and Lourenço Marques. More than 95 percent of Zambia's imports and all of its copper exports and coal (from a colliery in Southern Rhodesia) depended on this railway. In addition, almost all the electric power for Zambia came from the Kariba Dam on the Zambezi; the generators were on the south bank, under Rhodesian control. Large quantities of Zambia's consumer and other imports came from South Africa. The Zambians were further made vulnerable by the fact that many of the best trained personnel in Zambian civil service and private business were white, and often Rhodesian. It was alarming to see two hundred white railwaymen working in Zambia go on strike after UDI, almost crippling Zambian rail traffic. More alarming still was an act of sabotage against the main power line serving Zambia's industrial complex in the copper belt, apparently carried out by white Rhodesian sympathizers.

It is no wonder, then, that Kaunda and his advisers were unenthusiastic about Wilson's piecemeal economic tactics. It was essential, from the Zambian point of view, that the rebellion be put down as quickly as possible. Economic measures against the Smith regime would hurt Zambia nearly as much as they hurt the Rhodesian economy. The Zambians therefore pressed in the weeks following UDI for British military intervention. In July, 1964, Kaunda had offered Zambia as a base for British troops if they were ever to be used to assert British control in Rhodesia. He now renewed the offer and asked that British forces at least occupy the Kariba Dam, including the generators on the Rhodesian side of the river. He did not, however, want British ground forces on Zambian soil unless they were to be used against the Rhodesian regime. But the British would not use force against Smith and his supporters, and the Zambians were left with an RAF unit for defense and implied British threats against the Rhodesians if they cut off Zambia's power.

While the British refusal to quash the rebellion by force left Zambia on the horns of its economic dilemma, the stationing of an RAF squadron did relieve Kaunda of another difficult choice by deflating some of the African ardor for an OAU military force to do battle with the Rhodesians. Kaunda was saved from having to choose between allowing Zambia to become a battlefield and refusing the use of his territory to the soldiers of friendly African nations. By the time of the December 3 OAU meeting, Kaunda had been indicating that he would probably have to choose the latter. There could have been little doubt about the consequences for Zambia of an African assault on Southern Rhodesia, unsupported by the British. The Rhodesian Air Force included among its six squadrons between forty and fifty modern fighters and light bombers. Together with the well-trained Rhodesian ground forces, it was a formidable foe—especially if backed by South Africa's armed forces.

The penalties to the Zambians of the British sanctions program against Rhodesia became excruciating in early 1966. In addition to the damaging effects on the Zambian economy of measures taken by the British against the Rhodesians in November and early December, 1965, the mid-December oil embargo was a potential disaster for the Zambians. Zambia's oil came through Rhodesia. The British promised an airlift to tide the Zambians over while the embargo brought Rhodesia to its knees. The airlift, carried out by British, American, and Canadian aircraft until the middle of 1966, and continuing delivery of oil supplies by road along the "hell run" through Tanzania, met Zambia's oil supplies (with rationing), until August, 1968, when an oil pipeline from Tanzania was completed. Meanwhile, South African exports of oil to Rhodesia in early 1966 were making a mockery of British claims that a "quick kill" was possible, and the Zambians refused to sever all ties with the Rhodesians unless the British would guarantee enough assistance to make up for the economic damage it would cause. The British would not do so.

Clearly, the only long-term solution to the conflict in Kaunda's goals—all pressure possible against the Rhodesians but continued growth within Zambia—was to maintain no more than necessary economic relations with Rhodesia while reducing the scope of Zambian economic interdependence with Southern Rhodesia, particularly through developing an alternative to the Rhodesian railway. It appears that the Zambians have been succeeding; they have survived their period of greatest dependence on the Rhodesians. An essential factor was the allowance by the Security Council of necessary exceptions to the U.N. sanctions program. External assistance from Britain and elsewhere also helped the Zambians develop a more independent economy. Equally important, the road from Lusaka to Dar es Salaam, the Tanzanian capital, had by 1973 been tarred throughout its length, and the first four hundred miles of the Tan-Zam (Tanzania-Zambia) railway were already operational. Port facilities at Dar es Salaam were being expanded. It seemed possible that the railway, a major aid project of the People's Republic of China, could be completed within a year or two, providing Zambia with an alternative rail as well as road link to foreign markets and producers. Thus, when Smith closed his border to the Zambians on January 9, 1973, and then reversed course on February 3 and agreed to reopen the border, he was hoist with his own petard when Kaunda announced that the border would remain closed. The copper could be shipped over alternative routes.

Still, Zambia remains in a difficult position. Should it come to it, Rhodesian and South African military forces could punish Zambia heavily. Zambia still gets its electric power from Kariba. And, at least until the Tan-Zam railway is operating fully, the use of alternative transportation routes and the loss of trade with Southern Rhodesia must do some damage to the Zambia economy. Thus, Kaunda has joined other African leaders in the region in urging a peaceful settlement in Southern Rhodesia and in moving toward "détente" with South Africa.

Still heavily dependent on external assistance, still counting on Rhodesia's fears of international reaction if the Kariba power supply were cut off, still anxious to avoid giving London any excuses to wash its hands of the matter, the Zambians are unlikely to risk any fundamental rupture in their relations with the major powers over the Rhodesian issue. Kaunda's tightrope is not as high as it was in 1965 and 1966, but a tightrope it remains.

SOUTH AFRICA AND PORTUGAL: AMBIVALENCE

In the years following UDI, the South Africans and Portuguese performed their own balancing acts, as well. Both were ambivalent in attitude and approach to the Rhodesian problem. The Portuguese supported the Rhodesians in the United Nations, facilitated evasions of sanctions by Rhodesian and foreign businessmen, and indeed refused officially to support the sanctions, declaring instead their adherence to international obligations toward the rights of landlocked nations and their neutrality on what they considered to be an internal British affair and no business of the United Nations. Yet the Portuguese were obviously unhappy about UDI and eager that the issue be resolved between British and Rhodesian negotiators. The Rhodesian situation damaged Portuguese inter-

ests in a number of ways. There was the humiliating nuisance
of the Beira blockade, a symbol of the fact that the British
were willing to lean on the Portuguese more heavily than on
the Southern Africans. The Rhodesian rebellion also increased world attention to southern Africa as a whole, and this
was not in Portugal's interest.

With Portugal's decision to grant independence to Mozambique, its stake in the Rhodesian situation has been consid-
erably reduced. But an independent Mozambique makes Rhodesia all the more threatening to the South Africans. More
deeply involved in supplying Rhodesia than the Portuguese
ever were, they also found the disadvantages of the Rhodesian
situation potentially more damaging. South African support
has played an essential role in keeping the Rhodesian regime
alive in the face of the sanctions. It was aid, and particularly
oil, from South Africa which made impossible Wilson's hopes
for crushing the rebellion through economic strangulation in
the first half year after UDI.

The South Africans have also provided military support
to the Rhodesians. South African "police" units—which had
reportedly received paramilitary training—were observed in
Rhodesia as early as August, 1967. In mid-1973, South African helicopters were seen in Rhodesia. Intermittent meetings
between South African and Rhodesian military planners have
also been reported in the press.

And yet, for many of the same considerations that modified Portugal's rapture about UDI, the South Africans obviously would much prefer that the Rhodesian problem
quietly go away. Robert Good quotes Prime Minister Hendrik
Verwoerd as observing privately on the day of UDI, "I have
offered advice to three Rhodesian premiers. The first two
were wise enough to take it." An influential South African
newspaper bemoaned this "hot-headed and ill-considered action by Mr. Smith." [7] The South Africans have repeatedly
urged the Rhodesians to negotiate a settlement with the Brit-

[7] Good, *U.D.I.*,, p. 21.

ish. Even in the days immediately following the failure of the
Tiger talks in early December, 1966, Vorster made a strong
plea for a negotiated solution. His plea reflected South African dismay at the fact that the British, rebuffed in the negotiations, were then asking for a Security Council meeting at
which sanctions—a fearsome word in South African ears—
would be voted. After the Security Council had acted, *Die
Burger,* a newspaper which reflects the views of Vorster's Nationalist Party, sadly concluded that "Rhodesia's insistence that
she is an independent State has become an embarrassment to
her best friends." In 1968 the South Africans tried to help
make a success of the *Fearless* talks, but to no avail.

South African irritation with the Rhodesian problem and
the Rhodesians themselves was more clearly revealed when
Smith closed the Zambian border in early 1973. Ten days
after this ill-considered action, Vorster stated that his government had not been consulted in advance, and reiterated South
Africa's opposition to economic boycotts of any kind. It soon
became apparent that his government's opposition to Smith's
maneuver would be expressed by more than words. Hundreds
of tons of mining equipment and other urgently needed
goods from overseas were unloaded at Johannesburg to be
airlifted into Zambia during the following weeks. Of course,
the South Africans were not reacting in this fashion purely
through irritation at Smith or out of devotion to the principle
of free trade (or at least no sanctions); about $60 million
worth of South African exports had been reaching Zambia
through Rhodesia annually.

So the South Africans are trapped in their own Rhodesian
dilemma no less firmly than the British are still caught in the
consequences of their compromises of 1965–66. Vorster's government obviously fears the possibility that the Rhodesian situation could blow up and prejudice their economic and political relations with the British and others. The South Africans
no less than the British have a stake in their economic ties.
One South African leader was quoted in the *Christian Science
Monitor* on April 19, 1973, as having said, "Without America's

14% of our foreign investments we would still be okay. But without it and Britain's 61% we would be in real danger." Rhodesia can also play havoc with Pretoria's "outward-looking" foreign policies, through which the South African government hopes to improve its relations with African governments—to its own external and internal political as well as economic advantage. Worst of all, the South Africans must fear that war in Rhodesia could become a divisive and agonizing issue within South Africa.

Apparently, the South African whites would prefer letting go in Rhodesia and holding on in South Africa to getting bogged down in a Rhodesian quagmire. After a visit to South Africa during the summer of 1974, Gavin Young of the *London Observer* reported that Rhodesia "has already, in the opinion of Vorster's planners, 'gone black'." [8] As previously noted, this calculation has led the South Africans to put strong pressure on the Smith regime to settle the issue.

And yet, just as succeeding American presidents feared "losing" in Vietnam for domestic political as well as international reasons, so the South Africans could find it hard to let go completely in Rhodesia. And if Smith does not acquiesce in African rule there, South Africa will still be caught between the contradictory fears of either overinvolvement or a failure to support its white neighbors across its northern border.

Each of these compromises over the Rhodesian issue— British compromises, African compromises, South African compromises—has complemented the others. The result has been a persistent Rhodesian problem which continues to hound the members of the United Nations through the irritations and economic penalties of sanctions, and to diminish the stature of the United Nations itself.

[8] *Washington Post,* September 4, 1974. On May 29, 1974, the Johannesburg *Star* said in an editorial that "this is admittedly not the easiest time for Mr. Smith to reach a settlement . . . the point is that the best time is already past: from now on Rhodesia's chances are likely to worsen. The options are no longer fully open. Rhodesians must shake themselves out of their dream of perpetual white supremacy."

The British have compromised by taking harsh enough action against the Rhodesian regime to keep the Commonwealth alive and to satisfy partially the demands of African and more militant British opinion on the issue, while ruling out the reassertion of British control by military means. London has asked the United Nations to take action against Rhodesia—but not such strong action that Britain's economic ties to South Africa might be damaged. The result: The Rhodesian regime has been harassed, even shaken, by the sanctions, but it has survived.

The South Africans have given the Rhodesian regime enough material support to ensure its survival, and balanced this with diplomatic pressure in favor of a settlement—but not so much pressure as to create political splits at home. The result: The Rhodesian regime has not yet been forced to compromise in its insistence on white political supremacy.

The Africans, including Zambia, have pressed within the Commonwealth and at the United Nations for stronger British action and broader sanctions. But they have not dared damage their bilateral relations with the major Western powers when trying to persuade them to agree to firmer action by the United Nations. The result: The British, the Americans and others could the more easily pursue their compromises.

The consequence of all this has been more than a failure by the world community to resolve the Rhodesian problem. In addition, the United Nations has been misused. It has been asked to do a job but not allowed to do it.

A "Collective Measures Committee," formed by the United Nations in 1950 to study methods which might be used to strengthen international peace and security, concluded in a study of November, 1951: "If, despite its best efforts, the United Nations should again be compelled to make the grave decision to suppress an act of aggression or a breach of the peace, the success or failure of its action will depend then, as it does now, upon the will of its Members to accept danger and sacrifice for the sake of world peace. No previous preparation in the sphere of procedures, methods and machinery can take

the place of courage and steadfastness in meeting this supreme test."

This sensible injunction was disregarded in 1966. The
compromises in the foreign policies of the member states have
meant that the sanctions against Rhodesia were imposed
piecemeal, rather than at once; sanctions violators have rarely
been penalized; the threat, even, of further steps, i.e., force,
has been lacking. There was a fundamental inconsistency between the votes cast in the Security Council in favor of exercising an instrument which demands unrelenting pressure and
the mixed motives behind those votes. National policies of
compromise and muddle would limit from the start and inevitably undercut the effectiveness of the sanctions program.
The whole of the U.N. effort could not be larger than the sum
of its national parts.

Once adopted, the sanctions could not be abandoned. To
do so would be to abandon the international community's one
expression of concern that has had and will continue to have
an important, albeit not controlling, effect on the course of
events in Southern Rhodesia. It would be an admission of total
failure when the failure has, in fact, been partial. It would do
still more grievous damage to the concept of sanctions than
has already been done. The psychological effect on black Rhodesians would be devastating; the encouragement to white obduracy, tragic. Once it had been set on its course, the United
Nations could only follow it. And the course could offer no
early end.

As the United Nations was trapped by its member states,
so the states were trapping themselves. Once mandatory sanctions were adopted by the Security Council, member states
could not violate them without violating a treaty commitment.
Every member of the United Nations has an obligation under
Article 25 of the Charter to accept and carry out such decisions of the Council.

In retrospect, then, it seems clear that the major Western
powers that were present at the creation of the world organization—and will most influence its future for good or ill—

faced a hard choice in the sanctions votes of December, 1966, and May, 1968. They could push the sanctions to their logical conclusion, including action against the Portuguese territories and South Africa, and accept the damaging consequences to their own economies; they could refuse to ask the United Nations to resolve the problem unless it also had the means to do so; or they could wriggle out of their own dilemmas by adopting a compromise course. That they believed they had to choose this third course is not surprising. Only those who were prepared to sacrifice immediate and important national interests for the no less important, but less tangible future of the United Nations, and for the sake of Southern Rhodesia, would have acted otherwise. But on aesthetic grounds, if on no other, one might wish now that there had been less rhetoric in 1966 and 1968 about the majesty of the institution, while the United Nations was being so poorly used.

3

American Policy, 1965–1968 The Necessity for Compromise?

In his first annual report to the Congress on his foreign policies, in early 1970, President Nixon noted that in the period following World War II, Americans had acted around the world as "a do-it-yourself people—an impatient people." It was time, he suggested, to adopt a more modest vision of our responsibilities, to avoid overcommitment, to let other nations "deal with local disputes which once might have required our intervention." "Our objective, in the first instance, is to support our *interests* over the long run with a sound foreign policy," he wrote. "Our interests must shape our commitments, rather than the other way around." [1]

While many American policies in the postwar era did indeed reflect a general assumption of American responsibility even when American interests did not seem directly involved, the framers of American policies toward Southern Rhodesia in the first three years after UDI refused to commit the United States any more deeply than they thought it had to be. Their approach was to find and follow the course of least resistance. In this case, the United States would not try to shape events abroad; it would wind its way among conflicting international and domestic pressures on the issue, like the

[1] Richard Nixon, "U.S. Foreign Policy for the 1970's," February 18, 1970.

other nations involved. One should keep in mind that, despite bitter bureaucratic and congressional debate about Southern Rhodesia, no one at the highest levels of the American government (and very few Americans outside of the government) devoted much time or concern to the Rhodesian problem. In the words of one top official who served in the State Department in the mid-1960s, it seemed to most people at the Cabinet and sub-Cabinet level "just a little mess the British had on their hands," especially in comparison to the Dominican Republic and Vietnam crises that dominated American foreign policy councils in 1965, the year of UDI.

But the United States was nevertheless confronted with its own dilemmas as a result of UDI, most of them a paler reflection of the policy conflicts confronting the British. The result was that the United States, too, worked out a compromise policy and supported the British in using the United Nations to avoid more damaging choices. Its object was to keep free of responsibility, to prejudice as little as possible conflicting U.S. substantive stakes in the area, and to balance the opposing pressures of American advocates (within the government and outside it) who favored either more or less action against the Rhodesian regime by the United States, the United Kingdom, and the United Nations.

SUBSTANTIVE STAKES

Like the British, the United States has conflicting economic and political stakes in black and white Africa. By 1965, the wave of independence in Africa had washed over most of the continent. While independence inevitably brought with it massive economic and political problems for the young African governments, and individually few of them had much influence on the international game board of realpolitik, the United States had a stake both in their votes at the United Nations and in their attitudes toward American traders and investors. In 1945, of a total U.N. membership of 51 nations, 4 (including Egypt) were African. By 1965, 36 of the 115 members were African; 15 were Asian and 11 Middle Eastern. The State Department's working estimate in 1965 of direct American private investment in Africa north of the Zambezi came to more than $1.23 billion. In addition, there was the expectation that American investment in Africa would increase rapidly, as it has. There was also the potential stake in American investment in South Africa, the Portuguese territories, and Southern Rhodesia once they came under African rule.

On the other side of the coin, American investment in white Africa in 1965 was also significant: an estimated $650 million of American investments (including portfolio investments) in South Africa, $10 million to $20 million in South West Africa (a territory controlled by the South African government), and approximately $25 million in Mozambique and Angola, as well as flourishing American trade with South Africa and the Portuguese territories. Thus, American policymakers were less than enthusiastic about a response to UDI which would damage Washington's relations with Pretoria and Lisbon. There was also the favorable balance in approximately $33 million of annual American trade with Rhodesia itself to consider.

Some American analysts within and outside the government were also concerned with the military implications of the Rhodesian question. Conservatives tended to accept the Rhodesian view that the future of the white regime was crucial to the strength of the white redoubt in southern Africa in its stand against "Communist infiltration" of the African continent. They found evidence to support their concern in the aid given by Communist states to the various southern African liberation forces. There was also a more tangible American stake in cooperative arrangements between the American and South African military. (These included overflight and landing rights for American military aircraft; South African surveillance of Soviet shipping off the cape; use of Capetown by American naval vessels, later to be terminated; and a NASA tracking station which reportedly served military purposes.) And, of course, Portugal was a NATO ally.

On the other hand, liberals could argue in 1965 that the continuing existence of the Rhodesian regime damaged what security interests the United States had in Africa by creating a situation in which the Soviet Union and the People's Republic of China could score points by supplying the guerrilla forces. In this view, the longer Smith's illegal rebellion persisted, the greater the danger of growing Communist influence in the region. (Liberals were limited in the emphasis which they could place on this argument, since they also denied that the Communist threat in Africa was very real.) Perhaps of more immediate concern than the possibility of the Communists' insidiously working their way into Africa itself was the prospect that an ambivalent American position on Southern Rhodesia would allow the Soviets to score constant debating points off American representatives at the United Nations.

The Johnson administration also had a particular stake in the residual but still lingering "special relationship" between the United States and the United Kingdom. In addition to protecting a basic American interest in the close political, security, and economic ties with the British, American officials in late 1965 hoped to influence British behavior with regard to Vietnam and defense arrangements in Asia generally. The President laid great stress on getting "more flags" involved in Saigon's behalf, and American officials hoped to translate the verbal support which Prime Minister Wilson had been giving to American policies in Vietnam into more active involvement. While there is no evidence that there was ever an explicit deal under which the United States would support Britain's Rhodesia policy in return for Wilson's approving noises about American efforts in Vietnam, there could be little doubt that if Washington embarrassed London by breaking with it on Rhodesia, Wilson would think again about continuing to go along on Vietnam. American officials also hoped in late 1965 to persuade the British not to reduce the size of their military forces stationed "east of Suez" as drastically as the British planned to do.

These contradictory American stakes in the Rhodesian sit-

uation in 1965 had defenders within the American government: anti-Smith advocates of relatively stronger American action against the Rhodesian regime, advocates of any policy
which would preserve American economic and military interests in Africa (including especially white southern Africa), and
those senior officials who disliked the problem and simply
wished it and the advocates would leave them alone.

DIVISIONS WITHIN THE BUREAUCRACY

The first group included the State Department's Bureau
of African Affairs (AF), Bureau of International Organization
Affairs (IO), the Office of the Legal Adviser (L), the U.S. Mission to the United Nations (USUN), the Bureau of Intelligence and Research (INR), and (at the time of UDI) the
National Security Council staff in the White House. Officials
in these offices joined together, with varying degrees of enthu-
siasm and effectiveness, to provide the more anti-Smith impulses within the bureaucracy. The Bureau of African Affairs
was naturally most interested in preserving and promoting
American relations with the new African governments. In addition, Assistant Secretary of State for African Affairs G. Mennen Williams and his chief deputy, J. Wayne Fredericks, both
had deep personal commitments to the principle of majority
rule in Southern Africa. Williams had been appointed by President Kennedy before Secretary Rusk was, an act meant to
demonstrate Kennedy's interest in African affairs. A former
governor of Michigan, Williams had a strong civil rights record; his views on justice for American blacks carried over to
his views about justice for Africans in southern Africa. Fredericks had developed a strong personal antipathy to apartheid
in a previous incarnation as managing director of a Kellogg
plant in South Africa.

Both Williams and Fredericks were foiled more often
than they were victorious in their bureaucratic struggles to
stiffen American policy against the white regimes of southern
Africa. Williams brought to his work great personal decency,

charm and dedication, but he was not renowned for bureau-cratic shrewdness. Waldemar Nielsen notes in his first-rate work, *The Great Powers and Africa,* that within the bureaucracy, the pro-African viewpoint was often inadequately defended: "Assistant Secretary Williams, who swung an effective broad-sword in the area of general salesmanship and political speech-making, had neither the taste nor the talent for the fine épée work required in day-to-day internal staff debate. Within the government, he came to be opposed by virtually the whole old-line Foreign Service establishment and his influ-ence as a policy voice steadily declined. Outside it, he became the target of a sustained barrage of criticism by Republicans in Congress, much of the press, and certain influential Demo-crats outside the Administration." [2]

Fredericks was more persistent in bureaucratic infighting than Williams, but he was often too obviously an advocate to be effective in a bureaucracy which prefers the passive to the active voice and prizes the illusion of "objectivity" when ap-proaching foreign policy problems. Fredericks' efforts to re-duce the scope of American ties to South Africa gored so many oxen in such agencies as Defense, Commerce, and NASA that his views on Southern Rhodesia could be dismissed by officials in those agencies as special pleadings. Even within the African Bureau, some of his subordinates recall that he was "romantic" and asked for "too much, too fast" in believing that increasing American disassociation from the South Afri-can regime was possible or would make much difference within South Africa. Although one or two of the career of-ficials within the bureau were actually more militant than Fredericks when it came to the Rhodesian problem, most re-mained suspicious of this man who had gained a reputation for committing one of the most terrible of bureaucratic gaffes: He made no secret of his beliefs, and treated foreign policy problems as something more than technical issues.

Ambassador Arthur Goldberg, the head of the U.S. dele-

[2] Waldemar Nielsen, *The Great Powers and Africa,* (New York: Praeger, 1969), p. 293.

gation to the United Nations, was another leading advocate of
firm opposition to the Smith regime. Like Williams, the
former Secretary of Labor and Justice of the Supreme Court
brought a strong commitment to civil rights within the United
States to his approach to the racial issues of southern Africa.
In addition, Goldberg and the members of his delegation had
an institutional reason for advocating a strong American response to UDI. The African Bureau in the State Department
was naturally concerned that the Rhodesian problem might
damage United States–African relations; at the United Nations, the pressures were not potential, but real. While African
delegates seldom pressed the American delegation with any
real fervor in a bilateral context, their votes and rhetoric were
a source of concern.

Goldberg's advocacy, like Williams' and Fredericks', was
limited in its effect. Goldberg wrote the President and top officials in the State Department with some frequency about
southern Africa. He also pressed his views at meetings with
these officials during his periodic visits to Washington. Rather
like Fredericks, who put others on the defensive, Goldberg
could not help but be an irritant to senior officials who considered southern African issues a diversion from major issues
like Vietnam and Europe. And Goldberg's pleas for a more
flexible American negotiating position on Vietnam did little to
make his arguments on southern Africa more welcome.

Goldberg considered his closest ally within the Washington bureaucracy to be Charles Runyon, in charge of African
affairs in the office of the Legal Adviser at the State Department. He also received support from State's Bureau of International Organization Affairs. It shared Goldberg's interest in
promoting an American policy which would be as acceptable
as possible to the African delegations at the United Nations.
While disagreeing with Goldberg occasionally on his tactical
decisions and recommendations, the Bureau of International
Organization Affairs joined the Bureau of African Affairs and
the Office of the Legal Adviser in generally sharing the Am-

bassador's views. Joining these anti-UDI forces within the Department was the Bureau of Intelligence and Research.

The men in charge of African affairs on the National Security Council staff in 1965, Robert Komer and Ulric Haynes, Jr., were also sympathetic to Fredericks' and Goldberg's position. Komer, who was responsible for both the Middle East and Africa and would in early 1966 be placed in charge of coordinating the American "pacification" effort in Vietnam, had developed a close working relationship with both Williams and Fredericks. A CIA analyst before joining the National Security Council staff under President Kennedy, Komer had long held the view that independence throughout Africa was inevitable and that the United States should do what it could to identify itself with anticolonialism. On a number of occasions, Secretary Dean Rusk and other senior State Department officials objected to Komer's taking action for the White House on certain proposals by the African Bureau before Rusk or one of the Under Secretaries had had a chance to go over them. In the spring of 1964, President Johnson decreed that African issues would be considered at the highest necessary levels in the State Department before reaching the White House. At the time of UDI, therefore, the alliance between Komer and the African Bureau was less influential than it had been under Kennedy and in the early days of the Johnson administration.

In addition, there was only so much that Komer and Haynes could do within the White House. President Johnson did not want to be bothered with African issues, especially after the diversions of President Kennedy's time during the Congo crises of the early 1960s. (Johnson's views on the Congo problem had been notably less anti-Tshombe than those of President Kennedy and most of his advisers.) McGeorge Bundy, the President's National Security Adviser, was generally sympathetic to Komer's point of view but had little time to spare for African issues. Thus, while personally sympathetic to the AF-USUN-L-IO-INR lobby within the State

Department, Komer and Edward K. Hamilton (who took over African affairs on the National Security Council staff in 1966) were also concerned to keep southern African issues from becoming a time-consuming source of irritation to the President.

The second group of offices and individuals within the bureaucracy—advocates of an American policy that would take minimal risks, if any, with regard to our economic and military interests in southern Africa—included NASA and the Departments of Commerce, Defense and the Treasury. Commerce (and, occasionally, the Bureau of Economic Affairs at the State Department) took the position that American investment in, and trade with, southern Africa was an important element in efforts to improve the shaky American balance of payments position and should not be threatened. In the absence of African threats to penalize American businessmen if the United States equivocated on southern Africa, the only immediate threat to American economic interests in the continent was that the United States might go too far in opposing the white regimes, not that it would fall short. Defense officials were most concerned with the benefits of American military cooperation with South Africa and Portugal; direct American military ties to the rest of Africa consisted only of a modest military assistance program, bases in Morocco and Libya, an agreement for use of a military airfield in Liberia, and a large military communications facility at Kagnew in Ethiopia.

Treasury shared the concern of Commerce about the U.S. balance of payments problem, and was also interested in avoiding any damage to American relations with South Africa that might interfere with South Africa's role as a supplier of gold to the international monetary system. NASA opposed any policy which might threaten its tracking stations in South Africa. These agencies had a far less important stake in Rhodesia, however, than they did in South Africa. While they therefore often found themselves at loggerheads with the State Department's African Bureau over American policy toward the latter, they did not weigh in so heavily on the American response to UDI.

It was the third group—the senior officials who wanted a low-risk, low-cost policy that would let them get on with more important business—which smothered the advocacy of Goldberg, Williams, Fredericks, and their allies. Since the President was not much interested in the issue, and Secretary Rusk had little time for it, Under Secretary of State George Ball was a crucial figure. Ball was both a Europeanist who saw as America's first interest on southern African issues the preservation of our ties with the British, and a skeptic who doubted the ability of the United States to shape societies and events in the third world. Ball, engaged in continuing and deepening opposition to American overinvolvement in Vietnam, neither wanted to waste his bureaucratic ammunition on what he saw as a secondary issue nor wished to see what he thought could be unnecessary American meddling in Rhodesia. He also believed that liberalization of the societies of southern Africa depended on economic development, and ridiculed the concept of economic sanctions. As he was to write later in his book, *The Discipline of Power:*

Rhodesia is now caught in the movement of swiftly paced history and there is little that I can usefully say about it at this time, other than to express the feeling—which I have long felt—that economic sanctions are, in the modern day, a romantic delusion—a wishful expression of man's hope to find some means, short of direct military force, to compel nations and peoples to take the desired political decisions. . . . Where military power is not employed and the enforcement of an embargo depends merely on the agreement of nations—whether or not expressed in a United Nations resolution—the result will more likely be annoyance than hardship.[3]

Ball's view of the importance of subordinating strictly African considerations to the American relationship with the

[3] George Ball, *The Discipline of Power* (Boston and Toronto: Little, Brown, 1968), p. 245.

British and indeed of encouraging the Europeans to oversee Western interests as the United States would do in Latin America, was shared, not surprisingly, by the State Department's Bureau of European Affairs (EUR). But EUR, supported by officials of the Bureau of Intelligence and Research, was prepared to go further than Ball in supporting strong measures by the British. EUR had long opposed American support for rebellions against established authority in Africa— i.e., the European colonial governments—and was therefore against the supply of covert, nonmilitary aid to some of the liberation movements in southern Africa. But it was consistent when it also favored American opposition to Smith's rebellion against established British authority in Rhodesia. The major reason for EUR's support of such a policy, of course, was that it feared we might irritate the British if we dragged our heels on Rhodesia.

American policy at the time of UDI was shaped almost completely by these contending forces within the government and by their perceptions of the *potential* reaction to their decisions by groups and individuals outside the government. "Potential" is emphasized, for at the time of UDI, there was very little in the way of public attention to the Rhodesian question. Groups which had been active in opposing white rule in southern Africa had devoted most of their time to South Africa rather than Southern Rhodesia or the Portuguese territories; they would continue to do so until 1972.

OUTSIDERS' ATTEMPTS

The most active anti-apartheid group in the United States, the American Committee on Africa (ACOA), was formed in 1953 by a group of civil rights activists who felt the need for an American organization that would support African independence movements. Since its birth, the ACOA has tried to publicize the issue of southern Africa and to discourage all cooperation (particularly economic) between the United States and the region's minority regimes; to provide assistance and organize speeches and publicity for African nationalists visiting the United States and the United Nations; in the words of its Executive Secretary, George Houser, "to give active, tangible support to the liberation of Africa from colonialism, racism, and other social and political diseases of the same nature," including funds for the legal defense and welfare of political prisoners and their families; and to put pressure on the U.S. government to adopt stronger anti-apartheid policies. In 1965, the organization claimed around 16,000 members. Its effect on American policy toward southern Africa was limited because it focused, at least until the late 1960s, on New York and the United Nations rather than on Washington and the American government. And its tactics in approaching the government were flawed, for the ACOA concentrated much of the fire it brought to bear on the African Bureau of the State Department—the group within the bureaucracy which had views closest to its own. Consequently, it failed to put pressure on the offices and individuals which the African Bureau itself was trying to move and irritated the Bureau by pestering it to push for actions which could not possibly be sold to the rest of the bureaucracy. Thus, even on South Africa, the issue which the ACOA emphasized, its influence was very slight.

Nor, in 1965, was there significant pressure on the government from the black community. The ACOA had helped form, in late 1961, the American Negro Leadership Conference on Africa. Representatives of the NAACP, CORE, the Urban League and the National Conference of Negro Women decided to join forces on African issues through ACOA. But this effort to coordinate attempts by black American leaders to influence American policy did not prove effective. The Leadership Conference died a quiet death after holding its third conference in five years in 1967. Thus, although statements by individual black leaders on southern Africa were given some weight by American officials, the black community as such was paid little attention on African issues. It was an important failure, for this was the only anti-apartheid group with a natural interest in Africa which also had political clout. It was also an understandable failure, for black leaders had more pressing concerns at home in the United States.

On the other side of the fence, conservative groups and spokesmen within the United States had been developing an increasing interest in Africa. The Katanga lobby provided a natural base for continuing right-wing interest in Rhodesia. In 1965, the American-African Affairs Association (AAAA) was formed by a number of veterans of the China and Katanga lobbies. Almost a third of the people on its letterhead were writers or editors of the *National Review*. Its cochairmen were William A. Rusher of the *National Review* and recently of the television debate series, "The Advocates," and Dr. Max Yergan. In the late 1940s Yergan had been, with Paul Robeson, a cochairman of the Council on African Affairs, a black organization of decidedly unconservative views. By 1964, Yergan had closed the ideological circle, having become a Goldwater activist and a favored guest of the South African government.

The AAAA considered its main function to be the dissemination of public information rather than private lobbying, however, and it was not a factor in the government's deliberations at the time of UDI. (Nor has it since been very effective in selling its point of view publicly, since it has been limited in both its funds and its activities.) Conservative pressure was to become a factor, especially through Congress, in 1966 and later. But it played little role in the crucial two months after UDI at the end of 1965. American policymakers worried about potential pressure from American companies with investments in South Africa and feared they might lose some conservative congressional allies on Vietnam. According to the Department of Commerce, at least 63 American firms had subsidiaries and affiliates in Southern Rhodesia in 1964. Of these, the ones which had the most important stakes in the territory included American Metals Climax, Union Carbide and various American tobacco companies. Others included Goodyear, IBM, Eastman Kodak, Minnesota Mining and Manufacturing, Socony-Mobil, National Cash Register, ITT, and J. Walter Thompson.

While Union Carbide was caught with a heavy investment in its chrome mines within Southern Rhodesia, American Metals Climax also had a major investment in Zambia—which it had shrewdly moved to protect in the years before 1965. The company was a major stockholder in the Rhodesian Selection Trust, Ltd. (RST), which had extensive holdings in Zambian copper mines. The leadership of American Metals Climax had decided by the late 1950s that the RST (later to become the Roan Selection Trust when headquartered in Lusaka) should be on the side of interracism in the Federation. It built the first interracial hotels in the Federation, and top local company officials had orders to hold regular meetings with African leaders. These actions enraged the white settlers, but stood the RST in good stead after Zambia achieved independence.

Despite American investments in Rhodesia, American government officials who were working on the problem in 1965 can recall very little pressure from American companies. (A White House official recalls that when there were complaints from American businessmen, he would do his friends in the State Department a dubious favor and refer the complaints to them.) The pressure was more in the opposite direction, as American officials sought compliance by American companies with the voluntary sanctions program that was adopted by the government.

THE POLICY SETTING

The final factor influencing the immediate American response to UDI was the context established by previous American policies toward Africa and Southern Rhodesia itself. Official American interest in African issues began to grow in the late 1950s—the first years of the African rush to independence. Vice President Nixon visited the continent in 1957. The Bureau of African Affairs was created in the State Department in the same year. As the newly independent African nations gained admission to the United Nations, at the end of the decade, American policy and rhetoric at the United Nations shifted slightly on South Africa. In 1958, the United States for the first time recognized the competence of the United Nations to express itself on the situation there, although it still opposed any hint of sanctions against the South African regime. Still, the Eisenhower administration refused to come to grips with the colonial issue at the United Nations. In 1960, the United States abstained in the vote on The Declaration on the Granting of Independence to Colonial Countries and Peoples. The resolution passed by a vote of 89 to 0. Joining the United States in abstaining were Australia, Belgium, the Dominican Republic, France, Portugal, Spain, South Africa, and the United Kingdom.

In the presidential election campaign of 1960, Senator John F. Kennedy called for new attention to African issues. His election promised a new approach. Senior officials like Chester Bowles, Adlai Stevenson, and W. Averell Harriman, as well as G. Mennen Williams, were strongly pro-African. The ambassadors appointed by Kennedy to American diplomatic missions in Africa were applauded by Africanists. But the problem, particularly on southern African issues, was that as the rhetoric of American policy toward Africa took on a more elevated tone, the gap between word and deed became more noticeable. New American interest in Africa conflicted inevitably with traditional U.S. relations with the European allies (now caught up, for the most part, in the work of disengaging from colonial rule), and European interests continued to dominate American policy. For example, despite his anticolonialist rhetoric first as Senator and then as President, Kennedy refused to take a lead in pressing Portugal on its territories in Africa, for fear of losing the American bases in the Azores and of coming under Republican political attacks which would follow such a loss. According to Arthur Schlesinger, Jr., the President asked Ambassador Stevenson in a meeting on July 18, 1962, what the French position would be on a U.N. resolution pressing Portugal on the issue: "Adlai said that France, as usual, would seek the best of both worlds. The President said, 'Well, let us try that this time.' " [4]

In addition, the attention of top officials in the Kennedy administration was naturally preoccupied by crises in Cuba, Berlin and Indochina. In Africa itself, it was the Congo and not southern Africa which dominated these officials' time and thought. While American policy toward the Congo could be judged by the administration as essentially a success—integrity of the Congo was preserved by the actions of the United Nations from mid-1960 to mid-1964—it also become an irritant to American policymakers. They were under attack by the Katanga lobby, led by Senator Thomas Dodd of Connecticut, and they disliked having their attention diverted to an African issue. Between 1960 and 1964 it also became conventional bureaucratic wisdom that the Chinese and Russians would be unsuccessful in efforts to dominate the new nations of Africa; the official perception of American interests in the continent dwindled accordingly. Waldemar Nielsen convincingly argues that November 24–26, 1964, marked the end of the American honeymoon with Africa. Suddenly swooping on Stanleyville, American and Belgian armed forces carried out an airborne rescue of several hundred white hostages being held by rebel forces. "Even in the context of the tangled and emotionally charged history of the recurrent Congo crisis," Nielsen notes, "the operation aroused an astonishing volume of angry debate in Africa and throughout the world." [5] Although carried out with the permission of the Congolese government, the action was considered by many Africans to be a violation of African sovereignty. And the fact that American forces had joined with Belgian forces did little to make the Africans less angry at the United States.

President Johnson was reportedly hesitant about approving the operation, but had gone along with his senior advisers

[4] Arthur M. Schlesinger, Jr., *A Thousand Days* (Boston and Toronto: Little, Brown, 1965), p. 582.

[5] Nielsen, *The Great Powers,* p. 308.

despite the warnings of officials in AF and IO. As a consequence of his reluctant decision, the administration had been berated both by the Africans and by critics within the United States. The irony of the Stanleyville operation was that it helped persuade Johnson that the United States should avoid future "Stanleyvilles" anywhere in Africa, including Southern Rhodesia; yet in retrospect, to the Africans, it was proof that Europeans and Americans would intervene against black rebels in the Congo but would flinch from military confrontation with white rebels like Ian Smith.

Dwarfed by but linked to the problems of the Congo and South Africa, Southern Rhodesia seemed among the least of American problems in a problem-filled postwar world. According to Patrick Keatley, the Truman administration had given discreet support to the British in 1948 when they asked the Rhodesians to keep their franchise system nonracial in appearance. But this was apparently an exceptional bit of interest, and American concern over Rhodesia did not become evident until the early 1960s. As the breakup of the Federation drew near, official American policy was to support the British in what, after all, was "their problem." This was to be the central theme of U.S. policy until 1969. For example, during the Security Council's debate in September, 1963, over British plans to turn local military forces over to the Rhodesians, American representatives gave their British colleagues the most loyal support, arguing both that the Council should not act on the matter at that time and that the British terms for dissolution of the Federation would not produce a deterioration of the existing situation in Southern Rhodesia. The United States then abstained on a dissenting resolution while the British vetoed it. (Throughout the pre-UDI period, the United States generally abstained on measures regarding Southern Rhodesia. The British rarely voted, considering the problem none of the world organization's business.)

But internally, the American government was divided in its opinion of British policy in central and southern Africa. Wayne Fredericks and others believed that the stronger the position allowed the white settlers by the British, the greater would be the problems for the independent state to emerge from Northern Rhodesia. The African Bureau was also strongly concerned at indications of British ambivalence about Katanga. Secret meetings between Moise Tshombe, President of the rebellious province, and Sir Roy Welensky, the Prime Minister of the Federation, increased the fears of these American officials that an independent Northern Rhodesia could be strangled in the lines between an independent Katanga and the white settlers of Southern Rhodesia. Together with opposition from white settlers within Northern Rhodesia, such an alliance might have denied leadership to Kaunda and supported, in his place, African leaders less independent of white power in southern Africa. But the African Bureau's views were challenged by the European Bureau, and senior levels of the State Department supported the Europeanist view. No pressure was put on the British to be more steadfast in opposition to the Katangese rebellion.

Any independent government of Zambia, and especially one which was opposed by the white settlers in Salisbury, would require external assistance. American support for the new state was put to the test in 1965. In May, a meeting of British and American planners was held in Washington. They considered how much aid Zambia would need if the Rhodesians declared their independence and the Rhodesian-Zambian border were closed. The conclusion was that Zambia could survive, but alternative routes from Zambia to the outside world would have to be improved. It was also decided that more information was needed for more refined planning. By the time of UDI in November, the plans had not progressed much further.

While the planners wrestled with their contingencies in May, Kaunda also presented Washington with a request for assistance in constructing the Tan-Zam railroad. The request was hotly debated within the American bureaucracy. The African Bureau strongly supported the request, as did cables from American diplomatic representatives in Africa. Komer lent his voice, arguing that it was similar to the Egyptians' request in the mid-1950s for aid in building the Aswan Dam; Western refusal had forced Nasser to turn to the Soviets, and history could repeat itself now in central Africa. Surveyors from the People's Republic of China had already arrived in Tanzania. But these arguments failed. One American official who favored granting the Zambian request recalls: "What killed us was the money." AID, the Bureau of the Budget, and Treasury opposed the project. It would have cost about $400 million and there were technical questions about the economic value of the railroad compared to its cost.

Wayne Fredericks returned from a trip to Africa when the Zambian request was under consideration. He reported to Ball that the American ambassadors in East Africa and Zambia favored the Zambian request. One of Ball's associates told Fredericks the project was a "$500 million boondoggle." The problem was that whatever the merits of the proposal in terms of the politics of central Africa, the administration was having enough trouble getting its AID bills through the Congress without adding a new commitment to a project costing almost half a billion dollars. The President decided to refuse Kaunda.

The decision might have gone the other way in the early 1960s when the thought of Chinese laborers working their way into the heart of Africa might have seemed more threatening. By 1965, it was more obvious that independent Africa could survive non-Western assistance, and American resources were hostage to Vietnam. To take some of the sting out of its refusal to help with the railroad, Washington offered Kaunda a survey of the rough road between Lusaka and Dar es Salaam. American aid later contributed to the improvement and hard surfacing of a section of the route in southern Tanzania—one of the few American aid projects benefiting Zambia in the years after UDI.[6]

[6] After the Zambian-Rhodesian border was closed in early 1973, the government in Lusaka and a U.N. mission sent to study the situation appealed for aid to Zambia. In June, an American program loan of $5 million was approved; about $25 million of credit from the Export-Import Bank was

The United States would not commit itself to large-scale assistance to Zambia in the event of UDI, but it did tell the British it would take part in an airlift of coal into, and copper out of, Zambia, if need be. And during the summer and early fall of 1965 it adopted a diplomatic stance designed to support British efforts to head off a move to independence by Smith and his supporters. In May, American respresentatives announced that their government would not recognize a Unilateral Declaration of Independence. On October 5, the President asked Prime Minister Wilson to tell Smith that Washington opposed any such action by the Rhodesians. A message was conveyed directly to Smith on October 8, stating that the United States could not condone any political arrangement in Southern Rhodesia that was unresponsive to the interests of the vast majority of the population. On October 29, the President sent a personal message to Smith, stating that UDI would be a tragic mistake that would serve the true interests of no one. The United States, the message said, had to make known to Smith its strong opposition to any such decision. It would not change its course of firm support for the position of the British in opposing such a rebellious act. The President expressed the hope that Smith and his colleagues would avoid a course which, beyond its other consequences, would inevitably break the strong ties of friendship and understanding which bound the United States and Southern Rhodesia together in war and peace. (As drafted in the African Bureau, the American messages reportedly were more specific in their threats of dire consequences should the Rhodesians proceed. But the messages were softened at the top levels of the State Department.) At the United Nations, meanwhile, Ambassador Goldberg pledged that Washington would "take the necessary concrete steps" against any Rhodesian government that illegally declared its independence.

---

also made available. American aid to Zambia from 1946 to 1972 totalled $68.3 million, of which $34.7 million was in Ex-Im loans and $22.4 million was extended through the British to what was then Northern Rhodesia.

The United States also sent a message to the South Africans expressing the hope that they would discourage Smith from taking the leap; it followed and supported a rather tougher British demarche in Pretoria. Judging from Vorster's comment, quoted earlier, about the Rhodesian failure to follow his advice, these messages may have had some effect on the South Africans.

REACTION TO UDI

While American diplomacy was thus actively engaged just prior to UDI, planning for the event itself lagged. Although it had been clear for some time that there was a good chance Smith would defiantly proceed, when the day arrived on November 11, the American government had not yet decided on its response. For some months, there had been working-level consultations between American and British officials on contingency plans for a joint response to UDI, but the plans of each remained general in substance (especially on the British side). Nor had they been approved at responsible levels within the American government. As drawn up by State Department officers below the Assistant Secretary level, the plans reportedly included a review of those American ties to Rhodesia which might be cut, the kinds of logistic support the British might request in the unlikely event they decided to drop troops in Southern Rhodesia, and diplomatic scenarios which, according to some of those involved, included recommending to the British that they at least not continue to rule out the use of force in their public statements on the issue.

As it happened, President Johnson had scheduled for November 11, 1965, a full-scale foreign policy review with his senior advisers at his ranch. Secretaries Rusk and McNamara, George Ball, McGeorge Bundy, and Walt W. Rostow, then the chairman of the State Department's Policy Planning Council, were in Texas when the African Bureau at State began to consider the appropriate American response to the news of UDI. A telephone call was reportedly placed from the Bureau to

Rusk. His reaction was cautious. The contingency plans needed review and approval; they were immediately sent by plane to the ranch. Meanwhile, Rusk's public remarks on UDI that day consisted primarily of a holding action. Speaking to the press after the foreign policy review, which lasted about six hours, Rusk said that the American government deplored the "unilateral action of the white minority government of Rhodesia in illegally seizing power." The United States, he said, would recall its Consul General in Rhodesia and terminate the activities of the United States Information Service there. Further sanctions would be withheld, however, until Ambassador Goldberg stated the full American position on Rhodesia at the United Nations the following day, and "we see what Britain does."

Rusk's statement suggested that American policy on Rhodesia would remain within the old parameters: We would not get out in front of the British but would make the gestures necessary to keep the Africans and others from singling out the United States for particular pressure on the issue. Yet with UDI, the anxiety of American officials at the middle levels of the bureaucracy grew. The United States was to follow the British lead, yet too often—as now, at UDI—officials in Washington simply did not know where the British were leading them or what, specifically, London intended to do. Some British officials at the middle and senior levels who were concerned with the problem now agree that, in the words of one, there was "not enough coordination in advance and in the first days after UDI." In those first days, London was not asking Washington to offer real advice on the measures each would take. Rather, American embassy officials in London were being filled in at the foreign office on British plans as they were made, and the American government was asked to support them.

By the day following UDI, however, decisions as to the first full response of the United States had been made, and Ambassador Goldberg announced at the United Nations a series of American measures: A comprehensive embargo was being placed on the shipment of all arms and military equipment to Southern Rhodesia; American private travel to Southern Rhodesia would be discouraged; Americans were advised they could no longer be assured of normal protective services and that they must have British, not Southern Rhodesian, visas; U.S. quotas for the importation of Rhodesian sugar were being suspended; action on all applications for U.S. government loans and credit and investment guarantees to Southern Rhodesia was being suspended; and diplomatic status was being withdrawn from the Minister for Southern Rhodesian Affairs in the British Embassy in Washington and from his staff. Goldberg said that the United States was considering further steps as well.

These steps were considered by an interagency working group within the American government. It included representatives of Commerce, Treasury, Defense, the White House, and, from State, AF, IO, EUR, the Bureau of Economic Affairs (E), and William D. Rogers, representing Under Secretary Ball.

Ball brought Rogers, a member of a Washington law firm, into the Department at the time of UDI to serve as a special coordinator of American activities regarding Rhodesia. Ball had earlier told Prime Minister Wilson that he would appoint such a coordinator for Rhodesian affairs and had mentioned the possibility of asking Thomas K. Finletter, the former Secretary of the Air Force. President Johnson, who was notoriously sensitive about his role in making new appointments, reportedly killed the Finletter appointment when he learned of it. Ball had then approached Rogers, with whom he had previously worked. He is said to have told Rogers that Goldberg, Williams, and Fredericks were trying to push a harder policy than Ball wanted, yet he did not have time to control the course of bureaucratic events on the issue. Rogers agreed to take the job of acting as Ball's lid on the rest of the bureaucracy, on the condition that no cables issuing instructions for action on Rhodesia would be allowed to leave the Department without his clearance.

In essence, Ball, Rogers, and the other officials who were most influential in shaping policy toward Rhodesia—Williams, Fredericks, Goldberg, Anthony Solomon (Assistant Secretary for Economic Affairs), Joseph Sisco (Assistant Secretary for International Organization Affairs), and U. Alexis Johnson (Under Secretary for Political Affairs)—faced four questions about the American response to UDI. Should the United States support the British if they decided to use force, and what advice should be given to the British on the subject? What diplomatic stance should the United States assume, especially at the United Nations? What kind of economic measures should be taken against the Rhodesian regime? And what should be the private position taken by the United States in its talks with the British about Rhodesia, whatever its public protestations of support for London's policies? In general, the career officers in AF and IO supported Goldberg, Williams and Fredericks in pressing strong measures on Ball, U. Alexis Johnson, and Rogers.

With regard to the use of force, the judgment at higher levels was that, in the words of one former official, it would be "costly and ineffective." A paper by Rogers reaching this conclusion was given to British military planners who visited Washington in mid-December. The United States had consistently opposed the use of force by the British, partly because they would have required American logistical support. It would also have implied a further commitment of American assistance to the Zambians, since they were hostage to Rhodesian countermeasures (for example, the destruction of the power works at Kariba). Perhaps more important than the physical resources which the United States would have to commit to such an operation were the potential political consequences within the United States. President Johnson, no less than Rusk and Ball, had no desire to call down upon the administration the kind of harassment they had received from supporters of Katanga during the Congo crisis. Their view was initially shared by even the most militant middle-level officials. As one recalls, "At the time, everybody had the Congo very much in mind, and was very cautious about urging any kind of force that might blow up all over the place."

Within a few weeks of UDI, however, it was becoming clear that economic sanctions promised no quick end to the problem. While both the British and the American governments had publicly ruled out the use of force, discussion of military contingency plans between British and American working-level officials were continuing to take place. A number of American officials can recall that during this period British planners checked on available American logistic facilities—asking, for example, whether American fuel supplies held at Ascension Island might be available to the British for military purposes. It is clear that many officials in the State Department believed that there was life in the force issue at the beginning of December. The OAU was about to meet and decide whether an African military force would be dispatched. Kaunda was offering Zambia as a base for a British military attack. He also said at a news conference on December 3 that if Britain refused to dispatch troops at least to "neutralize" both sides of the Kariba Dam, "the alternative may be to send for American troops."

Within the State Department, AF, IO, L, the Bureau of Intelligence and Research (INR) and even EUR reached a consensus: Economic measures were not serving to keep events under control, and the United States should discuss with the British alternative plans for military action against Rhodesia. The preferred scenario would be for the British to drop troops on key facilities within Rhodesia including Kariba, bridges across the Zambezi, and the Wankie coal fields. British action against these facilities would avoid the bloodshed involved in an attack on Salisbury, and yet the Rhodesians would be under great pressure to settle quickly if they did not have access either to Wankie's coal or Kariba's power. Under Secretary Johnson killed the Bureau's recommendation, as he had previously vetoed other AF recommendations on southern Africa. Although couched always in terms of a discussion with the *British* of an action that the *British* would take pursuant to a *British* decision, even the suggestion of the possibility of using force was out of bounds. Senior officials, looking beyond the Rhodesian problem, refused to countenance anything which implied the possibility of American involvement in a military drama in Africa. The Rhodesians would fight; the outcome would be uncertain. And the Johnson administration was having enough trouble at home, as a result of Vietnam and the intervention in the Dominican Republic the previous spring, without helping to make Rhodesia any more of a front-page issue than it had to be. Occasional and informal conversations among the middle levels of the British and American bureaucracies on the subject of the public use of force were to continue into early 1966. But the issue was, for all intents and purposes, dead, as far as the American government was concerned.

The American position at the United Nations after UDI was decided upon quickly and with little argument. American statements would support the British and help them arrange the compromises with the African delegations that would allow the United Nations to act. On November 11, the General Assembly passed a resolution which condemned UDI, invited the United Kingdom immediately to implement previous United Nations resolutions on Southern Rhodesia, and recommended that the Security Council urgently consider the matter. The United States voted in favor of the resolution, together with one hundred other nations. South Africa and Portugal opposed it, France abstained and the United Kingdom did not vote. Charles Yost, speaking for the United States, stated that his government had voted for the resolution in order to express immediately its condemnation of the Rhodesian regime's "unlawful act." But he reminded the Assembly that the United States maintained its reservations about the previous U.N. resolutions on Rhodesia. In other words, the United States still opposed calls upon the British to use force.

Eight days later, on November 20, 1965, the Security Council acted. Resolution 217 condemned UDI and called upon the United Kingdom to quell the rebellion. It also called upon all states neither to recognize the Smith regime nor to entertain any diplomatic or other relations with it, to provide it with no arms or other military equipment, to do their utmost to break all economic relations with Southern Rhodesia, and to include in these efforts an embargo on oil and petroleum products. The Resolution represented a compromise between drafts submitted by the British and 36 African states. The African draft would have *imposed* an oil embargo instead of *asking* member states to cut off oil exports to Southern Rhodesia. It would also have included a provision for employing "all enforcement measures," which implied the use of force. Ambassador Goldberg played a key role in finding the compromise that helped the British avoid casting a veto. Goldberg, who had been ill with a virus infection and did not participate in the negotiations over the draft resolutions until the very last stages, suggested a key amendment to the African draft. The draft had stated that the situation constituted "a threat to international peace and security." Such a finding by the Security Council would have opened the way to the use of force or mandatory sanctions. Goldberg suggested rephrasing the statement to read that "the situation . . . is of extreme seriousness . . . its continuance in time constitutes a threat to international peace and security." The phrase "its continuance in time" allowed the British to interpret the resolution as calling for the possible application of Article 33. This section of the Charter provides that in any situation "the continuation of which" is likely to endanger peace and security, efforts be made to find a solution by negotiations and other peaceful means. The Africans, on the other hand, could interpret Goldberg's phrase to mean that, if the situation persisted, the Security Council could reopen discussion of the question of further sanctions or even force. Calculated and precise ambiguity often lies at the heart of successful diplomacy; Ambassador Goldberg's intervention was a model of its kind. Adding a rhetorical bouquet to the diplomatic assist he had given the British as they wriggled away from the veto, Goldberg's statement on the resolution praised the "gallant" and "prodigious" efforts made by Prime Minister Wilson to bring the rebellion to an end.

The Africans were disappointed, but UDI had at least made the British agree that the Security Council should be involved in the Rhodesian question. And immediately after the vote on Resolution 217, Ambassador Goldberg provided a small sweetener. He announced that the United States would do more than cancel the 1966 quota for sugar imports from Southern Rhodesia. It had since learned, he said, that "the entire 1965 sugar quota, amounting to approximately 9,500 tons is now on the high seas in transit to the United States." The President had ordered the suspension of the sugar quota for 1965 as well, and had directed that that "shipment from Southern Rhodesia would not be accepted."

Cancellation of the 1965 sugar quota was one of a number of further economic measures decided upon in the interagency group and approved by senior officials in the weeks following Goldberg's initial listing of measures on November 12. On November 13, it was reported that the State Department had halted the sale of 36 diesel locomotives to Southern Rhodesia. On December 8, the United States gave control of Rhodesian foreign exchange accounts in the United States to a new Board of the Rhodesian Reserve Bank which had just been appointed by the British government. The Rhodesian government thus lost control over the accounts; the total amount involved was estimated at about $1 million.

But these few American measures, and the measures taken by the British, were clearly not enough to head off what seemed to be a coming diplomatic confrontation with the Africans in December. And to American officials in AF and IO, the British seemed less concerned than they were themselves. The question was whether the British should be urged to take firmer actions. Senior officials would not allow any hint that the United States would favor the use of force. The issue to be discussed with the British, at the end of November and the beginning of December, was the possibility of an oil embargo, as called for in the Security Council's resolution of November 20.

A joint British-American working committee had been formed soon after UDI to coordinate existing economic measures being taken by the two governments. According to one official who participated in its deliberations, the committee studied the idea of such an embargo in late November, and reportedly concluded that it would probably be ineffective. There would inevitably be gaps in the embargo because of predicted South African and Portuguese nonparticipation. But the group thought it would still be worthwhile, for whatever marginal effects it would have on the Rhodesian regime and as a diplomatic device with the Africans. American officials urged that it be announced then, before the coming OAU meeting on December 5. But the British left their decision on the matter for the middle of the month, when Prime Minister Wilson was scheduled to meet with President Johnson.

A careful reader of the administration's statements concerning Southern Rhodesia on December 16, 1965 (the day Prime Minister Wilson was speaking at the United Nations and then flying to Washington to see the President) could have detected a continuing division in the government between those who thought the United States should press the British to move more quickly and those who wanted to see the United States support the British but do nothing that would let the United States get into an exposed position on the issue. Speaking at a meeting of the State Department American Legion Post, Assistant Secretary Williams emphasized the readiness of the United States to support further economic measures by Britain against the Rhodesian regime, and noted that the British had already applied a "broad range" of sanctions. Then he went further. "Speed is a critical factor in the situation, however," he added. "African nations already are impatient with Britain's choice of measures. Many of them are pressing for direct military action. And a few would consider turning to the Communists for help on the ground that the West is not moving fast enough. Obviously, the Communists would be happy to rush into this situation if they get a chance." On the same day, at a speech at a NATO conference in Paris, Secretary Rusk did not imply similar impatience while declaring American support for British measures against Rhodesia. A week earlier, Rusk had said in a news conference that the United States was considering an oil embargo—and then expressed doubt about its effectiveness.

Wilson had suggested at an impromptu news conference at Kennedy International Airport, on his arrival in the United States on December 15, that a final decision by his government on an oil embargo would be made after his talks with the President. The British had also, he said, been consulting with other nations about the possibility of such an embargo. The British Prime Minister obviously wanted to share the responsibility as widely as possible. On the same day, President Johnson was meeting with his advisers to go over the positions he would take with Wilson. Ball took William D. Rogers along with him to the meeting with the President and his senior foreign policy advisers. Most of the meeting was taken up by a long discussion of NATO burden-sharing. Defense issues were to be the main topic of the talks between the two leaders. The President's position on Rhodesia was worked out more quickly. It would be what it had been: a low posture, an effort to be both pro-British and pro-African, with the emphasis on the former. Pressing the British too hard might damage U.S.-U.K. relations and would, at the least, make Rhodesia another issue to which presidential energy and time might have to be devoted. But, according to a number of those who knew him during this period, Johnson was also very concerned with his standing with black leaders. Martin Luther King, Jr., among others, had strongly attacked UDI in a speech in early November. Johnson would not want to be caught lagging behind the British, and thus make himself vulnerable to criticism by black Americans or Africans over Rhodesia.

The meeting on the sixteenth went well. As the limousine

bringing Wilson from Andrews Air Force Base drew up at the
White House, Johnson came out to greet the Prime Minister.
As they shook hands, Wilson asked if the President had recov-
ered from his recent operation. As the President said he felt
"wonderful," Wilson exclaimed, "You look good; you look
fine; you look so well."

The Prime Minister is said to have made a bad impression
on the President in their earlier meetings, but his performance on Rhodesia at this encounter impressed the American
leader. Wilson described the problem clearly, and gave the
President the impression that he knew what he was doing and
understood the political implications of his actions. This reinforced Johnson's inclination to let the British call the tune,
within limits. From that meeting on, Johnson reportedly considered Wilson one of his friends among foreign leaders,
others notably being Ayub Kahn of Pakistan and Ludwig Er-
hard of West Germany. His personal relationship with Wilson
became another tie that bound stated American policy on
Rhodesia to Wilson's course, to the zigs as well as the zags.

The President agreed at their meeting to Wilson's request
for American support of an oil embargo, including American
participation in an airlift to get oil supplies to Zambia. (The
Rhodesians would inevitably prohibit the transit of oil to Zambia across their own territory, once under the embargo themselves.) The following day Britain announced its oil embargo.
The American government publicly "welcomed" the decision
and advised American oil companies to comply with the British order. On December 28, a formal embargo was placed on
the supply of U.S. petroleum and petroleum products to
Southern Rhodesia. At the same time, plans were being laid
for American participation in an airlift of oil supplies to Zambia. The first American plane (a chartered Pan American jet
transport) carrying 26 tons of oil landed at Elisabethville in
the Congo on January 4. From there the oil was carried by rail
to Zambia. The American airlift continued until April 30; it
carried a total of 3,639,028 U.S. gallons. The cost of tran-
sporting this fuel came to more than one dollar a gallon.

In the first months of 1966 the American government took other actions as well in support of Wilson's strategy of increasing economic pressures on the Smith regime. On January 10, the State Department announced that American manufacturers had agreed to discontinue imports of asbestos and lithium from Rhodesia. Imports of these products had amounted to $3,846,000 in 1964, out of total American imports from Southern Rhodesia of $10,470,000. On January 28, the government asked American chrome importers to stop buying Rhodesian chrome. This request followed a British order of January 20 banning the export of chrome and other products from Rhodesia. But the U.S. government's request to American chrome importers was undercut by an exception to the ban given by Her Majesty's government to British importers of chrome, under which 9,000 tons of high-grade chrome ore were shipped to England in the period January 20–January 26.

On February 9, the American government announced that it had "informed" U.S. tobacco companies of a British Order-in-Council of February 8 banning tobacco exports from Southern Rhodesia. American officials said they were confident the American companies would halt their imports of Rhodesian tobacco, which had been worth a relatively small $750,000 in 1965. On February 26, the Commerce Department announced that it would henceforth require licenses for virtually all American exports to Rhodesia. On March 18, it announced a ban on a wide range of exports which included almost any commodity of any value to the Rhodesian economy. This was legally possible under the Export Control Act; the government had to continue to rely on persuasion, however, when it came to imports from Rhodesia. With the exception of tobacco and sugar, a ban on imports would have required either new legislation or a mandatory ban on such imports ordered by the United Nations. The American government would then have had legal authority to act under the United Nations Participation Act, as was later the case. In addition to the measures just listed, the United States also as-

sisted the British, according to sources in London, by providing Her Majesty's government with *ad hoc* sporadic intelligence
reports on the Rhodesian economy.

RELATIONS WITH LONDON

But all of these measures were taken by American officials in the knowledge that the British program of economic
pressure on the Rhodesian regime was not working. American
officials within AF and IO and on the NSC staff were becoming increasingly irritated with the British, who "never seemed
to have done their homework on either economic or military
questions," as one former American official put it. By the
beginning of January, some American officials were beginning
to wonder what British intentions were. One remembers noting that there were two ways in which Wilson could achieve his
stated objective of bringing an end to the illegal regime. "You
could destroy it," he recalls telling his superiors, "or you could
legalize it." So, confused and suspicious about British policy
and uncertain of where events were taking them, American
officials continued to work in those first months of 1966 at
keeping public step with the British—but always a step behind
them. It was the safest diplomatic position to be in, but frus-
trating for officials who cared about what was actually happening in Rhodesia.

The question remained of what stance American officials
should take in private with the British. Should they push London toward more comprehensive sanctions? Should they say
nothing, and try to follow the ambiguous British lead as best
they could? Or should they adopt the lowest risk policy possible, and try to make sure that the British did not lead us into
a position which would prove costly to American interests?

Some American officials at the middle levels adopted the
first position in their informal talks with their British opposite
numbers. These British officials, in fact, shared the frustration
of their American friends. But it was clear to both that they
had lost their respective bureaucratic struggles for more forceful action, and were simply commiserating with each other.

The official American position—the third course—was conveyed to the British by Under Secretary Ball and others. The British Ambassador in Washington, others in the British Embassy and high-ranking officials in the foreign office were told by the Americans that Wilson's "quick kill" strategy could not work. In fact, their prediction was self-fulfilling, since the United States was not prepared to offer the vast amounts of aid to Zambia that Wilson's strategy would have required and that the British were certainly not prepared to offer if the United States would not share the burden. Indeed, the American message to the British was still more limiting than that. Speaking officially, Ball told British officials that they could not count on America's bailing them out if they took measures against Rhodesia that seriously damaged their own balance of payments position—already in a shaky position. This meant, of course, avoiding any action that might bring Britain into economic confrontation with South Africa. Ball's thinking was that economic sanctions were simply driving Smith into total obduracy. No embargo of this kind could work effectively unless it were backed with force, and the use of force was impossible because of Southern Rhodesia's geo-political position. Why, therefore, encourage the British to proceed in a direction which could exacerbate the United States' own balance of payments problems, when such a course could not succeed? At the same time, the United States had to support the British in the efforts they did make, since a failure to do so would have made the situation worse and placed the onus for a failure of those measures on the United States. And in any case, Ball believed that one should try to support an ally even when one disagreed with its approach. Hence the thrust of his message: "We are behind you, but don't go too fast." It may have been unnecessary, since Wilson seems hardly to have been of a mind to open the throttle.

On April 9, 1966, the British gained the authorization of the Security Council to use force in order to prevent oil from reaching Southern Rhodesia by sea through Beira. The British had requested the authority on an emergency basis, since the tanker *Manuela* was nearing the port with a full load of oil for the Rhodesians. African draft amendments to the resolution that would have committed Britain to use force to overthrow the Smith regime and to cut off Southern Rhodesia's land communications with South Africa and Mozambique were defeated. The resolution, as it was finally passed, made no reference to the oil that was being sent into Southern Rhodesia by rail and highway from South Africa.

Ambassador Goldberg lent support to the British position, saying that the United States was convinced of London's sincerity and advising the members of the Council to "proceed practically to do what we can agree on." Goldberg also argued that the resolution did not preclude further action by the Security Council: "And this Council, as before, remains seized of the problem so that the additional measures which become necessary, if they do become necessary, can be ventilated here, debated here and decided upon here."

Despite such support in public for the United Kingdom, the Beira embargo made American officials of all persuasions on the Rhodesian problem still more concerned about British handling of the matter. Some were complaining to British journalists that they were uninformed about British strategy and tactics. While Goldberg and the African Bureau still wished for a more active British policy, other senior officials feared that the British were drawing the United States into a widening problem. The Security Council resolution had noted its grave concern at the arrival of one oil tanker at Beira and the approach of another and had determined that "the resulting situation constitutes a threat to the peace." The Security Council is authorized by Article 39 of the Charter to make such a determination; once it is made, the Council is obligated to take such mandatory enforcement measures as it deems fit under Chapter VII to deal with that threat to the peace. In this case, the threatening situation was specifically the shipment of oil to Beira. But it was also a precedent: This was the first time that the Security Council had found that any element of the Rhodesian crisis presented a "threat to the peace." According to a report filed on April 13 by the Washington correspondent of the *Financial Times,* there were grave doubts at the highest levels of the American government about the British decision to invoke Chapter VII, since it could lead to increased pressure for mandatory economic sanctions that might be extended to Portugal and South Africa. As a result, American policy would become more cautious still. The article predicted that the United States would continue to support British sanctions, but if they were extended to South Africa and Portugal the United States would be a "most unwilling partner." Yet if Lord Caradon, the British representative at the United Nations, vetoed such an extension of the sanctions, it would be extremely doubtful that he would find Goldberg publicly behind him. (And, in fact, an American official was sent by President Johnson specifically to tell the British that the United States would not join in vetoing such a measure.) If the British used force, the article noted, Washington might privately approve but the British could not expect overt help. And if Wilson entered negotiations with Smith, Washington would not endorse the deal lest the Africans be offended.

Within two weeks, the British announced the beginnings of what became the *Tiger* talks with the Rhodesians. The United States adopted a very careful public stance of restrained support for the negotiating effort but silence as to its view of the terms which might be worked out. (A British "sell-out" could then have placed Washington in a very difficult position.) At the United Nations, as the Africans pressed in May, 1966, for a new resolution asking Britain to use force, Goldberg joined Caradon in urging the Security Council to forgo further pressure on the Rhodesian regime that might impede British efforts to find a "just and peaceful solution." (The resolution failed to gain a majority.) Goldberg even suggested that the United States arrange a meeting on Rhodesia between Prime Minister Wilson and African diplomats at the United Nations, at which Wilson could describe his diplomatic efforts. The African delegates turned Goldberg down, reportedly because many of them feared that they might be compromised by any meeting that seemed to imply African approval of whatever deal was cooked up by the British and Rhodesian negotiators. On October 23, 1966, the General Assembly passed a resolution, by 86 votes to 2 with 18 abstentions (including the United States, Britain and France), which declared that the talks between the British and Rhodesians jeopardized the rights of Rhodesia's black population. While the American delegation abstained on the vote, they attacked the resolution on the grounds that it prejudged the question and imputed motives to London that the American delegation believed did not exist.

American support for the British against African attacks at the United Nations was balanced by the general rhetoric of American leaders on the Rhodesian question. On May 26, 1966, President Johnson invited a group of African ambassadors to the White House to observe the third anniversary of the founding of the OAU. In the first major speech by an American President devoted exclusively to African questions, Johnson blasted "the narrow-minded and outmoded policy which in some parts of Africa permits the few to rule at the expense of the many. . . . The government of the United States cannot, therefore, condone the perpetuation of political or racial injustice anywhere in the world. . . . We are giving every encouragement and support to the efforts of the United Kingdom and the United Nations to restore legitimate government in Rhodesia." But the President did not commit himself to any new, specific action on the issue—except further aid to Zambia, which was not soon forthcoming. After his speech, official spokesmen tried to emphasize its importance while denying that it contained any departure from existing policy. Johnson's specific criticism of the Rhodesian regime was contrasted by reporters with his failure to mention South Africa by name. The spokesman tried gently to suggest that Johnson meant, in fact, to be critical of the South Africans. But the spokesman's assertion of this fact was as convoluted and cautious as American policy toward southern Africa generally: "I would say that the President is not trying to be undisturbing."

On September 22, 1966, Goldberg re-stated at the United

Nations, America's objective with regard to Rhodesia: "to open the full power and responsibility of nationhood to all the people of Rhodesia—not just six percent of them." His statement implied (as he could never state explicitly) what was, in fact, the case: that most American officials were opposed to a British sell-out in the *Tiger* negotiations. London had reportedly approached Washington during the summer about the possibility of yielding further to Smith, and the American reaction had been cool.

SANCTIONS

Limited in the concessions he could make by the United States as well as the Africans and anti-Smith opinion within Britain, Wilson had to hope that he could instead wrest significant concessions from Smith. He could not, and by the end of November it seemed likely that the talks would fail. Sir Saville Garner of the Commonwealth Relations Office left for Washington and Ottawa on November 29, 1966, to discuss British plans to take the Rhodesian issue to the United Nations again. His trip was meant to signal to the Rhodesians that the British would stand by their commitment to the Commonwealth to ask for mandatory sanctions by the United Nations if a negotiated solution could not be found.

He found that key American officials were quite prepared to commit the United States to the support of mandatory sanctions ordered by the United Nations. And they were prepared to go further than the British with regard to the scope of those sanctions. The American position reflected some shifts within the bureaucracy. Ball had just resigned as Under Secretary, and had been replaced by Nicholas Katzenbach. Williams had left in the middle of the year and had been succeeded by Joseph Palmer II, a career Foreign Service officer. Palmer was both highly competent on the substance of African issues and more conscious of bureaucratic nuance than Williams. But he was less of an advocate, and his more cautious style of operation meant that Joseph Sisco and his Bureau of International

Organization Affairs took an increasingly assertive lead on
southern African issues. The African Bureau remained on the
same side of the bureaucratic debates, but its voice was somewhat muted, as Palmer increasingly was forced to devote his
attention over the next few years to the growing crisis in
Nigeria.

The Treasury and Commerce Departments reportedly
were not in favor of United Nations sanctions against Rhodesia. Treasury officials are said to have argued that a sanctions
program against Rhodesia could not prove successful and
would damage the concept of sanctions. This could, in turn,
interfere with Treasury's sanctions programs against Albania,
Cuba, the People's Republic of China and other Communist
nations. Treasury was also concerned about the effect on the
American balance of payments and gold position if American
relations with South Africa became involved. The CIA, like
Treasury, doubted that sanctions would succeed. (On at least
one occasion, its analysis of the situation incurred Goldberg's
and Sisco's wrath.) But the weight of opinion within the American government was cautiously in favor of sanctions—
provided they did not mean total confrontation with South
Africa. While American officials in the African Bureau had
suggested informally to British colleagues during 1966 that
comprehensive sanctions would be a good idea, this was not
yet the official American position. Argument between the
British and Americans during Garner's visit to Washington
centered, instead, on three issues: whether oil (and especially
South African oil) should be included in the United Nations
selective mandatory sanctions program; whether the British
should except South Africa from penalties for violating sanctions; and, more generally, what British strategy and tactics
were to be in coming months.

The issue of imports from Rhodesia was not a great problem. The British had already sent a draft resolution covering
most Rhodesian commodities, and American officials had no
real problem with it. The items covered by the draft were not
of real concern to South Africa, and yet the program would

have some bite to it. The problem lay in the embargo on exports to Rhodesia. The British were intrigued by the idea of embargoing oil from Mozambique to Rhodesia but allowing the continued flow of South African oil to the Rhodesians. American officials, especially Ambassador Goldberg, would not accept such a distinction, since it would create major problems in the voting at the United Nations. On December 5, Smith rejected Wilson's settlement terms; the next day, George Brown, the British Foreign Secretary, left for the United Nations to ask for selective mandatory sanctions. The British press reported that he was taking two drafts with him, one including oil and one not. It was the draft including oil which had been discussed with American officials during Garner's visit to Washington, and in the course of his consultation with interested delegations at the United Nations, Brown was told by Goldberg that the British should not dilute their proposal. Under strong pressure by the African delegations, the British allowed oil to be included in the list of embargoed items.

Beyond the question of whether oil would be included was the issue of what the British would say at the time of the Security Council vote about South African responsibilities with regard to the sanctions program. During their meetings with American officials, Garner and the officials who had accompanied him reportedly proposed that the British make it clear at the United Nations that they were not prepared to extend sanctions to South Africa and—anticipating a proposal for the extension of sanctions to any nation which broke them—that Britain was not prepared to agree that the South Africans were liable to penalties for violations. American officials argued that the British would, in effect, be providing the South Africans with a broad exception. Such a statement would mean recognizing in advance that sanctions would not work. Sisco argued that it would be obvious to all the world that the British were picking on weaker Portugal and excepting the most important country involved—South Africa. It would be better, he suggested, not to say anything about what

Britain would do if the South Africans violated the sanctions. During the debate in mid-December, the British did not make a major point of their position, but it still was clear from what was said that London had no stomach for any kind of penalties against Pretoria if it refused to go along.

The third point of disagreement between Britain and American officials concerned British strategy and tactics in general. A number of American officials recall pressing the British for some indication of what they thought would happen in the following year and what they wanted to have happen. One recalls posing to the British a series of questions which went something like this: "Unless sanctions are also brought against South Africa, is it not true that they probably will not work? What will happen then? What events are you counting on to resolve the problem? If the sanctions *include* South Africa as well as Southern Rhodesia, our as well as your economic interests will be damaged. Therefore, the confrontation should be short and dramatic, and something should happen to get us both off the hook. What would that something be?" The British had no good answers. It is doubtful that their American questioners could have supplied any.

The doubts of most American officials about the course the British were pursuing were intensified during the days before the Security Council vote on December 16, 1966, when they were able to obtain only the most general responses to their questions about the meaning of specific sections of the British draft resolution. But the United States was publicly committed to Britain's support, and there seemed no alternative to going along with the next step. So senior officials put aside their reservations about the Security Council's invoking Chapter VII and finding the Rhodesian situation as a whole to be "a threat to the peace," and Smith's more militant opponents within the bureaucracy set aside their reservations about the limited nature of the sanctions. Goldberg supported the British in debate on the measure and expressed his optimism about the future: "If every state does its duty in the work that now lies before us, our action will not only exert a profound

effect in Salisbury; it will do much to build respect for the
United Nations as a force for peace and justice in Africa and
throughout the world."

Goldberg was also careful to note, however, that Southern
Rhodesia remained a British problem: "We do respect the fact
that it is the United Kingdom that has borne and still bears
this responsibility." One official who was at the Security Council that day recalls being instructed by a high official in Washington to make sure that the United States did not get in front
of the British in any way during the debate and vote. He was
told to keep his eye on Goldberg, and to tell him that he could
put his hand up only after the British representative lifted his
in the vote on the sanctions. Prizing his relations with Goldberg more than his informal instructions, the official did not
pass along the message.

Resolution 232 (1966) determined that the situation in
Southern Rhodesia constituted a threat to international peace
and security and ordered all Members to embargo the import
into their territories of a number of Rhodesian commodities
including asbestos, iron ore, chrome, sugar, tobacco, and copper. It also prohibited any activities which promoted the
supply to Southern Rhodesia of arms, other military equipment, aircraft, and motor vehicles. Nor could oil or oil products be shipped to Southern Rhodesia.[7]

The next step for American officials was to issue an Executive Order implementing the sanctions. This was left to the
Treasury and Commerce Departments and the Office of the
Legal Adviser in the State Department. There was little argument among agencies or bureaus over the text of the order,
which listed the various prohibited activities and assigned responsibility for implementation of the American sanctions
program among the Secretaries of State, Commerce and Treasury.[8] The only controversy came when the order was issued
on January 5, 1967. The White House press release, apparently drafted in the Treasury Department and not widely

[7] See Appendix I.
[8] See Appendix II.

cleared within the State Department, announced that implementing regulations would be issued by the Departments shortly, and would be effective as of the date of the Executive Order. The news release then stated: "A violation of an Executive Order is a criminal offense. Provision will be made in the regulations to deal with cases of undue hardship arising from transactions commenced before the date of the Order." A similar reference to a hardship exception was contained in the subsequent Treasury Department press release that accompanied the Department's sanctions regulations. A hardship exception was not mentioned anywhere in the Executive Order. But this *ex post facto* definition of such an exception was to become the basis for claims by Union Carbide and the Foote Mineral Company of the right to import certain allotments of Rhodesian chrome. Union Carbide was to claim that it had paid for approximately 150,000 tons of chrome after passage of the U.N. resolution but before the issuance of the Executive Order, and that it would be a hardship on the company not to be allowed to import the chrome it had purchased.

American policy toward Rhodesia was now set. The major policy decisions had been made at the end of 1965 and in April and December, 1966; from then on, it was primarily a question of implementing the sanctions. There was little controversy or internal debate over the American vote for Security Council Resolution 253, which ordered comprehensive sanctions in May, 1968.[9] Through 1967 and 1968, middle level State Department officials consulted with their counterparts at Commerce and Treasury over items as diverse as bull semen and tapes of the "I Love Lucy" television program. For the first months of 1967, the most important questions of interpretation were referred to Under Secretary Katzenbach. This became increasingly rare. There were arguments among the bureaus over the extent to which the United States should press its allies over their violations of the sanctions; these were usually resolved in favor of discretion over valor, although

[9] See Appendix I.

representations were occasionally made to such nations as France and Japan.

By 1968, American trade with Rhodesia had dropped to $3.7 million, a drop of about $29 million since 1965. The government's performance on sanctions in 1967 and 1968 was generally meticulous. Indeed, State Department officials working on the sanctions program were surprised to discover that the British interpreted the December, 1966, resolution more liberally than did the Americans. The American government, for example, initially interpreted the sanctions as governing the activities of American corporations wherever they were based. The British said that they would only apply them to British corporations in England. As a result, the Americans accepted the more liberal British definition. But minor differences remained, and American businessmen would occasionally complain to State Department officials that the United States government was being tougher than the British. One State official recalls that "American businessmen would say, 'Well, even the British aren't asking that under their law,' and we could only say, 'Oh,' and fumble and start to stutter. It was very embarrassing."

PRESSURE FROM THE RIGHT

While American policy was being decided and implemented within the administration during 1966 and 1967, opposition was growing on the outside. The challenge came not from supporters of the United Nations and independent Africa, but from conservative quarters. It took about three months for Smith's supporters in the United States to get organized. At least fifteen organizations sprang to life after UDI, most of them in the South. If, as one suspects, there is a secret office within the government which does nothing but invent new acronyms for old and new programs, and then finds words to match the letters, its most active members were moonlighting for Smith's supporters in late 1965 and early 1966. FAIR (the Friends in America of Independence for

Rhodesia), RIGHT (the Rhodesian Independence Gung Ho
Troops), HISTORY (Hooray for Ian Smith, Titan of Rhodesian Yearning) and other small groups soon withered away.
Three organizations sporting less flamboyant names were
longer-lived. They were the Rhodesian Information Office,
the Friends of Rhodesian Independence, and the American–
Southern Africa Council.

Easily the most effective of the pro-Smith groups operating in the United States since UDI has been the Rhodesian Information Office (RIO). It was established and registered with
the Justice Department under the Foreign Agents Registration
Act on February 3, 1966. The office immediately became very
active in churning out information on the glories of independent Rhodesia, in making sure this information got to other
pro-Smith groups within the United States, and in organizing
tours of Rhodesia for Americans who seemed likely to approve of what they saw there. The first publication it distributed, one of a series of newsletters written by the Rhodesian
Ministry of Information, Immigration and Tourism entitled
"Rhodesian Commentary," attacked British "fiddling" in
Africa.

The presence of the RIO confronted the American government with three closely related issues: the status of the office itself, the legal status of its Rhodesian employees, and the
financing of the office's activities. The status of the office itself
was quickly established. On February 25, Thomas C. Mann,
the Under Secretary of State for Economic Affairs, sent a letter to Henry J. C. Hooper, who was then the head of the RIO,
about his personal status. The letter insisted on a distinction
which allowed the American government to permit the continued operation of the office. The RIO could not portray itself as representing the "Government of Rhodesia," since the
United States recognized no such government. Officials of the
RIO could not remain in the United States "on the basis of a
purported official capacity." But the office could operate,
Mann's letter implied, if it were identified as the agent—not of
a government—but of a foreign principal, or group. It would

thus become similar in status to the representatives of other foreign groups which claim themselves to be governments but which are not so recognized by the United States.

Mann's letter also suggested that Hooper apply to the Department of Justice for an adjustment of his personal status in the country. Hooper did so, and was able to satisfy Justice that he would not make further claim to official status within the country. But his personal status, and that of Kenneth Towsey (who became Hooper's superior at the RIO in March, 1967), have remained an issue to the present day. Both Towsey and Hooper had entered the United States as foreign government officials, attached to the British embassy. Towsey had arrived in May, 1964; Hooper in September, 1965. With UDI, both lost that status, as their connection with the British embassy was severed. Once they had satisfied the State Department that they were not portraying themselves as official representatives of a foreign government, they did not face deportation and through the remainder of 1966 and part of 1967 simply remained in the United States without any resolution of their formal status. Since this allowed them to continue their work for the RIO, they apparently saw no need to rock the boat. But the problem was that they could not leave the United States and be sure of readmittance unless they were allowed to adjust their status to that of permanent residents. On May 4, 1967, Towsey applied for such an adjustment; his application was approved by the Immigration and Naturalization Service (INS) on December 27, after the State Department had advised the INS that it had no objection. He became a permanent resident alien on January 4, 1968. He has visited Rhodesia for about a month every year since 1968, accompanied in 1969 and in 1973 by his wife and daughters.

Towsey's status was granted after some argument within the government. IO officials favored denial of his application as a means of forcing the RIO out of the country. AF favored approving it on the grounds that there was no clear legal requirement that it be refused, that the Rhodesians might kick out the American consultate in Salisbury if Towsey were ousted, and that his removal might create another "Struelens case." (Belgian-born Michael Struelens was the head of the Katanga Information Office in the United States during the Congo crisis. After he was accused in December, 1961, of attempting to bribe the Costa Rican delegation at the United Nations, the State Department invalidated his visa for engaging in activities outside the information work specified in his visa. State also contended that his propaganda work for Katanga was at odds with U.S. and U.N. policy. Its action was strongly attacked by the Katanga lobby in the United States, and by others on the grounds that he had violated no U.S. statute and that his right to free speech was being violated. Struelens voluntarily migrated to Canada in August, 1963. In addition to AF's hesitations, the Bureau of Security and Consular Affairs in the State Department took the position that the United States should not use its visa power to deny the free expression within the country of points of view with which the government might not agree, including Towsey's.

Hooper did not fare so well. He applied for a similar adjustment of status on March 5, 1968, two months after Towsey had received his. Within almost three months, while his application was still under review, the Security Council adopted Resolution 253 which, while ordering comprehensive mandatory sanctions, required all states to "take all possible measures to prevent the entry into their territories of persons whom they have reason to believe to be ordinarily resident in Southern Rhodesia and whom they have reason to believe to have furthered or encouraged, or to be likely to further or encourage, the unlawful actions of the illegal regime in Southern Rhodesia . . ." While the American government decided that this resolution did not apply retroactively to Towsey, the State Department concluded that it would rule out adjustment of Hooper's status. According to a letter from the State Department to the INS on March 13, 1969: "He is despite assertions he may make to secure permanent residency here 'ordinarily resident in Southern Rhodesia.' He obviously 'furthers or en-

courages the unlawful actions of the illegal regime.' He is paid
by the regime to do so. In addition to regularizing his status in
the United States, adjustment of his status would permit Mr.
Hooper to travel freely between the United States and Southern Rhodesia to consult with the Smith regime about his activities in the United States. These activities are directly contrary
to the objectives of the Security Council Resolution. For the
Attorney General to exercise discretionary authority to grant a
change of status would waive a 'possible measure' of inhibiting
his travel and could not be reconciled with the requirements
of the resolution." [10]

In addition to the legal problem, the British asked the
American government not to grant Hooper his request.
(Prime Minister Wilson sent Secretary Rusk a letter on the
subject.)

On the other hand, Senator Eastland and other congressional supporters of the RIO weighed in with both the State
Department and the INS, both before and after the accession
to power of the Nixon administration.

The INS was in a quandary. On the one hand, the State
Department's recommendation was that "the Department of
Justice deny the application for adjustment of status." On the
other hand, a member of Senator Eastland's Senate Judiciary
Committee staff called the INS asking that no action be taken
to deny Hooper's application. (Hooper had himself raised the
matter with the Senator's staff.) The only way out was to sit on
the application. Even the State Department agreed, in March,
1973, after both an oral and a written plea from Eastland to
Secretary Rogers, that the Security Council's action did not
"require Mr. Hooper's deportation." It adopted this position
in a letter to the INS. Thus, Hooper's status is likely to remain
for some time, in the words of an INS official, that of "an
applicant for adjustment of status to permanent resident."
When asked at hearings of the House Subcommittee on Africa

[10] Hearings before the Subcommittee on Africa of the Committee on
Foreign Affairs, House of Representatives, May 15, 17, 1973, p. 35.

in May, 1973, by the Committee's counsel, how long Hooper's application might remain pending, the INS official intimated the possible immortality of the case:

Mrs. Butcher: "In other words, you could wait forever?"
Mr. Green: "Conceivably, yes." [11]

The third problem posed by the RIO was its financing. Soon after the issuance of the Executive Order implementing Resolution 253, in 1968, the Treasury Department froze the bank accounts of the RIO in the United States. It did so because these accounts were being funded from Swiss accounts, and thus violated one of the provisions of the Executive Order. Towsey's and Hooper's personal accounts were also frozen. An immediate wave of criticism by conservative congressmen and journalists forced Treasury to remove the restrictions on these personal accounts. The RIO's official accounts remained frozen, however. A new funding system was therefore arranged through "free accounts" at banks in New York. Under this system, the RIO draws on the dollars paid into these accounts by various religious and other groups which are legally transmitting money to Rhodesia for charitable purposes. The Rhodesian government pays equivalent amounts in Rhodesian currency to the recipients of these contributions.

Thus, thanks to the intervention of its friends like Senator Eastland and its skill in finding a way to receive its funds from the Smith regime, the RIO has been able to continue to operate as the best informed and most effective lobbyist for the Rhodesian cause in Washington.[12]

While members of the RIO, according to a number of sources, privately dined and worked with the leaders of the conservative American organizations founded to support the Smith regime and have occasionally quoted statements by them in the RIO's newsletters, they have generally been care-

[11] *Ibid.,* p. 42.
[12] Chapter 5 includes a description of its activities.

ful to keep an arm's length from them publicly, for the sake of the RIO's image with the moderate Americans whom it wishes to influence. Thus, Lawrence Feinberg noted in an article in the *Washington Post* on December 26, 1967, that although the RIO offices displayed a small stack of fund-raising pamphlets for the American–Southern Africa Council, Hooper explained that "sometimes your friends may support you for some of the wrong reasons."

The Friends of Rhodesian Independence was founded in 1966 with the financial backing of the very conservative Liberty Lobby. Its membership included a number of John Birch Society stalwarts. By June, 1967, the Friends of Rhodesia claimed 122 branches in the United States with 25,000 members. But while its reported activities included organized tours to Rhodesia and banquets in the United States, the organization was "never more than a paper organization," according to Wesley McCune of Group Research, Inc. It was disbanded in 1971.

The American–Southern Africa Council was also founded in 1966, to carry out public relations work for the Friends of Rhodesian Independence. By 1969, the leaders of the two organizations were reportedly on poor terms, and both were in financial trouble. A new chariman, Michael Jaffee, tried to rebuild the Council as a new organization, separate from the Liberty Lobby and its Friends. But in 1972, the Council was forced to sell its mailing lists (to pay off outstanding debts) and disbanded.

During its best years between 1966 and 1968, the Council's activities were quite varied, although they revolved around two dominant purposes: fund-raising and support for Smith. The Council twice threatened to go to court against the sanctions. In 1967, it spoke of obtaining an injunction against President Johnson's implementation of the embargo. In 1968, it asked its members for money for the court case of one Robert Wyckoff, a Louisiana businessman and cochairman of the Friends of Rhodesian Independence. Wyckoff had purchased in Rhodesia $5,000 worth of copper plaques to be used for the purpose of "building bridges with a friendly nation." The Treasury Department refused to allow them into the United States. The Council's challenge to the legality of Treasury's action apparently never went to court.

Another of the Council's fund-raising activities was the Southern Africa Gift Shop. It advertised, in the Council's newsletter, selected Rhodesian products whose purchase would help "our allies overcome the hardships of sanctions." Advertised items included Ian Smith neckties, witch-doctor bottle openers, and handcrafted copperware items including copper elephant plaques.

Among several trips by Americans to Rhodesia reportedly sponsored by the Council, a congressional task force in 1967 was among the least successful, as described in an article by Robert J. Havel in the Cleveland *Plain Dealer* on January 24, 1968. Using the names of nine Congressmen, including Dan Kuykendall (R.–Tenn.) and John Ashbrook (R.–Ohio), who had supposedly accepted the Council's sponsorship of this "fact-finding" trip to Rhodesia, Acord sent out at least two newsletters soliciting funds. The first anticipated cost was a "desperately needed" $66,670 for an expected entourage of twenty Congressmen and six newsmen. The second solicitation asked for less ($32,500), since the (now nine) Congressmen had reportedly decided to fly economy. However, the Congressmen had only tentatively accepted the Council's offer, and after discovering the use of their names for solicitation purposes only two of them, John Rarick (R.–La.) and Thomas Abernathy (R.–Miss.), accepted. They were accompanied by two newsmen.

The American-African Affairs Association, described earlier, was better known and more respected among conservative Americans. Although it was founded in September, 1965, it did not become active on Rhodesia until the following year. In January, it sponsored a fact-finding mission to Southern Rhodesia which included Max Yergan, Ralph deToledano, a conservative writer, and Congressman Ashbrook. They met with Smith and others, and, in Ashbrook's words, "came away with very definite ideas." "Rhodesia is one of the finest countries I have ever visited," he said. "Its people are of the very highest quality, their motives are good, their outlook is humanitarian and, above all, there is an effort to make improvement." In May, 1967, another fact-finding mission sponsored by the AAAA, including columnist James J. Kilpatrick, Rene Albert Wormser, and Dr. Walter Darnell Jacobs, reported on the "tranquility" of life in the cities and the "peacefully primitive" countryside to which many of the "Rhodesians of African descent still cling." The Africans, the mission said, were "a simple child-like people still blinking from the darkness of the cave."

Another arm of the Rhodesian lobby has reached a much wider audience. A number of conservative radio commentators have made Rhodesia one of their most favored causes. Dan Smoot, Melvin Munn, Clarence Manion, Carl McIntyre, and others have thundered from their electronic pulpits against sanctions and in favor of the embattled, little, anti-Communist nation of Rhodesia. In June, 1967, Professor Vernon McKay estimated that "right-wing radio talks are heard each week on more than 10,000 broadcasts averaging more than fifteen minutes each, not including the major network programs of Paul Harvey and Fulton Lewis III." [13]

Perhaps the most committed and effective of the pro-Smith radio commentators has been Fulton Lewis III. Lewis inherited Fulton Lewis Productions from his father in August, 1966. He had worked as a research analyst for the House Un-American Activities Committee and served as a member of the board of directors and the "national field director" of the Young Americans for Freedom. In 1967, Lewis traveled to Rhodesia and broadcast a series of interviews with Smith, his ministers, and local chiefs. On May 16, he reported from Salisbury his conclusion that "Rhodesia has adopted a non-racial approach—instead of the apartheid philosophy." Lewis was later to work hard for the passage of the Byrd Amendment.

[13] Vernon McKay, "The Domino Theory of the Rhodesian Lobby," *Africa Report,* June, 1967, p. 57.

None of these groups or individuals was of much concern to officials within the Executive branch. They could be dismissed as an automatic source of discomfort rather than representatives of a block of opinion which could damage President Johnson politically. It was unlikely that many of these friends of Ian Smith in the United States had voted for Johnson against Goldwater.

But questions about the American decision to go along with the British in asking for mandatory sanctions by the United States were raised by more moderate Americans, as well. Editorial opinion ran about six to four against the sanctions; the majority view was shared even by the *Washington Post*. On December 14, 1966, the *Post* restated its opposition to the Smith regime but dismissed some of Ambassador Goldberg's arguments at the United Nations in favor of sanctions as "nonsensical." Even limited sanctions, it argued, were unwise. "There is no reason to believe they will be effective. They set a questionable precedent. They amount to interference in the domestic affairs of another country merely because of the form of government practiced there. Moreover, the effort to impose them ignores the purpose and injures the prestige of the U.N." The *New York Times,* in an editorial the same day, gave the sanctions its lukewarm approval as "simply the least dangerous of available courses in a highly explosive situation."

ACHESON VS. GOLDBERG

The most important attacks on American policy in late 1966 and 1967, outside the Congress, came from former Secretary of State Dean Acheson and his former State Department associate, Charles Burton Marshall. In a letter to the *Washington Post* on December 11, 1966, Acheson warned against U.N. sanctions on legal grounds. He argued that the only "threat to the peace" was the threat by African members against Rhodesia simply because they did not like what was going on within its borders. It was the African members,

therefore, who might transgress against the "First Command-
ment of the United Nations" that all members shall refrain "in
their international relations from the use of force against the
territorial integrity or political independence of any state."
Acheson went on to heap scorn on the logic behind sanctions.
"Since Rhodesia by doing what it has always done and with
which the United Nations cannot constitutionally interfere, in-
cites less law-abiding members to violate their solemn obligation not to use force or the threat of force in their international relations, Rhodesia becomes a threat to the peace and
must be coerced.

"If this reasoning leads the reader to ask with Mr. Chan-
ler, 'Who's loony now?,' don't blame Rhodesia. Blame the Security Council and Harold Wilson."

Acheson was raising one of a number of legal objections
to the sanctions that were to be laid out in some detail by
Professor Marshall in March, 1967, in his cleverly written
Crisis Over Rhodesia: A Skeptical View.[14]

Ambassador Goldberg quickly replied to Acheson in indirect terms, in a speech supporting sanctions on December 13
at the United Nations. His direct answer to Acheson came in a
long letter to the *Washington Post* on January 8, 1967. Since
Goldberg raised and answered many of the legal arguments
made by Acheson, a number of conservative Congressmen,
and subsequently by Marshall, his letter is worth summarizing
rather fully.

Goldberg first considered the argument that the sanctions
violated Article 2, Paragraph 7 of the Charter, which reads:

Nothing contained in the present Charter shall authorize the
United Nations to intervene in matters which are essentially
within the domestic jurisdiction of any state or shall require the
Members to submit such matters to settlement under the
present Charter; but this principle shall not prejudice the application of enforcement measures under Chapter VII.

[14] Charles Burton Marshall, *Crisis Over Rhodesia: A Skeptical View* (Baltimore: Johns Hopkins University Press, 1967).

Goldberg disposed of this argument by pointing out that Rhodesia was not a "state"; that the situation in Rhodesia was not "domestic," since it involved "the international responsibilities of the United Kingdom under the Charter relating to nonself-governing territories"; that the Security Council's action did not "constitute intervention," since it had acted at the request of the legitimate sovereign, the United Kingdom; and that Article 2, Paragraph 7, explicitly does not apply to the application of enforcement measures such as the mandatory economic sanctions just voted by the Council.

Goldberg next turned to the argument that the sanctions represented a denial of the principle of self-determination. He rebutted this point by recalling that UDI denied self-determination to over 94 percent of the Rhodesian population and the United Nations action was an effort to protect their rights under that principle.

He then took exception to the argument that the Rhodesian situation posed no threat to international peace. This he answered by pointing out that Article 39 gives the Security Council the power to make such a determination and that it had done so in a legal manner. It was the Council's best estimate of the future that there were great risks of violence involved in the suppression of the fundamental rights of the great majority of the Rhodesian population. (Central to Goldberg's argument was the fact that the Security Council has a broad legal authority to determine that a threat to international peace exists in a *situation;* it does not have to pin the threat to a certain regime.) Thus, with regard to the argument that the sanctions could not be applied against Rhodesia since the threat to peace originated from other African states, Goldberg suggested that the point was that the threat inherent in the Rhodesian situation lay in Rhodesia itself.

Finally, Goldberg considered the argument that the United Nations action created a dangerous precedent for similar sanctions wherever violations of human rights might occur. "This argument," he wrote, "overlooks a number of elements which are quite unique in the Rhodesian situation. Here we have witnessed an illegal seizure of power by a small minority on racial grounds bent on perpetuating the subjugation of the vast majority. Moreover, in this situation the sovereign authority with international responsibility for the territory has asked the United Nations to take measures which will permit the restoration of the full rights of the people of this territory under the Charter."

The concluding paragraphs of Goldberg's letter made a more general and more positive argument for the sanctions. Our domestic principles, he argued, demand our support for human rights abroad. Indeed, he stated, the United States has a treaty obligation to support the provision of the United Nations Charter concerning human rights and self-determination.

There was thus a fundamental difference between Goldberg's and Acheson's approaches to the problem under international law. While Acheson emphasized the rights of states to manage their domestic affairs as they wished, Goldberg was asserting the obligation of the United Nations to defend individual human rights, even against the abuses of their own leaders. In a speech at the annual meeting of the Association of American Law Schools on December 29, Goldberg had stated his affirmative concept of international law: "Law must operate to eliminate discrimination, to assure human rights, to feed the hungry, to educate the ignorant, to raise up the oppressed." The Ambassador declared, "It must foster in the international realm the same creative and positive values which nations, at their best, have fulfilled in their own domestic life."

Acheson continued the debate with Goldberg through 1968. In writing to the *Washington Post* on June 4, 1967, he compared Goldberg's and Britain's Rhodesian policies to, respectively, Andrei Vishinsky and the Soviet Union's policies with regard to South Korea. In a speech in May, 1968, Acheson accused Britain and the United States of conspiring to overthrow the government of Rhodesia—a government, he said, which threatened no one. When asked to comment by newsmen, Goldberg said that Acheson was "a very distinguished man, but what he has said is sheer nonsense."

ARGUMENT IN CONGRESS

The debates between Acheson and Goldberg paralleled debates within the Congress over Rhodesia. Smith's supporters on Capitol Hill included, most notably, Senators Eastland, Fannin and Goldwater, and Representatives Utt, Gross, Ashbrook and Waggonner. In August, 1966, Eastland introduced a resolution calling on the administration to cease immediately its "inhumane, illegal, arbitrary, unfair, harmful, and costly policy of economic sanctions against Rhodesia." It died in the Foreign Relations Committee. On the first day of the Ninetieth Congress, January 10, 1967, Utt introduced a resolution directing the President to pull the United States out of the United Nations sanctions program. Several similar measures were introduced by other Representatives in succeeding weeks. Eastland also reintroduced his resolution. None passed.

Conservative congressional rhetoric on the issue emphasized a number of themes: the illegality of the sanctions; the anti-Communist friendship of the Rhodesians for the United States; the inability of the Africans within Rhodesia to govern themselves, as proved by the experience within other African nations; the danger of letting the United Nations and particularly its Afro-Asian bloc dictate international policy; and the incongruity in supporting the British over Rhodesia when British vessels were carrying materials to North Vietnam. Eastland, for example, pointed out that Rhodesia had repeatedly offered military assistance to the United States in Vietnam. He also raised a legal argument which Goldberg's letter had not deigned to answer. The Security Council's vote, Eastland argued, was not legal, since Article 27 (3) of the Charter required decisions of the Security Council to be adopted with the concurring votes of the Permanent Members. Since both France and the Soviet Union had abstained on the sanctions vote of December 16, 1966, the resolution had been adopted illegally. Eastland's argument failed to note that, by custom, this provision was not so narrowly interpreted by the Council itself. Various Permanent Members had abstained on many of the Security Council's previous 231 resolutions. Indeed, the United States had traditionally supported this broader interpretation, lest the Security Council be hamstrung.

Eastland had a better argument when he pointed out that before UDI, Britain had consistently taken the position that Rhodesia was not a nonself-governing territory, and therefore the Rhodesian question did not concern the United Nations. But the situation had changed after UDI when the British asked the United Nations to vote mandatory sanctions. Whatever Rhodesia's status before UDI, the British retained legal sovereignty over the territory and thus, according to the American government, at least, retained the right to determine whether the United Nations should become involved.

On January 12, 1967, Senator Fannin argued, as others have, that it was unfair to pick on Rhodesia since less than half of the members of the United Nations have governments clearly based on majority rule. An argument similar to this noted that other colonies had received their independence without objections by the United Nations, although ruling tribes were denying political rights to the majority of their countrymen.

Yet Rhodesia is a special case. The denial of rights there is based on relations between black and white, an issue with worldwide implications. And South Africa, another former British territory which formally bases its political, economic and social systems on racial distinctions, achieved its independence long before the United Nations came into existence. Thus, Rhodesia is one of a kind.

The anti-British argument was most strongly put by Representative H. R. Gross (R-Iowa) on May 2, 1966. "Rhodesia is friendly to the United States. It is strongly anti-Communist," he said. "Compare this with the treacherous record of Britain. Through the years and down to the present, the British carried on unlimited trade with Communist China, Communist North Vietnam, and Communist Cuba. Whenever it is possible to make a fast dollar, there the unscrupulous British are to be found and it seems to make no difference whether the source of profit is friend or foe."

Representative Joe D. Waggonner, Jr. (D-La.) combined anti-Communist and anti-African (i.e., racial) themes in a statement on April 5, 1966: "Three generations ago, a group of resourceful white men went into the jungle of what is now Rhodesia and carved a civilized land by the sheer force of their brains and management ability. The lesson of history was crystal clear then as it is now: the natives were not capable of producing any semblance of what we call civilization. Now that the white man had led them out of savagery, the Socialist, left-wing camp is up in arms to turn the country back to them. This is, of course, a not too subtle way of building a Socialist bridge from democracy to Communism." Waggonner's statement reminds one of an earlier statement by Theodore Roosevelt when he said, "The settler and the pioneer have at bottom had justice on their side; a great continent could not have been kept as nothing but a game preserve for squalid savages."

In December, 1967, Senator Goldwater, in an interview with Harvey Ward broadcast from Salisbury over Rhodesian radio, expressed his admiration for Smith: "We need more men like Ian Smith, I think, in the world today. We have too few leaders, and I'd like to see him multiplied a little bit, and spread around." Goldwater disapproved of American policy toward Rhodesia: "Well, I hate to say this, but I think the so-called Afro-Asian bloc has a great deal to do with my country's attitude. I think this is unfortunate, not that we should completely disregard the Afro-Asian block, whatever that might be or wherever it might be, but I do not think we should allow what is essentially a minority of the United Nations to effectively control the United Nations. Now, we have some local political reasons for this, let's face it. While I don't for one moment believe that the Negro problem in America can in any way in the world be equated with the so-called Negro problem of Rhodesia and South Africa and Mozambique, I do know that the Negro in the large American cities can be a balance of voting power, and I hate to say this, but I think this Administration in my country has been influenced by that."

On the other side of the issue, the administration also had its critics among members of Congress who were strongly anti-Smith. Representative Benjamin S. Rosenthal (D-N.Y.) criticized the administration for shying away from confrontation with South Africa. Speaking on April 28, 1966, he argued: "I submit, then, that the United States must face up to the question of whether or not it is doing all it can to bring down Smith, and equally important, to convince South Africa that it is against her interest to aid the rebellion. This country, after all, is not without power in South Africa. Indeed, we are often told that the United States maintains relations with South Africa in order to exercise creative influence there. I would suggest that it is time to do just that, to spend a little of our accumulated credit with Verwoerd, and put it on the line: the South Africans isolate Rhodesia or the United States takes steps to isolate South Africa. Such a step would be the beginning of a new invigorated American policy."

On the same day, Representative Donald M. Fraser (D–Minn.) suggested that the United States should move immediately to mandatory sanctions: "We should not wait until we are pushed by the African and Asian nations and then try to achieve the weakest possible compromise." Within the Senate, Senator Edward Brooke (R–Mass.) became the leading advocate of stronger American efforts against apartheid in a major speech on Africa in April, 1968.

But the volume of rhetoric on Rhodesia in the late 1960s was far stronger from the right than from the left. Goldberg, concerned Congressmen, and Joseph Palmer (who made a particularly forceful speech on February 28, 1967, attacking the idea that UDI could be equated with the American Declaration of Independence) did not strike a responsive public chord. Perhaps because of their natural obsession with American policy toward Vietnam, leaders of liberal American thought very seldom spoke up on Southern Rhodesia.

American officials were not much concerned, however, with the attacks on Rhodesia from the right or the left. Even the American businessmen with whom they were in frequent contact about the sanctions did not have much influence over general policy in the years between UDI and January 1969. The outcry on the far right was easily dismissed. Congressional debate established general limits to further U.S. action, but American policy had found the easy middle between the two groups on Capitol Hill who seemed interested in the issue. Senator Eastland was influential in preserving the status of the Rhodesian Information Office, but the conservatives lost on another issue, when Ian Smith was denied a visa to visit the United States in March, 1968.

In early January, 1967, Secretary Rusk was reportedly told in an executive session with the House Foreign Affairs Committee that there could be no American military involvement in the Rhodesian situation. But this warning represented a congressional delivery of coals to Newcastle. If anyone in the Johnson administration still thought there was any chance of American military involvement there, which is unlikely, all doubt was dispelled in early 1967 when Congress reacted with great indignation to the dispatch of three C-130 transport planes to the Congo for use by the Congolese government in ferrying supplies and men to its battle against marauding white mercenaries. After this incident, President Johnson issued an order that the United States would not again get so involved in Africa, except out of the most overwhelming necessity.

Thus American policy wound its way between conflicting domestic as well as international pressures. Until 1969, this policy was remarkably successful, in the terms of the senior officials who made it.

The Africans were occasionally irritated, but never so seriously as to lead them to jeopardize their relations with

Washington. The United States helped the British, with economic measures against the Rhodesian regime and diplomatically at the United Nations, but carefully avoided becoming a focal point for African recriminations. It was a British problem, and the United States helped keep it that way. Recall, for example, the American message to the British warning that we would not join them in vetoing African sanctions proposals, even if we agreed that the proposals went too far.

While thus taking advantage of the fact of British responsibility for the Rhodesian problem, American officials privately helped shape and limit British efforts to resolve it. On the one hand, they privately opposed a negotiated "sell-out" and any sanctions proposals which too obviously made a special exception for the South Africans. But, on the other hand, Washington also kept a loose rein on London lest it go too far and cause a real confrontation with Pretoria. The United States would not offer economic support either to the Zambians or to the British if it would cause serious damage to the American economic position, much less support for the use of force. This, of course, limited Wilson's options, although it may be doubted that American actions were as limiting as Wilson's own calculations of domestic and international advantage.

An American policy of compromise reinforced a British policy of compromise. The costs of this caution, beyond the psychic wear and tear on concerned British and American officials, did not fall directly on the United States or the United Kingdom. It penalized the Africans in Rhodesia, who were confronted with a drawn-out struggle for their rights while apartheid grew within the territory. It meant that Zambia would face at least seven or eight years of economic difficulty. And it allowed the United Nations to be used as a dumping ground for a problem that neither limited economic measures nor limited diplomatic concessions had been able to resolve. The United Nations was stuck with sanctions. Robert Good, formerly the American Ambassador in Zambia and, before that, during the early 1960s, the Director of the Office of

Research and Analysis on Africa, recalls that he wondered, when sanctions were voted, if the "world organization wasn't destined to wander aimlessly and endlessly in some irrelevant orbit with insufficient power to complete its journey and no guidance system for turning back."

Edward K. Hamilton, the National Security Council staff member responsible for African affairs from 1966 to 1968, tersely summarizes the tragedy of the world community's response to the Rhodesian problem: "Some day Rhodesia and the rest of southern Africa will blow up. But no one could do anything at a price anyone thought he could afford."

A new, more active chapter in American policy toward Rhodesia would unfold in 1969, with the advent of the Nixon administration. The new White House thought it would try to "do something" about southern Africa, and at a price it could easily afford, since in the process it would be doing something as well for American business interests there. American policy would no longer be so completely made-in-London, for good or ill.

4

"Tar Baby"
The Shift in Approach,
1969–70

To those observers outside government who care about American policy toward Africa, 1969 seemed even less eventful than the two preceding years with regard to Washington's approach to the Rhodesian problem. Yet behind the scenes, a protracted bureaucratic battle was shaping a new American policy. By the first month of 1970, President Nixon had decided that the United States would now emphasize "communication" with the white minority regimes of southern Africa, both in word and deed. The new policy was designed largely with South Africa in mind. Southern Rhodesia was included despite and without sufficient attention to the important differences between the two.

The infighting within the government and the President's decision took place in great secrecy, although anyone who cared enough to ask was told that a general review of American policy toward southern Africa was taking place. The President's decision memorandum was withheld even from the working levels of the State Department. This apparently was done not for national security reasons—officials agreed at the time that there was no vital American security interest involved in the area—but to avoid embarrassment to the administration, both domestically and with the Africans. The fundamental shift in policy did not become public knowledge within the United States until Terence Smith wrote a long article which appeared on the front page of the *New York Times* on April 2, 1972, revealing that the Nixon administration was quietly pursuing a policy of "deliberately expanded contacts and communication with the white governments of southern Africa." Smith went on to describe the course of the policy review and the decision memorandum which ordered the new approach. His article did not cause much of a stir in the United States or in Africa. One thus wonders why such great secrecy had enshrouded the events Smith described. Far from inspiring an embarrassing but democratic debate over the general course of American policy toward southern Africa, an open shift in approach by the administration, somewhat openly arrived at, might have inspired more public yawns than yowls.[1]

The following account of this policy review and its consequences was pieced together from extensive interviews with a number of the participants.

The policy review began in the spring of 1969. The new administration was carrying out a general review of American foreign policies, and Dr. Henry A. Kissinger was flooding the State Department with requests for new policy analyses and options. Roger P. Morris, who had succeeded Edward Hamilton in the new administration as the National Security Council staff member responsible for African affairs, recommended to Kissinger a review of southern African policy. Kissinger quickly agreed, and ordered the review on April 10 in National Security Study Memorandum (NSSM) 39. He is reported to have believed that the State Department had been exercising too much control over American policies in Africa generally. The Interdepartmental Group (IG) for Africa, an interagency, Assistant Secretary–level committee chaired by David Newsom, the Assistant Secretary of State for African

---

[1] The news might have had greater impact in 1970 than in 1972, but not necessarily; 1972 was a presidential election year, and some leaders of the black community in the United States were proclaiming their interest in African issues.

Affairs, had responsibility for preparing the response to
NSSM 39.

The African Bureau suggested that a National Policy
Paper (NPP) on southern Africa developed between 1966 and
1968 be used as a basis for their response. National Policy
Papers were invented by W. W. Rostow while in the State
Department in the early 1960s. From the beginning they were
generally regarded as theoretical, rather than practical, policymaking exercises. The NPP on southern Africa was reportedly
no exception—through drafting and redrafting, clearing and
reclearing, it had become less than precise in delineating any
possible shifts from existing policy. Indeed, one source claims
it was a classic example of the typical "options" paper dealing
with any problem for American policymakers: (1) war, (2)
humiliating withdrawal, or (3) the preferred option—present
policy. It reportedly had very little to say about Southern Rhodesia. The NSC staff (i.e., Hamilton and his subordinate, Morris) had been unwilling in 1968 to clear it as an agreed analysis, and Secretary Rusk had decided that it should be held
over for the new administration.

The White House found the NPP as unacceptable in 1969
as it had in 1968. Through the rest of the summer, the IG
argued out a fair description of the various options. While
each agency's representatives maintained in these meetings a
pro forma commitment to objectivity in developing these options, their points of view clearly emerged. Two fundamen-
tally conflicting views tended to dominate the course of discussion.

The first view, held by the Africanists in the State Department, opposed any basic shift in policy toward southern
Africa. State's concern was based partly on its assumption that
the National Security Council staff would support a Defense
Department effort at moving American policy toward a "normalization" of relations with the white minority regimes. It
based this fear on the memoranda reporting the President's
remarks to representatives of Portugal and South Africa at the
beginning of his administration, when they were visiting

Washington to attend President Eisenhower's funeral. The
President's posture in these conversations had appeared to
State Department officials to be excessively friendly to the Por-
tuguese and South Africans.

The second point of view was pressed by the National Security Council staff (Morris), supported by Defense (represented by Richard Kennedy, later to become an NSC staff
member). They argued for more communication with, and a
partial relaxation of, American measures against the white minority regimes and cooler rhetoric on the issue at the United
Nations and elsewhere. (The Defense Department itself also
reportedly favored more "normal" relations with the governments of southern Africa than the NSC option provided.)
The NSC/Defense view was grounded in two beliefs. The first
was that such an American stance *could* do more—at least in
theory—to promote peaceful change within southern Africa
than hostile actions which lacked real force and simply made
the whites of southern Africa more obdurate. The second
belief was that it was wrong, especially for an administration
with the constituency of the Nixon administration, to penalize
American businessmen in the name of a policy which was not
working.

But there were many unanswered questions. Was it possible for the United States to exert any influence over the
course of events in southern Africa? Could it do so in a way
that would promote the possibilities for peaceful change
there? Was such change possible, whatever the nature of
American policy, or was violence inevitable? What would be
the reaction of black African governments to an American
policy of gradual accommodation? In general, State Department representatives argued that the chances for peaceful
change were so slight, and American influence was so limited,
that it did not make sense to prejudice our standing with the
African nations north of the Zambezi to test some theory of
effective "communication." The NSC staff and Defense
argued that peaceful social and political change could flow
from economic advancement, as more and more African la-

borers came into the industrial economy. It made no sense, therefore, to try to limit both economic development and the liberalizing role American businessmen could play in the region, while heaping insults on the white leaders whose policies we were trying to moderate. In defending this view, Roger Morris drew on an article by Norman MacRae in *The Economist* of June 29, 1968, entitled "The Green Bay Tree." In this article, MacRae suggested that South Africa, "right across the surprising board . . . is a country where richer and securer generally means lefter: which is one reason why efforts to make it less rightist by boycotting it into greater insecurity and poverty would not seem to make any very evident sort of progressive sense."

Most of this general argument about assumptions concerned South Africa—the directions of its economy and society and the history of American relations with it. Southern Rhodesia thus became something of a tail on the South African dog. The administration's approach toward Rhodesia was to be shaped largely by conclusions about South Africa, although the two countries differed greatly and did not have the same status under international law.

The IG conclusions about the Rhodesian situation tended to support the positions of the NSC staff. The group concluded that sanctions were not having enough effect on the Rhodesian economy to bring Smith to terms and yet were slowing the pace of economic advancement. The implication was that while the sanctions induced pleas by Rhodesian businessmen for a negotiated settlement, they also were adding to economic problems which could speed a trend toward violence. The IG also concluded that international observance of the sanctions would continue to erode. The United States would therefore gain little by fighting for a program which penalized American business, when the program would probably run out of steam in any event.

The group's conclusions about potential African reaction to American policy toward southern Africa also seemed to support a move toward increased cooperation with the white regimes. It observed that African reactions would continue to vary widely, and that most African representatives acted more forcefully on the issue at the United Nations than in their private conversations with the American government.

It should be noted that State's representatives did not accept these arguments. For example, they agreed that the sanctions program was eroding, but argued that the United States had no business contributing to the erosion. The economic benefits of doing so were outweighed by political and legal considerations. And, they argued, the sanctions were effective, to some extent at least, in hampering the growth of the Rhodesian economy.

The IG's response to NSSM 39 was completed by mid-August. It laid out five options. The first, the so-called "Acheson" option, after the views of the former Secretary of State, called for normalization of American relations with the white regimes.[2] The second option called for a partial relaxation of American measures against these regimes, together with increased aid for black Africa, especially South Africa's neighbors like Botswana, and diplomatic efforts to resolve tensions between the white governments and their neighbors. The third was very similar to existing policy: maintain relations with both white and black African governments along existing lines and sustain a stated policy of opposition to both racism and violence. A fourth option included decreased contacts with the white regimes. And a fifth suggested the possibility of simply severing U.S. ties in the area to avoid having a stake in either side should the situation blow up. The second and third options were, of course, the key ones. The first (although it

[2] Acheson had urged such a policy on the President in a written memorandum as well as orally. He also, in mid-November, 1969, ran afoul of Prime Minister Wilson. After Acheson publicly stated that Britain's policy was based "not on principle but on malice," Wilson responded in Parliament, on November 20, that Acheson was "a distinguished figure who has lost a State Department and not yet found himself a role"—a reference to Acheson's famous phrase about Great Britain's lack of a role after its loss of empire.

had its proponents) served to make the second appear more moderate, a purpose which the fourth (also with its own earnest advocates) served for the third.

In damning the second option of partial relaxation, the State Department argued that, once adopted, the policy would prove sticky. The United States would be unable to abandon it if it did not work. Hence, the label given this option by its State opponents: "tar baby."

At the end of the year, meetings of the NSC Review Group and the National Security Council considered the various options. The State Department reportedly proposed a last-minute compromise between the two real options, in a last-ditch effort to find a bureaucratic ploy which could head off what it knew would be the White House decision. This "compromise" would have maintained the current policy while American diplomats made soundings of black African opinion to see how a relaxation would be greeted. The compromise was attacked at the review group meeting by the National Security Council staff, on the grounds that it would simply postpone a decision and make it harder to shift course. There would be a big difference between asking the Africans how they would react to such a policy—they would, of course, oppose it—and leaving the initiative for complaints to them as the outlines of a new policy gradually became evident. The compromise option received only minimal attention in the subsequent NSC meeting.

None of our recent Presidents has liked to use NSC meetings as a forum for decision. To do so would have limited his own freedom of action; it would have allowed policy to be made by committee rather than by the President himself. The Council is an advisory group. To try to make it more than that would be, in the words of one official who served on the NSC staff in the mid-1960s, "impossible in intramural politics—the Director of the Office of Emergency Preparedness would have a voice equal to that of the Secretary of State."

The National Security Council meeting in December, 1969, on southern Africa was no exception, and the quality of

debate reportedly was not high. Vice-President Agnew is said
to have delivered a lengthy disquisition on "South Africa" in
which he described how they had attained independence; how
their declaration of independence was modeled on our own;
how they, indeed, were very like us; and how it would be better simply to leave them alone and let them settle their own
problems. At the end of his remarks, the President is said to
have leaned across the table and gently asked, "Ted, you mean
Rhodesia, don't you?" The Vice-President looked again at his
notes, and agreed that that was what he meant.

According to some who can recall it, a memorandum
from Kissinger to the President on January 2, 1970, recommended adoption of the NSC option, with a few minor modi-
fications. The United States should, he argued, adopt a posture of relaxation in relations with the white regimes along the
general lines of the second option considered at the NSC
meeting in December. And it was no surprise that President
Nixon followed that recommendation.

Thus the President approved a policy under which the
United States would quietly improve official relations with
South Africa, including a partial relaxation of the arms embargo and avoidance of the issue of illegal South African control of Namibia (South West Africa) in a bilateral context;
eschew pressuring the Portuguese; modulate American rhetoric on southern Africa at the United Nations; and, to balance
these moves, increase its aid to black African nations.

The public was spared revelations of the new policy.
White House officials reportedly preferred that it not be revealed because it was to be a quiet, long-term relaxation of
American relations with the white minority regimes. It should
only become evident over time. The shock of a sudden announcement might call forth congressional and even public
reaction in the United States, and African governments might
feel forced into protest by such a sudden shift. The State
Department had its own reasons for keeping the new policy
obscured from public view. Beyond its concern about African
reaction, the Department apparently preferred to believe that

the President's decision was not all that meaningful. To announce it (or even to distribute his decision memorandum widely within the Department) obviously would have made it harder to continue to express American opposition to apartheid and white racism in southern Africa. As a result, during the following year, the speeches and background interviews of State Department officials seemed oddly unsynchronized with those of the White House; the former acted as if nothing had happened, while the latter were silent or evasive with American reporters.

In February, 1970, Jim Hoagland of the *Washington Post* noted that while white Africa found reason for cheer in President Nixon's foreign policy report to the Congress, "parts of black Africa [were] more sympathetic to the words uttered by Secretary of State William P. Rogers during his just-completed tour of Africa." [3]

At the same time, a report in *Africa Today* sensed the policy shift, but did not know it had already occurred.[4] It stated that the review of American policy in southern Africa was proceeding, and it was unclear what the conclusions would be. An NSC aide for Africa had said, it continued, "that U.S. rhetoric was likely to be scaled down to better coincide with actual policy. This means that if no firm steps are taken to disengage from South Africa, the U.S. government is also likely to sit mute in the United Nations and elsewhere when the issues of southern Africa are debated."

On April 1, 1970, the *Star* of Johannesburg reported an exclusive interview on United States–South African relations with a "State Department official." The reporter summarized the interview: "The overall impression he left was a somber one—a vista of difficulties and dangers in which change would be painful and improvements in the general climate could, in the short term, be minuscule at best for as long as apartheid continued." On September 19, the same correspondent reported that the State Department had issued a "distillation" of

[3] *Washington Post*, February 24, 1970.
[4] "Washington Letter," *Africa Today*, January–February, 1970.

the President's February foreign policy report which shifted its emphasis "from the need to avoid violence to the aim of achieving racial equality—and qualifying statements which White House sources gave great weight in February have been omitted." According to this story, it was an "open secret" that senior officials of the State Department's African Bureau would like to have gone "even further."

On November 8, 1970, Hoagland reported that the White House appeared "to be opting . . . where useful . . . [for] small but increasing accommodations with white minority governments." He also sensed the State Department's continuing opposition: "Such a policy," he stated, "would be at odds with what the State Department has been seeking." Thus, ten months after the President had reached a general decision on U.S. policy toward southern Africa, probably the best U.S. reporter on African affairs—after two weeks of Washington interviews—had found only that the White House "appear[ed] to be opting," not that it had, in fact, "opted."

In January, 1971, John Chettle of the South Africa Foundation described the President's difficulties in controlling the bureaucracy. He concluded, "It is small wonder that a high policymaker of the Nixon administration was reported to have said that the ambition of the administration's southern Africa policy was to cover itself so thickly with grease that nobody could get hold of any part of it." [5]

The first press report on the existence of "tar baby" came from Ken Owen, Washington correspondent of the Johannesburg *Star,* on February 11, 1971. Owen, a consistently well-informed reporter on American policy toward southern Africa, described how "Nixon Plumped for Option 2." Obviously drawing on NSC sources, he described the policy shift in some detail. Surprisingly, the American press did not pick it up. Indeed, it was not until late 1974 (when Jack Anderson "revealed" NSSM 39 in his column) that the policy shift received widespread comment in the press.

[5] *South Africa International,* January, 1971.

By the autumn of 1971, the thrust of the new policy was receiving stronger public support from the State Department, although the fact that it was *new* was still obscured. State officials seem to have regretfully concluded that they ought to make the best of a bad thing. In September, a speech by Assistant Secretary Newsom stated—in very strong terms—the reasoning behind "communication": "Isolation can breed resistance to change. Open doors can accelerate it." Indeed, in his flat prediction that "economic and demographic pressures" made change in South Africa "inevitable," Newsom was expressing a certainty which went beyond the strong hopes of the framers of "tar baby."

Terence Smith's article in April, 1972, more than a year after the Owen article, provided the first public description in the United States of the relationship between a series of practical steps taken by the administration toward closer relations with the white minority regimes and the fact that a fundamental shift in approach had taken place more than two years earlier. These steps, not all of which were directly related to the policy review, included a redefinition of embargoes on military equipment for Portugal and South Africa, which permitted the sale of two Boeing 707 airliners to the Portuguese government and the authorization for sale of executive jet aircraft to the South African military; [6] a new agreement with the Portuguese government on American bases in the Azores (reached largely for reasons unrelated to Africa) and authority for the Export-Import Bank to loan Portugal up to $400 million; a new agreement covering the sale of South African gold to the International Monetary Fund on terms highly favorable to Pretoria; and a series of abstentions and negative votes at the United Nations on measures condemning apartheid and the white regimes of southern Africa.

It is important to emphasize the basic difference between "tar baby" and the previous American approach to southern Africa. As defended by Morris and its other creators, the new

[6] Ironically, after the administration had made this gesture, the South Africans failed to purchase any of these aircraft.

approach was designed to assist peaceful change in the area. The danger was that if it failed to meet its purpose, the new policy would simply provide a thin excuse for normalization of relations with the white regimes. And to make a policy of "communication" succeed would require a series of delicate judgments about how specific U.S. actions would affect the situation in southern Africa. This would depend on high-level attention and a commitment at all levels of the government not to let the policy simply become a screen for easy accommodation. An examination of the government's performance in 1969 and 1970 on the three issues concerning Southern Rhodesia involved in the policy review suggests that such a commitment did not exist. While Morris (and Kissinger, to the degree the issue interested him at all) looked at the problem in foreign policy terms—however wrong-headed, in the view of the State Department—other parts of the White House and political appointees elsewhere in the Administration seem clearly to have supported the shift in policy because of the benefits to American business interests and to the Defense Department.

The three issues were the status of the American consulate in Southern Rhodesia, American votes at the United Nations on Southern Rhodesia, and an exception to the sanctions requested by the Union Carbide Corporation.

THE CONSULATE

On June 27, 1969, Morris sat down to lunch at the Occidental restaurant with Kenneth Towsey, the head of the Rhodesian Information Office in Washington. Over martinis, steaks, and baked potatoes they discussed the future course of American policy toward Southern Rhodesia. The meeting had been arranged by John Jordi of the South African Argus Press. Jordi had previously complained to Morris that American officials lacked any real communication with the Rhodesians in Washington and that this was a mistake. Morris agreed, knowing that Kissinger had been pressing his staff members to get to know people of all persuasions who had something to say about the substantive areas in which the staff members worked. Morris said that he and Towsey could meet on an informal basis, neither officially representing his government. Morris wanted to hear what Towsey had to say.

What was said at the lunch must have been of more interest to Towsey than to Morris. The National Security Council staff member told the Rhodesian that the administration was in the process of reviewing its policy toward southern Africa and that all options were being explored. While it was unlikely, given the political realities of Washington, to result in tremendous changes in the American approach toward Rhodesia, certain subtle changes were possible. They would depend on the approach of the Rhodesians. Morris reportedly said that the United States could never be considered a friend of the Rhodesian government, since its racial policies were a direct affront to a sizable segment of the American population. But some accommodation on specific issues might be possible, if they served some useful purpose.

This brought Morris to the question of the American consulate in Salisbury. A week earlier, on June 20, the Rhodesian electorate had voted overwhelmingly that Rhodesia should become a republic. While Smith had not yet declared the republic, Rhodesia's final break with Britain was assured. On June 24, London withdrew its residual mission in Salisbury. This raised, of course, the question of the continued status of the American consulate there. Its removal or retention would make little actual difference, but it was a symbol of American policy to the Rhodesians, the British and others. The continued presence of the consulate would affirm a continuing American interest in events within Rhodesia; it would also imply American unwillingness to accept Britain's complete jurisdiction over Rhodesian affairs.

As the lunch proceeded, Morris came to the point about the status of the consulate: If the United States were to keep the consulate in Salisbury, despite the predictable pressures by the Africans for its removal, would the United States then be in a position to effect any kind of mediating role between the British and the Rhodesians? Towsey, also speaking personally, thought that it might be possible. He must have been seizing on a means of encouraging continued U.S. presence in Salisbury more than he was seriously supporting American mediation, an unlikely prospect. Morris reportedly then left Towsey with the thought that while this administration might be less susceptible to African opinion than its predecessor it could not ignore the Africans or the position of the British and black Americans. So one could not be sure what the American approach to Southern Africa and to the consulate would be. But there was some chance that it might be kept if it could serve some useful function.

Morris informed Kissinger of his meeting. However, there is no evidence that the State Department was told about it. Morris saw Towsey again in August, and then in October at a party given by Jordi. Towsey reportedly said that his government would not raise the issue of the legal status of the consulate. The United States government was welcome to stay there as long as it wished. Even as a republic, Rhodesia would not insist that the consulate be accredited to it; the United States could maintain the "fiction" of accreditation to the British or even to the Matabele kingdom, if it wished. The important thing was that some contact be maintained. Morris reportedly informed Kissinger and the President of these conversations, suggesting that the Rhodesians were not going to push the United States consulate out of Salisbury but that at some point the legal issue would probably arise with Britain.

Thus, in the fall of 1969, the Rhodesians could understand a number of things about American policy. They knew that there was a policy review under way which could result in a more flexible approach to the Rhodesian question. They knew that the White House would prefer to keep the consulate in Salisbury. They probably recognized that it would have to be withdrawn if the British threatened to make a legal issue of the matter. And they knew that Morris, at least, appeared to believe that one purpose of maintaining the consulate in

Salisbury would be to facilitate negotiations. In his remarks to Morris, Towsey encouraged the adoption of a more flexible approach to the Rhodesian question by noting that his government was ready to negotiate a settlement with the British, and that it had representatives in London who were discussing the possibilities of such a move with the Labour government.

The State Department, meanwhile, was beginning to press strongly for closure of the consulate. The African Bureau favored such a move as soon as the British withdrew their residual mission. The Bureau of International Organization Affairs, Ambassador Yost at the United Nations, and the Legal Adviser's Office all agreed. Secretary Rogers was at first equivocal. He was reportedly concerned, for example, about the withdrawal of consular services for the approximately eleven hundred Americans in Southern Rhodesia (of whom about nine hundred were missionaries). He was reassured by the Legal Adviser's Office that alternative ways could be found to provide such services and protection—for example, by appointing a Salisbury law firm in place of the consulate.[7]

U.S. Consul General Paul O'Neill returned to Salisbury in mid-September after a home leave in the United States. According to a story by R. W. Apple, Jr. in the *New York Times,* many Rhodesians rejoiced at his return. One official privately told a visiting American, "I can't think of anything that would have been a better morale booster for us at the moment." O'Neill, who himself had recommended the closure of the consulate, had become a symbol for white Rhodesians of their importance to the United States. Another Rhodesian official was quoted by Apple: "I know some people in the world would like to pretend that we don't exist, but as you can see, we do exist, and no amount of bullying will make us cease to exist."

[7] When the consulate was finally closed, Southern Rhodesia simply became part of the responsibility of American consular officials in South Africa. An employee of the American Embassy in Pretoria, himself a Rhodesian, made periodic visits to Salisbury to deal with passports, visas, birth and marriage certificates, etc., for the Americans still living in the territory.

Rogers was soon arguing more strenuously for closure. His conversations with African leaders in late September at the United Nations, he said, demonstrated their concern over the issue. But his advocacy failed. Nixon, Kissinger, and Morris thought that there were a number of reasons for refusing to move so quickly. One element of the Southern African policy review, then nearing completion, would be prejudged. Retaining the consulate until pressures for its removal became greater would allow the White House later to give something both to the Africans and to the State Department. If the administration should decide to allow Union Carbide the exception to sanctions it had requested, the decision could be balanced by removal of the consulate then. In the meantime it served as a useful listening post. Its presence in Salisbury was consistent with a policy of "communication" with the white governments of southern Africa. And, in any case, neither British nor African pressures for its closure were yet all that great. Morris went through the Secretary's memoranda on his conversations with African leaders; they were then forwarded to the President to show that, in fact, for the most part the Africans seemed to accept the presence of the consulate. The issue had not come up in most of his meetings; when it had, the Secretary had raised the issue more often than the Africans.

The White House not only thought it good policy to postpone a final decision on the consulate, but it was also, according to the press reports at the time, under pressure on the issue from Southern Congressmen and lobbyists representing Union Carbide and Foote Mineral. According to a number of sources, Vice-President Agnew and his foreign policy assistant, Kent Crane, and possibly some of the President's domestic advisers, also went out of their way to indicate their belief that the consulate should be retained.

The National Security Council meeting on southern Africa in December and the President's subsequent decision memorandum did not resolve the issue—despite previous statements to the press by American spokesmen that a decision would be reached once the policy review was completed. The "tar baby" option included a decision to retain the consulate and even to move eventually to recognition of the Smith government; the State Department option called for closing the consulate immediately. The President's decision was a compromise: no immediate action would be taken. The United States would retain the consulate, subject to strong legal objections by either the British or the Rhodesians. In any case, it would go if its presence came to imply recognition of the Rhodesian regime.

In January, Morris reportedly told Towsey about the National Security Council meeting and the President's decision on the consulate. They were, by now, lunching regularly to exchange their general views of the situation. Towsey continued to do, or rather say, what he could to keep the consulate in Salisbury, as he had during the autumn. The pressures on the White House to order O'Neill to close shop now began to grow much stronger, however. Secretary Rogers was preparing for a trip to Africa in February, and he urged the White House to remove the consulate as an issue; its continued presence could sour his meetings with African leaders. In mid-January, prompted by the Sanctions Committee, Secretary-General U Thant sent letters to the governments still maintaining consular and other representation in Salisbury, asking them, in effect, to pull out. Security Council Resolution 253 of May, 1968, which had ordered comprehensive mandatory sanctions against Rhodesia, had recommended that all consular and trade representation in Rhodesia be terminated.

But far more important than U Thant's message was the fact that the British soon began more seriously to urge the United States to move on the matter. Prime Minister Wilson visited Washington in late January. According to American officials, in the course of British-American discussions at the White House, the British briefly raised the status of the consulate. Wilson was reportedly told that no decision had yet been made. The policy review could no longer, of course, be the excuse for delay. The new American position was that the

President was awaiting Secretary Rogers' report on his forthcoming trip to Africa before making further decisions on African issues.

Following Wilson's visit, one of the more bizarre episodes
in the history of American policy on Southern Rhodesia took
place. The American government began to get signals from
London which were no less conflicting than the signals the
Rhodesians had been getting from Washington. Just as Towsey could see that the White House and the State Department
were at odds, the American government in February and
March, 1970, was getting two very different messages from
London: one from the Labour government and the other
from the Tory opposition.

As it became clear near the end of February, 1970, that
Smith would formally declare Rhodesia a republic at the
beginning of March, Wilson's government decided that the
American consulate had become too great an embarrassment.
Other governments which maintained representatives in Salisbury were looking to the United States for their cue on what
to do, and Wilson was being taunted by the Conservatives for
this failure to make the Americans leave. On February 24,
1970, Wilson rejected a Tory charge in Parliament that the
United States had rebuffed his representations to Nixon on
the issue, claiming, "I made no representations to him on the
matter at all." Privately, meanwhile, the British embassy in
Washington formally conveyed to the State Department a
request by its government that the United States remove the
consulate immediately. The request fell on receptive ears in
the Department, but the White House was still holding out.
On the morning of February 27, spokesman Ron Ziegler told
the press that the United States would maintain the consulate
and that its presence did not imply recognition of the Smith
regime. He apparently misspoke, for later that afternoon,
Ziegler made his morning remarks inoperative by stating that
no decision had been made. The administration was "reviewing the situation in the light of rapidly developing events in

Southern Rhodesia." The *Times* reported in London that the State Department knew nothing of Ziegler's two statements until the transcripts of his remarks were released.

The refusal of the White House to bow to British pressure was due partly to other extraordinary messages it was getting from London. According to a number of sources who recall the episode, some time early in 1970 President Nixon had sent a private message to Sir Alec Douglas-Home (who was later, in June, to become the Foreign Secretary in a Conservative Cabinet), expressing the President's admiration for Home and inviting him to choose a time to come privately to Washington for a black tie dinner at the White House. (The Nixon White House reportedly preferred the Tories to the Labour government on personal as well as doctrinal grounds. The President is said to have particularly admired Home since the 1950s.) Home subsequently accepted the President's invitation for later in the spring.

Meanwhile, a personal, private message on Rhodesia from Edward Heath, the Leader of the Opposition, was sent to the President in February. A member of Heath's personal staff told an officer at the American embassy that a Tory government would make a determined effort to reach a settlement with Smith, although no one should be overly optimistic, since the obstacles to such a settlement would be great. This was no surprise. Heath and Home were taking the same line in public in the months before the June, 1970, general election which brought them to power. But the fact that a member of Heath's personal staff was making a point of saying this gave the message particular significance.

Then, near the end of February, a more explicit Tory message was conveyed to the embassy. An embassy official was asked to meet with Heath's private secretary. At this meeting, he was given a secret and personal message for the President. Heath wanted Nixon to know that when the Conservatives won the general election, they would as a matter of policy reestablish a residual mission in Salisbury (i.e., some kind of official British presence on the ground in Southern Rhodesia). This message was not, apparently, distributed within the State Department.

Thus, while the White House was under increasing pressure from the British government to close the consulate, the Conservative opposition in London was quietly but directly trying to influence the White House in the opposite direction. And this at the same time that it was ridiculing Wilson in Parliament for his inability to persuade the President to act! As the Tory campaign against Wilson gathered force before the June election, Rhodesia became a still more bitter issue, with Wilson accusing Heath of undercutting his policy by allowing numerous contacts between his Conservative supporters and the Smith regime. There is no sign that Wilson knew during this period how the opposition had undercut him in Washington.

At midnight, March 1–2, 1970, Smith formally declared Rhodesia a republic. Yet the American position on the consulate still did not change. The State Department spokesman said that the matter was "still under active consideration." Secretary Rogers, who had returned from Africa in late February and had submitted another memorandum to the President urging the consulate's withdrawal, continued to press the White House. In London, British officials at the working level raised the issue with the embassy, referring to the fact that it was the British and not the Rhodesians who had provided the consulate with its exequatur. The White House would not move.

In the end, it took bigger British guns to dislodge it from its position. On March 5, Foreign and Commonwealth Secretary Michael Stewart called Ambassador Annenberg to the Foreign Office to discuss the situation. Stewart gave Annenberg a formal, clear message. If the United States did not withdraw the consulate, the British would, in the very near future, consider withdrawing the exequatur. Similar messages were being passed to the other nations which retained representation in Salisbury. Faced with an open break with the British, the President gave in. On March 9, Secretary Rogers happily announced that the consulate would be closed on March 17.

In Rhodesia, the news was received with anger and dismay, although the Rhodesian government reassured the public that the closure would make no difference. The American decision was a symbolic defeat that dashed the Rhodesians' slim hopes of international recognition of the new republic. The British press carried stories which claimed that the United States had violated a secret agreement with the Rhodesians over the consulate. On February 3, 1970, Smith had told the Rhodesian Parliament that his government was "more than happy" with a deal under which two convicted spies had just been released. It was widely believed in Salisbury that the two men were American spies, and that the "deal" to which Smith was referring was an agreement with the American government that retention of the consulate would be traded for the freedom of the two men. Now, the British press speculated that the United States had double-crossed Smith. The facts of the matter have not become known publicly. But generally very well-informed and reliable sources state flatly that this tale of a secret "spy" deal is "hogwash."

In London, the British press gave the American decision banner headlines. American newspapers barely mentioned it. But Smith's supporters here, who had been following the issue, were disappointed with the President's failure to stand up to the British, come what may. On March 11, Senator Eastland introduced a resolution in the Senate calling for recognition of the Smith government. "Once again," he said, "we are dancing to the tune of Whitehall's Pied Piper in a game of follow-the-leader diplomacy. We are courting disaster when we let tiny African nations, through London, dictate our decisions." It was "one of the Administration's most colossal follies." The next day, the *Evening Star* of Washington, a supporter of Rhodesian independence, argued that withdrawing our Consul would undercut opposition to Smith within the European community in Rhodesia.

Smith's strongest American opponents, on the other hand, welcomed the announcement but gave little credit to the administration for its decision. One week after the consulate was closed Robert Good, who had left the State Department and was then a professor at Johns Hopkins University, told the House Subcommittee on Africa: "The 1970s in Africa, Mr. Nixon asserts, will be years of hard choice. Evidently he is right. He equivocated for eight months over the decision to close our consulate in Rhodesia when it was an open secret that his Secretary of State strongly advised that it be closed and a patent fact that the British urged its closure. If Mr. Nixon found in that issue a hard choice, one can only wonder how he will respond should the going really get rough in southern Africa."

The White House staff reportedly did not enjoy the appearance of a State Department victory, even if it knew that the consulate had been withdrawn more because of the British near-ultimatum than the Department's pleadings. But it did no harm to let the State Department believe it had won, since the White House could use that *quid* later to justify other *quos* on southern Africa. The decision to close the consulate was to be Nixon's first and last half measure of devotion to the cause of majority rule in Southern Rhodesia. This was to be demonstrated in the decisions on American votes on Southern Rhodesia at the United Nations and on the Union Carbide exception.

THE DOUBLE VETO

On March 17, the day that Consul O'Neill left Salisbury, the United States cast its first veto at the United Nations—on a resolution concerning Southern Rhodesia. While it was an accident that the two events occurred on the same day, they symbolized the administration's intention to give in no more on Southern Rhodesia.

With Smith's declaration of a republic at the beginning of the month, African delegations at the United Nations had begun to urge again that the British use force to crush the rebellion. A tough resolution along these lines was drafted; it included also the mandatory withdrawal of foreign consulates from Salisbury. On March 6, the British introduced their own resolution, designed once again to finesse the Africans, which called on all countries neither to recognize the Rhodesian republican regime nor to give it any assistance. The Africans, with their Asian allies, went ahead with their draft. As presented to the Security Council, it extended sanctions to Portugal and South Africa, condemned the British for their refusal to use force, and called for the severance of all communications and transportation ties between Rhodesia and the outside world.

The British and American delegations at first thought that no veto (i.e., a negative vote by one of the Permanent Members of the Security Council) would be necessary, since it appeared that the draft resolution would have only eight affirmative votes, one short of the necessary majority. But the draft's sponsors gained Spain's support by allowing the Spanish to vote against, and thus gain the deletion of, the section applying sanctions to Portugal. No longer inhibited by loyalty to its neighbor, Spain agreed to vote against the British. In doing so, they apparently calculated that they would both improve their relations with the Afro-Asian world and pick up support for their position against the British on Gibraltar.

The Spanish defection meant that a veto would be necessary to defeat the Afro-Asian draft resolution. It seemed likely that the British, who had previously exercised the veto over Rhodesia, would do so again. Should the United States join them? For some time, officials both in the American delegation at the United Nations and in the State Department had been in the process of coming to two conclusions about American votes at the Security Council. The first was that the United States was placing too high a value on its record of never having cast a veto. The value of the debating point which had been made by American representatives for twenty-five years—that the United States remained pristine while the So-

viet Union blocked the Council's business with its "nyets"—
had lost its force. Perhaps it was time that the United States
begin to act like the other Permanent Members of the Council.
The second conclusion concerned southern Africa. Even
many of those officials within the State Department who had
supported removal of the consulate and had opposed "tar
baby" felt that it was time that the United States come out
from behind Britain's skirts and show the Africans at the
United Nations that the use of force, the extension of sanctions to South Africa and Portugal, and the severance of communications links to Rhodesia were simply not in the cards.
Both the African Bureau and the Bureau of International Organization Affairs reportedly agreed, therefore, that the
United States should join the British in their expected veto.

As is customary on major U.S. votes in the United Nations, the final decision was left to the White House. After the
Spanish move, time was short, however; as the White House
considered the State Department's recommendation, time
began running out at the United Nations. A British request
for a delay of twenty-four hours was defeated by six votes to
seven. While he awaited his instructions, to be relayed to him
from a staff member waiting by an open telephone line to
Washington, Ambassador Yost was therefore forced into delaying tactics—requesting, for example, consecutive rather
than simultaneous translation of his remarks. The instructions
came through just before an American proposal that the vote
be delayed half an hour was defeated.

The British had also taken longer than expected to make
up their own minds. On the morning of the vote, American
embassy officials in London were unable either to tell British
officials at the Foreign Office what the United States would do
or learn if there would be a British veto. This seems to have
led to some suspicion on each side that the other might let it
bear all the burden in blocking the Afro-Asian draft resolution. The American delegation in New York learned the British would also be voting negatively only a short time before
being told by the White House to cast the first American veto

in the history of the United Nations. Ambassador Yost and Lord Caradon, the British representative, joined in killing the measure. The American veto was thus unnecessary; but it probably would have been cast even if American officials had known all along that the British would act as they did. The United States lost its virginity at the United Nations, it seems, out of choice rather than necessity.

While there was some public criticism of the veto, including an editorial in the *New York Times* on March 21, it centered not on the veto *per se,* but on the facts that it was (1) unnecessary and (2) on a southern African issue. The American delegation at the United Nations was relieved to discover that African reaction to the American move was less intense than it had feared. And most American critics of the administration's southern African policy and of the veto itself accepted the substantive arguments made by Ambassador Yost in explaining the American position.

By mid-1973, the United States had vetoed four more measures in the Security Council. The fourth again concerned Southern Rhodesia, and again the United States acted with the British. They struck down a draft resolution which would have limited the purchase by all states of any products from South Africa and the Portuguese territories to the quantitative levels prevailing in 1965 and would have extended the Beira blockade to cover the commodities and products traveling between Southern Rhodesia and the port of Laurenço Marques. The draft resolution would also have had the Council urge the British to implement fully the extension of the blockade and to seek the cooperation of other states in doing so. There was little question within the government what the United States should do. A decision to veto was reached at the Assistant Secretary level in the State Department, and cleared with the National Security Council staff. Higher levels in the Department were informed in advance. Explaining on May 22 why the United States was joining in the veto of this measure, Ambassador John Scali said, "While we can well understand the sentiment behind the draft resolution, we consider it unrealistic to call for broader sanctions until the full membership of the United Nations has demonstrated its willingness to take more seriously the sanctions already in force."

As it had in March, 1970, the United States then voted for a resolution which strengthened the sanctions in less dramatic ways.

Between these two vetoes, the United States abstained while the British vetoed a number of measures in the Security Council which would have limited the flexibility of London's negotiating position with Smith. The United States made a distinction between such diplomatic issues, which it continued to regard as Britain's responsibility, and the question of the nature of sanctions, which involved American interests directly. Some half a decade after American officials had told the British that the United States would not take the heat with them on the issue of the scope of sanctions, Washington was finally taking the responsibility for a position which it had clearly held all along.

AN EXCEPTION FOR UNION CARBIDE

Perhaps the most complicated Rhodesian issue facing the President as he made his decisions after the National Security Council meeting on southern Africa in December was the problem posed by the requests of three American firms for exceptions to the sanctions. Union Carbide, Foote Mineral, and Corning Glass had all applied for such exceptions under the terms of the "hardship" provision of the press release accompanying the President's Executive Order of January, 1967, and a Treasury Department press release of March 1, 1967. The Treasury release had stated that, "in general," Rhodesian goods which had been paid for but not exported before January 5, 1967, would be licensed for import into the United States, if it were a case of "undue hardship." Corning Glass's application for a license to import petalite clearly did not meet this criterion, and could be dismissed, although its president, Robert Murphy, was a friend of the President and had personally presided over the foreign policy aspects of the transition between the Johnson and Nixon administrations.

The other two cases were more complicated. Foote Mineral had transferred to its Rhodesian subsidiary, the Vanadium Corporation, funds with which to operate its chromite mines at a minimal level in order to avoid their becoming flooded. As a result of these operations, 57,000 tons of chromite was mined in 1967 and 1968. During the Johnson administration, Foote's application for licenses to import this chrome was denied—its transfer of funds to its Rhodesian subsidiary had been approved on the condition that the chrome which would be mined could not be imported into the United States. In 1967, Foote therefore decided that it made no economic sense to continue to operate the mine if it could not get the chrome, and discontinued its financial assistance to the Vanadium Corporation. In 1968, the Rhodesian government took over effective control of the subsidiaries of both Foote and Union Carbide.

According to one Foote official, their application was denied because they lacked all of the documentation they needed to prove that a part of the chrome which they wished to import had been mined before the January, 1967, Executive Order. Foote, he says, budgeted in advance, and did not send specific orders to its subsidiary as it sent the money. "We just sent over monthly installments regardless of whether any ore was shipped or not." As a result, Foote could not prove that it should receive even part of the 57,000 tons. While its argument was apparently never formally denied by the Nixon administration, Foote could not get its chrome until it had helped Senator Byrd shoot the necessary hole in the American sanctions program.[8]

Union Carbide had a better, although still difficult, case. In November and mid-December, 1966, the American company had transferred approximately $3 million to a South African subsidiary, Ruighoek Chrome Mines. On December 21,

[8] See chapter 6.

five days after the United Nations had passed its mandatory embargo against Rhodesian chrome (among other minerals), Ruighoek sent $2,680,000 to another Union Carbide subsidiary, Rhodesian Chrome Mines, as payment for 150,000 tons of chromite. Union Carbide officials claim that some of these 150,000 tons would have been imported before the mandatory sanctions had been voted if they had not agreed to observe the voluntary sanctions program of 1966. They say they had believed the American officials who had told them through 1966 that voluntary sanctions would work quickly, and had thus been faced with an undue hardship when the United Nations moved to make the sanctions mandatory.

During the last two years of the Johnson administration, lobbyists for Union Carbide and Foote met with State Department officials some twelve to twenty times to discuss their separate complaints. Meetings were also held with Treasury officials. State officials strongly opposed their case. While Foote went ahead and formally applied, despite the handwriting on the walls of the State Department, Union Carbide shrewdly waited. Its formal application for an exception was filed only after a new administration, more sympathetic to its position, had taken power in 1969.

The Nixon White House was, of course, far more sympathetic to business generally than the Johnson administration. And Union Carbide itself was in good odor. President Nixon's new ambassador to Bonn, Kenneth Rush, after teaching Nixon at Duke Law School, had served in important positions at Union Carbide for more than thirty years. Rush did well in Bonn, and in January, 1972, he became the Deputy Secretary of Defense; he was later Deputy Secretary at State and then Economic Coordinator at the White House. While Rush and other officials deny that he actively pressed Union Carbide's case within the government, his association with the company cannot have hurt it in the eyes of the President and his subordinates in the White House.[9] A number of these White House

[9] According to Bruce Oudes, writing in the *Observer* on May 13, 1973, and Laurence Stern, in the *Washington Post* on May 19, 1973, Rush drew a yearly

officials made little secret within the bureaucracy of their sympathy for Union Carbide's case.

Much of the discussion on Rhodesia in the 1969 Southern Africa policy review concerned the requests of Union Carbide and Foote for exceptions. The IG reportedly concluded that Foote's application could not be granted under the terms of either the President's Executive Order of 1967 or the hardship provision of the subsequent Treasury Department press release. The Union Carbide case was less clear. While it fell under the prohibitions of the Executive Order and would violate the intent if not the letter of the United Nations sanctions resolution of December, 1966, granting the exception might still be justified publicly on hardship grounds. The various departments were split on the issue, with State strongly opposed to the exception and Treasury and others in favor. The legal office of the State Department stated that "in strictly legal terms," the Union Carbide request fell under the provisions of the Executive Orders on Rhodesia and clearly violated the intent of the Security Council's sanctions. During the course of the National Security Council meeting, Kissinger reportedly suggested a compromise. The President agreed. Since it involved complicated legal issues—particularly with

pension from Union Carbide of $50,000 after joining the government. In addition, according to Stern, Union Carbide paid into a "blind trust" for Rush some $26,000 a year in "dividend equivalents." In early 1973, when he was confirmed as Deputy Secretary of State, Rush held approximately $1.2 million worth of Union Carbide stock. Thus, while Rush's personal income was not directly dependent on Union Carbide's fortunes, since the pension was at a set amount, Rush's future fortune continued to depend on Union Carbide's income. The blind trust would be terminated, and Rush would have access to its funds, once he left government. At the time of his State Department confirmation hearings, Rush assured the Senate Foreign Relations Committee that he would maintain a policy of "neutrality" on the Rhodesian issue and specifically on the Byrd Amendment. State Department officials say that Rush was meticulous in taking no part in State's decisions on American policy toward Rhodesia, and that his "neutrality" did not mean that he would disassociate himself from whatever positions the Department might take on the subject. In 1973, however, he reportedly refused to help present the Department's case in favor of repealing the Byrd Amendment.

regard to whether the payment of funds to subsidiaries could be counted as payment to Rhodesia—and all the evidence about what Union Carbide had actually done in late 1966 was not clear, why not submit the issue to an interagency group for further study?

The exception now became further intertwined with a broader issue: the Administration's general approach to American participation in sanctions. Following the NSC meeting, the President reportedly ordered two studies by the bureaucracy. One would specifically concern the legal merits of the Union Carbide case, with the Justice Department to resolve interagency differences. The second study, to be completed after the Union Carbide decision was made, would take a look at various American options should other nations continue to slide away from the United Nations sanctions program.

According to well-informed sources, the first study was quickly written by Richard Kleindienst, Deputy Attorney General, approved by Attorney General John Mitchell, and submitted to the President in early February, 1970. Kleindienst recommended approval of the Union Carbide request. The other agencies involved—Treasury, Commerce, State, and the Office of Emergency Preparedness—submitted their own positions. State opposed Kleindienst's recommendation on the ground that inconsistencies in Union Carbide's presentation of the facts required clarification before a decision was made. This seems to have caused enough uncertainties to keep the White House from making a decision, for the Union Carbide case was then folded into a more general review of American sanctions policy.

On March 9, a new decision memorandum from the White House directed a review of this policy, especially with regard to chrome imports. (The memorandum also reported the President's decision that the consulate in Salisbury would be closed.) A working group, including representatives of State, Defense, the National Security Council staff, Treasury, Commerce, Justice, and the OEP, was to examine alternative revisions of the sanctions program designed to minimize penalties to U.S. business while meeting American legal obligations under the U.N. sanctions program. A report was to be submitted to the President within three weeks. The group would be chaired by the State Department representative.

The committee was unable to complete its job before the end of April. Meetings were reportedly stormy. A number of sources state that during these sessions, as during the meetings before Kleindienst's early February report, a strong hostility developed between Kleindienst and the State Department representatives. Officers representing State's Legal Adviser and the Bureau of African Affairs argued strenuously that the exception for Union Carbide would both be illegal and not worth the price to be paid with the Africans. Kleindienst reportedly argued that it was the job of the group to find ways to accomplish what the administration wanted. He reportedly told the State Department lawyers that if they could not find legal ways to grant the exception, other lawyers could. It was the job of diplomats to find diplomatic ways to accomplish what the United States wished to accomplish. If the State Department wished to oppose the exception, it should not argue to the President that it was illegal, since that could later haunt him if he accepted the judgment of other departments to go ahead.

Treasury reportedly argued that since the Rhodesians had the money, there was no point in letting them keep the chrome as well—and that there were precedents for such hardship exceptions in the history of the American embargo against trade with Cuba and China. Treasury also supported Justice in its opinion that the exception was legal.

At the very end of April, Secretary Rogers transmitted the group's report to the White House. Rogers was reportedly unenthusiastic about the State Department's position, repeating to his staff the point which had by then become a cliché: "Why let them have both the chrome and the money?" But he was persuaded to sign the memorandum to the President which had been prepared for him. It recommended that all licenses continue to be denied; that the Union Carbide exception be denied for foreign policy reasons, since it would damage us in Africa and embarrass the British government shortly before an election (an argument hardly likely to sway the Tories' friends in the White House); and that the United States should make a more strenuous effort, together with the British, to gain more uniform observation of sanctions by other nations. If, after six months, it was clear that these efforts to strengthen sanctions were having no effect, the whole issue should be re-examined in detail. (As it had the previous December, when it suggested checking with the Africans before adoption of "tar baby," the State Department was forced to fight a delaying action in the face of superior strength.) After years of strict compliance with the U.N. sanctions program, Rogers argued, the United States should try to avoid doing anything which would lay it open to blame for a failure of that program.

The report of the group itself, transmitted by the Secretary's memorandum, indicated unanimous agreement on a number of points. American national security, it said, was not adversely affected by the sanctions at the present time. (The last phrase was reportedly needed to gain concensus on the statement.) American observation of sanctions should be consistent with anti-apartheid and pro-sanctions American policy statements, and with U.S. treaty obligations in the United Nations to observe sanctions. The document also reportedly included an analysis of the U.N. sanctions to that date, including a listing of violations by South Africa and others.

With regard to the Union Carbide application, the report described the split among the agencies. State opposed the application on legal grounds, basing its argument on the fact that Union Carbide had paid for the chrome after the Security Council had voted the mandatory sanctions. The Executive Order specifically prohibited any such import. The Justice Department, supported by Treasury; the Office of Economic Planning (OEP); Defense; and Commerce argued that the exception would be consistent with the spirit, if not the letter, of the U.N. sanctions program, and would be consistent with the Treasury Department's March, 1967, press release.

The National Security Council reviewed the issue on August 7. The President subsequently decided that if Union Carbide established to the satisfaction of the Treasury Department that it had paid for the chrome before the date of the January 5, 1967, Executive Order, the license would be issued. The decision was also reached that American firms with assets in Southern Rhodesia could sell those assets freely. This meant that certain American subsidiaries could be sold to Rhodesian as well as to South African and Portuguese buyers, an action which the State Department had opposed. The White House memorandum recording these decisions was reportedly issued in November. The Union Carbide decision was quickly made, however, by the Treasury Department. The exception was granted on September 18.

There was some argument within the State Department about how the decision should be released publicly. Some officials wanted to delay the news as long as possible; others thought it should be announced within a broader context before Union Carbide leaked it. American posts in Africa were told in early September to take the line that the exception was consistent with American sanctions obligations and that the United States wished to minimize any unnecessary adverse effects to American firms as those obligations were met. On September 17 in a speech in Chicago, Assistant Secretary Newsom quietly announced, "A special difficulty concerns firms which legally paid for goods in Rhodesia *before* the U.S. government prohibited such imports. At the time our implementing regulations were published, the Treasury Department announced that such transactions would be licensed under a 'hardship' provision. If any American firm can demonstrate that it did legally pay for the goods prior to the Executive Order—and only one has to date—we consider that it may complete the transaction, thus denying to Rhodesia the benefit of keeping both the foreign exchange and the goods. The U.N. sanctions committee will, of course, be formally advised of any such transactions." Union Carbide was to be the one.

The November decision memorandum reportedly went beyond the Union Carbide exception and the decision to let United States firms sell their Rhodesian assets to all comers. It also reaffirmed American participation in the U.N. sanctions program. While this probably represented an effort to provide the State Department with some frosting to make up for the cake it had lost, the fact that such a point was made suggests that there had been, during 1970, a chance that a key part of the original "tar baby" concept might have become a reality: as originally framed in the IG discussions a year before, this option had included a gradual relaxation of American sanctions, including the exception for chrome.

"Communication," then, had become, by late 1970, a conceptual cover for a series of moves that favored the Smith regime. It also included American advice to Salisbury. In the early fall of 1971, the United States indicated to Smith its interest in a negotiated solution. As Smith was negotiating the terms of his agreement with Home, now Foreign Secretary, the President sent a secret message to the Rhodesian leaders through an intermediary in South Africa. The message stated that the United States believed a settlement was in the Rhodesians' interest. It did not endorse or suggest specific terms. When the Home-Smith agreement was announced, American spokesmen took a neutral position, indicating the acceptability of the deal to Washington if the Rhodesian parties agreed. They did not, of course, as the Africans overwhelmingly rejected it.

The American effort to influence Smith in the direction of some sort of compromise was consistent with a policy of "communication" as it was first designed in the summer of 1969. But the failure of the Home-Smith agreement demonstrates the fact that the white Rhodesian regime must go much farther than it has ever suggested it would in meeting African demands, if there is to be an agreement between black and white leaders that can provide a lasting and peaceful solution. And an American policy of "communication" which consists of potentially bigger carrots and smaller sticks can only provide Smith with more comfort than concern.

The next chapter suggests that Rhodesian officials must be greatly comforted by the American performance in a number of areas where U.S. sanctions regulations are either vague or attractive to the eye of a corporate lawyer who thinks he spies an ambiguity not evident to the layman.

5

Business As Usual Assorted Activities Violating Sanctions

The Union Carbide exception was just that—an exception. In general, the performance of the American government in barring the illegal import or export of prohibited goods has been quite meticulous. (Since passage of the Byrd Amendment in late 1971, of course, a variety of Rhodesian minerals has been allowed into the country; see chapters 6 and 7). But the government's performance on prohibited activities not directly involving trade is much less impressive.

American implementation of the U.N. sanctions has been based upon Executive Orders 11322 and 11419 of January 5, 1967, and July 29, 1968, respectively. These Orders have the force of law. Under Sections 5(b) of the U.N. Participation Act, any person "who willfully violates or evades or attempts to violate or evade" such an Order is subject, upon conviction, to a fine of not more than $10,000, imprisonment for not more than ten years, or both.

The Executive Orders prohibit, with certain humanitarian, educational and other exceptions:

1. "Any activities by any person subject to the jurisdiction of the United States which promote or are calculated to promote the export from Southern Rhodesia, after May 29, 1968, of any commodities or products originating in Southern Rhodesia and any dealings by any such person in any such com-

modities or products, including in particular any transfer of funds to Southern Rhodesia for the purposes of such activities or dealings";

2. Activities which "promote or are calculated to promote" the sale of any commodities or products "to any person or body for the purposes of any businesses carried on in or operated from Southern Rhodesia";

3. Transfer of funds directly or indirectly to any person or body in Southern Rhodesia; and

4. "Operation of any United States air carrier or aircraft owned or chartered by any person subject to the jurisdiction of the United States or of United States registration (i) to or from Southern Rhodesia or (ii) in coordination with any airline company constituted or aircraft registered in Southern Rhodesia."

The Orders give to the Treasury Department the responsibility for enforcing the restrictions on imports into the United States of Rhodesian goods and for preventing illegal transfers of funds. The Commerce Department has the responsibility for implementing the restrictions on American exports to Rhodesia, and the carriage in American vessels of prohibited commodities. The Department of Transportation is responsible for ensuring compliance with the Executive Orders by American air carriers. All of them are to consult with the Department of State as they perform these duties.

The Treasury Department, which has also implemented the American embargoes of Cuba, Albania, and other Communist countries, has, by most accounts, been properly stringent with regard to imports of Rhodesian goods, despite some general qualms within Treasury about the merits of U.N. sanctions against Rhodesia. Any American can apply for an import license; unless it is for a commodity allowed entry under the Byrd Amendment, a license for a Rhodesian product is almost automatically denied. Government officials like to recount the fury of a few big-game hunters who have even been forced to relinquish to American customs officials the heads of the Rhodesian animals they had slaughtered. Trea-

sury has also used its power over currency transfers to bar or
strip the profits from illegal trade. For example, in early 1973,
Treasury officials instructed an American bank not to act on a
letter of credit held by a foreign supplier who had shipped
elephants to the United States with documents purporting to
show that the beasts had been captured in Mozambique. An
investigation revealed that the exporter had acquired a
number of baby elephants from Rhodesia at the same time. In
another case, Treasury blocked $337,000 in a South African
bank's account in New York which was to be used to pay for
an illegal shipment of anhydrous ammonia.

Because of the humanitarian exceptions to sanctions allowed under the U.N. Security Council Resolutions, the Commerce Department must make frequent decisions about the
purposes of export goods for which American exporters seek
licenses. It allows licenses for exports which would go to humanitarian, religious, medical and educational institutions.
Use of an item by such institutions is usually considered proof
that those items are in fact used for medical or humanitarian
purposes. In the words of one Commerce official, "If a missionary wants to fly an aircraft, he can get an aircraft." The
trickier questions arise when nonhumanitarian institutions ask
for goods which they state will serve humanitarian purposes.
What, for example, of a chemical agent designed to wipe out
the larvae of a disease-carrying insect, to be supplied to a local
commercial distributor? If the disease affects human beings,
the license would probably be granted. If the chemical were
purely for use in preventing disease that afflicts only animals,
the license would probably be denied. Rhodesia exports beef,
and a chemical that prevented disease in its cattle would
strengthen the Rhodesian economy without serving a strictly
humanitarian purpose. But to split this fine hair further, if the
meat of diseased cattle caused human disease, then a license to
export the chemical would be granted.

Commerce decides on about 75 percent of the applications for licenses without reference to other agencies. On bor-
derline cases, it consults informally with the State Department,

and occasionally with agencies which can offer technical advice, like Interior. The State Department is reportedly more strict in its interpretations than Commerce, and its views are usually accepted, since according to a Commerce official, "it is a foreign policy problem." (It is not surprising that Commerce Department officials are less restrictive than their State counterparts; they work in a department whose general mandate is to expand, not limit, American exports. Commerce officials who deny export applications are not ingratiating themselves with their bosses.) In late 1972 or early 1973, State and Commerce reportedly disagreed over a piece of safety equipment for a Rhodesian coal mine. After checking with the Interior Department's Bureau of Mines, Commerce favored approval of the license since the equipment would enhance the safety of the miners. State argued that the same safety procedure which the equipment would facilitate could be carried out with more labor, and that the equipment was not therefore necessary. Labor is something Rhodesia does not lack. State won.

In addition to the decisions of Treasury and Commerce on licensing and financial transfers, three cases of sanctions violations have been prosecuted in American courts. These were among the few cases to have been brought against violators anywhere in the world. On March 31, 1970, William H. Muller & Co. was indicted by a federal grand jury for allegedly importing Southern Rhodesian chrome concentrate worth $367,782. The company pleaded guilty, and a federal court judge immediately imposed the maximum penalty, $10,000. The judge said that it was unusual to inflict the maximum legal punishment on a firm which had never before been in trouble with the law, but he was doing so because the case involved a violation of "an important part of United States foreign policy." In June, 1972, two corporations and three individuals [1] were fined $131,750 for planning to build a $50 million chemical fertilizer plant in Rhodesia and for en-

[1] Margas Shipping Co. of Panama City, Panama; IDI Management, Inc. of Cincinnati; Herbert Hamilton, president of IDI; Conrad E. Wysocki, an IDI engineer; and David J. Patterson, a Coral Gables, Florida, businessman.

tering into a secret agreement with the Smith regime to ship $5 billion worth of ammonia there. One of the individuals was placed on probation for a year as well as fined; all had pleaded guilty. In late 1973, a subsidiary of Reynolds Metals Company was indicted by a federal grand jury on charges that it had imported from South Africa 197 tons of petalite ore that originated in Rhodesia. (The case was reportedly brought to the attention of the U.S. government by a note from the British.) The company pleaded guilty, and a Reynolds spokesman said, "We deeply regret that this constitutes a violation of the law, and have taken steps to prevent such mistakes in the future." The spokesman also said the material imported was "a sample quantity of petalite ore for research purposes." One must suppose that it was a rather large research project.

As a result of the government's efforts to implement the U.N. sanctions program, American trade with Rhodesia was reduced from approximately $33 million in 1965 to $600,000 in 1970, all of it, according to government officials, in permissible items such as pharmaceuticals, books, etc. But some questions remain.

One issue is the degree to which the United States helps the United Nations to implement sanctions. The American government informs the United Nations of all shipments of goods between Rhodesia and the United States, but it could do more. Representative Donald Fraser (D.–Minn.) has expressed the view that the Central Intelligence Agency might pursue sanctions violations by other nations and provide the information it uncovers to the United Nations. Although this might be difficult in practice or even unacceptable in principle, there is room for more regular American information sharing at the United Nations about sanctions violations.

The American government could also do more in raising sanctions violations which have come to its attention with the governments concerned. Violations of sanctions within the jurisdictions of a large number of countries, including Belgium, France, West Germany, Holland, Italy, Japan, South Korea,

Luxembourg, Portugal and Switzerland, have been widely alleged. Government sources indicate that the United States has raised possible violations during the past seven years with a number of governments, including the Italians, French, West Germans and Japanese. But the United States has apparently never made much of an issue of such complaints and has refused to point the finger publicly at its allies. Nor, since the passage of the Byrd Amendment, has it been in a position to do so.

The passage of Security Council Resolution 333 on May 22, 1973, presented the American government with a further challenge, one which it could meet only in part. The resolution approved a list of recommendations prepared by the Sanctions Committee on ways in which sanctions could be strengthened. (The American representative abstained on the measure, and government officials indicated that Washington would be unable to comply with some of the requests which the Council made to all States.) Some raise domestic legal problems; others raise problems of implementation. For example, the resolution called upon states to inform the Sanctions Committee of their sources of supply of chrome, asbestos, nickel, pig iron, tobacco, meat and sugar. To determine whether any American imports of such goods from third countries were actually from Rhodesia would require massive testing procedures of doubtful efficiency. And it is practically impossible to determine the origin of some of the items listed, such as pig iron. However, according to then Secretary of the Treasury George Shultz, in a letter to Congressman Diggs on September 3, 1973, the American government has carried out a number of tests of suspect imports. Specifically:

(1) All tobacco imported into the United States from African countries is subjected to laboratory analysis.

(2) All chrome ore imported into the United States from South Africa was subjected to laboratory analysis up until the time when it became legal to import chrome ore from Rhodesia pursuant to the Byrd Amendment.

(3) All ferrochrome imported into the United States from South Africa and Japan was subjected to laboratory analysis until the passage of the Byrd Amendment. (Some tests were reportedly carried out by American experts who traveled to Japan and South Africa for that purpose.)

(4) Test analyses and expert examinations were made of random samples of chrome ore from the USSR in connection with allegations that Russia was buying Rhodesian chrome and re-exporting it to the United States, falsely labeled as being of Russian origin. (The tests did not substantiate the allegations.)

Despite these precautions, it is very difficult to prevent the entry of Rhodesian goods into the United States through third countries. Similarly, the American government has been unable completely to block the export of American goods to Rhodesia, in some cases even when the goods fell under specific export restrictions. In late 1972, the sale of a DC-8 to AFRITAIR, an airline registered in Gabon but with ties to Rhodesian businessmen, was allowed after AFRITAIR reportedly gave assurance that the airplane would not be used to transport Rhodesian goods. In the late summer of the following year, the DC-8 was reported to have been carrying Rhodesian beef from Salisbury to Gabon, Greece, and other nations in Europe. By the end of 1973, the American government moved to prevent the export of spare parts for the aircraft—which seemed to be missing one wheel.

The Gabon connection thus gave the Rhodesians another air link to the outside world. Another link was forged in dramatic incidents in Switzerland and West Germany in September, 1973. Three Boeing 720s (similar to 707s) were put into service for Air Rhodesia, and by year's end they were flying the Salisbury-Johannesburg run.

The three aircraft had been part of Eastern Airlines' fleet, operating in America, from 1962 to 1970. In 1970, Eastern sold them back to Boeing as trade-ins for new aircraft. They then became the objects of a series of complicated deals which allowed them finally to be flown from Europe to Salisbury. According to investigations by Peter Deeley and Bruce Oudes recounted in the *Observer*,[2] Boeing sold the three 720s, together with two others, to one Carl Hirschmann, a Swiss millionaire with large banking and business interests in Europe, Africa and America, for between $3.5 and $4 million. On the same day, Hirschmann sold the planes for about $10 million to a company in which he had an interest. The planes then sat for three years at the Basle-Mulhouse Airport, for the company which owned them had failed. By April, 1973, Boeing was preparing to reclaim four of the aircraft, since it held a lien on them for about $2.5 million. Hirschmann made Boeing an acceptable offer for two of them, acting through a different company. And, through a series of intricate paper deals, he gained control of the fifth. He then sold the three aircraft he controlled to Mervyn Eyett, the deputy general manager of Air Rhodesia.

One of the export licenses Hirschmann had been granted by the American government covered his purchase of the jets from Boeing in 1970. That license included the standard clause that a foreign purchaser of American aircraft must obtain the authorization of the United States government before reselling it. (Hirschmann also obtained, some time during the first half of 1973, an export license for the purchase from Boeing of hundreds of thousands of dollars worth of spare parts for the planes.) Sources in the American government state that the transfer of the aircraft to Rhodesia was never authorized. The government therefore tried to prevent the sale of spare parts to Air Rhodesia, and in January, 1974, Hirschmann's company lost the "station license" which had allowed it to buy aircraft and parts from American companies without close scrutiny from the Commerce Department.

According to Oudes and Deeley, Hirschmann claims that he did not know that Eyett was an agent for Air Rhodesia. Eyett, he claims, said he was acting for a South African company—although the South African company he names does

[2] The *Observer*, "How Smith Got His Boeings Through the Blockade," Peter Deeley in London and Bruce Oudes in Washington, September 30, 1973.

not appear in trade or telephone directories, and Boeing says that it is aware of Eyett's position with Air Rhodesia. Boeing also says that it is "in the clear" over the transaction. However, the Africa Bureau in London has reported that shortly after the three aircraft were delivered to Rhodesia, Air Rhodesia personnel attended a Boeing instruction course in South Africa. Air Rhodesia employees had previously attended Boeing courses in Denver, Colorado, according to this report.[3]

The Boeing case should not obscure the generally good performance of the Executive Branch in implementing the regulations with regard to the flow of embargoed materials. But the trade embargo is only part of the sanctions program. The government's performance when it comes to other activities, about which the regulations are sometimes arguably ambiguous, has been remarkably lax. And it apparently has even overlooked activities by American air carriers which seem flatly in contradiction of the Executive Orders.

A review of these cases leads one to the inescapable conclusion that the American government has usually done what it was legally required to do in implementing sanctions, but it has made no effort to do any more than that. If it had the political will to implement sanctions to the fullest extent allowed by the law, rather than to the minimum extent legally required, it apparently would have ample grounds to act in a number of areas. It apparently does not have this will.

As a result, if you live in the United States, you can:

—receive mailings about Southern Rhodesia from its information office in Washington, or pick up tourist brochures at the New York office of Air Rhodesia and the Rhodesian National Tourist Board;

—read paid advertisements for Rhodesian firms and investment opportunities printed in an American newspaper;

—make a hotel reservation or reserve a rented car in Rhodesia through a representative of Pan American in the United States;

—reserve an automobile there through an American rent-a-car office here;

[3] *Newsbrief Rhodesia '73*, September, 1973.

—stay at a Holiday Inn in Rhodesia;

—pay for your air tickets and rent-a-car with one of a number of American credit cards;

—or visit Rhodesia as part of a package African tour managed by an American travel company;

—and, until the late summer of 1974, even make reservations to fly on a Rhodesian airline through airlines registered in the United States.

RHODESIA'S REPRESENTATIVES IN THE UNITED STATES

The House Foreign Affairs Subcommittee on Africa launched in 1973 an investigation of the activities of the Rhodesian Information Office (RIO) in Washington. There are only two or three such offices maintained by the Smith regime throughout the world. One other, the Rhodesian Information Centre in Australia, has been under pressure from the Australian government to reduce or close out its activities. Unlike the RIO in Washington, the Australian office is managed by local citizens. The Rhodesians also claim to have an information office in France. In addition, Rhodesia has had official representatives in South Africa and Portugal. And the Rhodesians reportedly have unofficial, *sub rosa* offices managed by local citizens in a number of other nations.

The House subcommittee's investigation of the Rhodesian Information Office apparently was seeking to answer more than the general question of why the United States should allow such an office to operate here when so few other nations will have anything to do officially with the illegal regime in Salisbury. The subcommittee was looking into possible violations of American law and the U.N. sanctions resolutions with regard to allegations concerning the Rhodesian Information Office's promotion of trade by publishing lists of Rhodesian products and by supporting the passage in 1971 of the Byrd Amendment; its activities as, in effect, a diplomatic agent of the Smith regime; its encouraging immigration to Rhodesia; its performance of consular functions; the visa status of the two Rhodesians who maintain the office; and the supply of goods and services to it by American companies.

A brief review of each of these areas suggests that while there may not be an open-and-shut case that the RIO has violated American law or the Security Council's sanctions resolutions, there are questions both of fact and of interpretation of the law which could be pursued by the American government if it had the political desire to remove the office from this country.

There is nothing illicit about the RIO's disseminating general information about Rhodesia. That is, after all, what it is here for. It distributes *Rhodesian Commentary,* published in Salisbury, which covers news about developments in Rhodesia. *Rhodesian Viewpoint,* published in Washington, reviews American comment on Rhodesia; supportive comments are played up in it, of course, and negative comments are disputed. Both publications are sent to thousands of newspapers and editors, individual journalists, former visitors to Rhodesia and interested individuals (almost all of them pro-Smith), as well as officials within the Executive Branch and all members of Congress. In addition, films about Rhodesia have been shown throughout the United States. Those privileged to see them have included American servicemen in at least twenty-one Army, Navy and Marine facilities in the United States. One film has even been shown at the Department of Justice in Washington.

While the RIO may have the right to distribute general propaganda so long as it is allowed in the United States at all, the American government, if it wished, could pursue the question of whether some of this information has served purposes contrary to its sanctions program. For example, in acting as a kind of central clearinghouse for local newspaper editorials supporting passage of the Byrd Amendment, was the RIO promoting trade with Rhodesia, since such trade in certain commodities was the purpose of the Amendment? When it disseminated copies of the publication *Products of Rhodesia,* was it promoting trade in those products? There is no doubt about the intention of the RIO itself. In a report on file at the Justice Department, Towsey has stated that the RIO's activities "include the promotion of Rhodesian government policies in the United States with a view to improving relationships between the two governments to the ultimate end that there will be full and free diplomatic and *trading* exchanges between Rhodesia and the United States." (Emphasis added.)

Support by the RIO of passage of the Byrd Amendment went beyond the pleadings of *Rhodesian Viewpoint.* During the course of debate on the Amendment, Towsey and Hooper were in close touch with its congressional supporters and the business lobbyists who were pressing for its passage. Neither Towsey nor Hooper have made any secret of the fact that they have been active on Capitol Hill. Witness the following excerpts from RIO registration statements:

> Both officers . . . were involved in frequent visits to the Capitol clubs and private meetings where they made themselves available for talks with Congressmen, Senators, members of the press and officials interested in Rhodesian/U.S. relationships.
> . . . Close contact is kept with Members of the U.S. Congress and their staff when legislation affecting the situation is being debated or considered.
> Officers have attended Congressional hearings on the Rhodesian situation and have met at their request with Congressmen, Senators, members of the news media, officials and diplomats who have expressed interest in the Rhodesian situation.[4]

They argue, however, that this activity is not lobbying. As Towsey has said, "Certainly, we were not in the business of seeking to solicit votes from Members of Congress in support of the Byrd Amendment."[5] Simply providing information when asked and keeping in touch with interested parties does not, in Towsey's view, constitute "lobbying." Hence, the RIO was not promoting the Byrd Amendment and trade with Rho-

[4] Hearings before the Subcommittee on Africa of the Committee on Foreign Affairs, May 15, 17, 1973, p. 22.

[5] *Ibid.,* p. 39.

desia. It comes down to a question of degree and interpretation. Did the RIO so actively press its information on the members of Congress as to have been lobbying? While the House subcommittee pursued the question, the Executive Branch has not.

A related question concerns those activities of the RIO which might be interpreted as "diplomatic" in nature. Security Council Resolution 277 (March, 1970) provides that "member States shall immediately sever all *diplomatic, consular,* trade, military and other relations that they may have with the illegal regime in Southern Rhodesia, and terminate any representation that they may maintain in the Territory." (Emphasis added.) Were Towsey and Hooper, in their contacts with members of Congress, acting as representatives of the Rhodesian government? The Department of State says "no." A legal memorandum to the House subcommittee states: "The Department of State regards the contacts by representatives of the Rhodesian Information Office with Members of Congress as analogous to the private contacts by proponents of other interest groups with such Members and does not consider the contacts to fall within the meaning of Resolution 277." [6] In addition, the FBI reviewed the files of the RIO in 1973. It found, according to a report sent to the subcommittee on April 30, 1973, "no sign of actual direction or close control from Rhodesia." Nor did its examination show that Towsey had initiated in writing his contacts with Congressmen; his letters to them followed "a previous personal contact by Mr. Towsey of a social or possibly business nature with Members of Congress or their staff members, or as a result of requests for information relative to Rhodesia initiated by Members of Congress or their staffs." [7] Thus, the FBI's investigation showed neither that the RIO was acting under orders from Salisbury nor that it was engaging in "lobbying activity on behalf of the Byrd Amendment." The FBI investigation, which was carried out under the Foreign Agents Registration

[6] *Ibid.,* p. 82.   [7] *Ibid.,* p. 33.

Act, should not be considered, however, the equivalent of the kind of investigation that the government would make if it were intent on forcing the issue. The FBI agents reportedly made an appointment in advance for their visit to the RIO offices to review the files which were presented to them. Some questions remain. What of Towsey's 1969 meetings with a National Security Council staff member, Morris, during which Towsey discussed the position of the Rhodesian government on the American consulate? While the meetings began on an informal basis, were not the two of them actually dealing with each other as official representatives? Towsey must surely have been reporting to Salisbury what Morris said, as Morris was reporting to his superiors. And what of a recent registration statement which shows that the RIO still considers itself part of the government of Rhodesia, despite the insistence of the American government since early 1966 that it is not? The RIO statement asserted that the "registrant is a permanent agency of the Ministry of Information of the Government of Rhodesia. Its fees and expenses, including the remuneration of its staff, are allocated by the Rhodesian Treasury as part of the Rhodesian government budget which is subject to approval each year by the Rhodesian Parliament. The Rhodesian Information Office, as an arm of the Government of Rhodesia, is staffed by members of the Rhodesian Public Service and certain locally recruited personnel in clerical capacities." [8] If the RIO considers itself part of the Rhodesian government, should not the American government agree? And if so, does its presence violate Security Council Resolution 277?

The RIO also acts as a "post office" for Rhodesian students and others who seek renewal of their passports. It apparently does not actually validate the passports. It has also occasionally seemed to act for the Rhodesian government with regard to the entry of Americans into the territory. In January, 1971, Towsey interrupted a press conference held by Congressman Diggs to inform him that the Rhodesian regime

[8] *Ibid.,* p. 12.

would not allow him to visit Southern Rhodesia. Did this imply that the RIO was acting as an official consular representative of the Rhodesian government in violation of Security Council Resolution 277?

If the American government were to pursue these lines of questions and to decide that the RIO had done nothing to violate sanctions, other issues would still remain. For example, consider the activities of the RIO with regard to immigration into Rhodesia. Security Council Resolution 253 calls upon all members "to take all possible measures to prevent" anyone in their territories from encouraging emigration to Southern Rhodesia. The RIO receives about a dozen requests a month for information about emigration; some are referred to the RIO by the Air Rhodesia office in New York City. The RIO supplies this information, but reportedly does not then pursue the matter with those individuals. One of the pamphlets it has distributed, *Employment in Rhodesia,* provides glowing descriptions of "a Land of Opportunity." The brochure states that the reader will learn in it "what [he] may expect to earn, the scope of various fields of employment and . . . working conditions generally." It concludes with the address of the Department of Immigration Promotion in Salisbury. The RIO argues that the pamphlets it issues on industrial and agricultural conditions in Rhodesia "are only given out as part of the Office's information function if specific inquiry is made." Does this clearly mean that conveying this information to potential emigrants is not "encouraging" their emigration to Rhodesia? In allowing the RIO to do this, is the American government taking "all possible measures" to prevent such encouragement, as it is asked (but not required) to do by Security Council Resolution 253?

Towsey's and Hooper's visa status was reviewed in chapter 3. Hooper's continuing position as an applicant for permanent resident status perfectly symbolizes the approach of the American government to the RIO. The questions just listed about its activities do not mean that the American government is flatly required by law to move against the office.

But if it decided that the continued presence of the RIO in the United States contradicts the spirit if not the letter of the American obligation faithfully to observe sanctions, it would have numerous avenues along which to proceed. Acting against the RIO would incur the wrath of Senator Eastland, and it would violate the principle that Americans should not fear expressions of any point of view. But Rhodesia is a very special case; its regime is the only regime against which the United States is legally obligated to carry out sanctions. If it wished to, the American government could decide the issue of the RIO as easily as it could decide Hooper's visa status.

One witness, Barbara Rogers, at hearings held by the Diggs subcommittee on May 15, 1973, suggested a further issue. She argued that supply of communications facilities to the RIO by RCA, ITT and Reuters, Ltd., as well as the supply of other goods and services by American companies, may violate paragraph 1(d) of Executive Order 11419, which prohibits the "sale or supply by any person . . . to any person or body for the purposes of any business carried on in, or operated from, Southern Rhodesia of any commodities or products." Since the RIO is an agent of the regime in Salisbury, it would, as Barbara Rogers pointed out, "appear likely to fall within the definition of a business operated from Southern Rhodesia."

The same point also applied to the office of Air Rhodesia and the Rhodesian National Tourist Board in New York City. In May, 1974, the Treasury Department blocked the accounts of the Air Rhodesia office after it was discovered—through information supplied by a former employee—that the office had been carrying out "unauthorized transactions" for at least three years. How Treasury had failed to discover and crack down on these transactions while they were taking place remains unexplained.

Congressman Diggs and other opponents of the Smith regime in the United States have concentrated most of their fire on the RIO and the office of Air Rhodesia and the Rhodesian National Tourist Board. But some firms are conducting what amounts to business as usual with Rhodesia, and they have received less attention. They include U.S. airlines, American rent-a-car companies, and an American newspaper. Their actions raise the possibility of violations of American law.

FLYING TO SALISBURY

Flying to foreign countries can be a trying experience. Visas and shots and tickets, delays and complications—all can make travel to most areas of the world something less than an unadulterated pleasure. A trip to Southern Rhodesia, however, is a breeze. No visa is required, just one or two inoculations, a passport, and a confirmed onward reservation. Air travel reservations? Until late summer, 1974, one could drop by a ticket counter here in the United States, and in seconds the computer would confirm a space on an Air Rhodesia flight from Johannesburg, South Africa, to the Rhodesian capital of Salisbury.

Such has been the experience, at least, of many Americans who have traveled to Rhodesia during the past few years. It was all very convenient. The trouble is that when Pan American, TWA, and other American carriers helped make the going great to Salisbury, they apparently did it illegally.

On July 15, 1973, Stephen Park, a student at the University of Oregon and I went to the Pan American offices in Washington and made a reservation on Air Rhodesia flight 876 for October 7, 1973, from Salisbury to Blantyre, Malawi. (Reservations were also made for other flights in a planned journey from Washington to Salisbury and back.) The reservation was confirmed within seconds by Pan American's computer. On August 8, a reservation was made at the TWA office in Washington for travel to Africa and back. It included Air Rhodesia flights 873 and 731.

The tickets for all the flights from Washington to Salisbury and back could be paid for in Washington by major American credit cards. Pan American also requested a reservation at a hotel in Salisbury, confirmed it later, and offered to reserve a Hertz or Avis rent-a-car there.

We asked both Pan American and TWA if there would be problems getting into Southern Rhodesia because of the sanctions program. In neither case did their ticket agents seem particularly aware of the sanctions. Both offices assured us that all that was required to enter Southern Rhodesia was a valid passport, an onward reservation, and a smallpox vaccination (according to Pan American) or a yellow fever inoculation (according to TWA).

We made the inquiries at Pan American and TWA because of their leading role among American carriers in service to the African continent; they are used here as examples. In fact, as suggested below, most if not all American carriers were cooperating with Air Rhodesia. They were acting in violation of two sections of Executive Order 11419. Section 1(g) of the Order prohibits "operation of any U.S. carrier or aircraft owned or chartered by any person subject to the jurisdiction of the United States or of United States registration (i) to or from Southern Rhodesia or (ii) *in coordination with any airline company constituted or aircraft registered in Southern Rhodesia.*" (Emphasis added.)

The Executive Order was defined in greater detail by Special Federal Aviation Regulation No. 21, promulgated September 18, 1968, by the Federal Aviation Administration: "No U.S. air carrier may operate any aircraft. . . . In coordination with any airline company constituted, or aircraft registered, in Southern Rhodesia, whether by *connecting flight, inter-line agreement, block booking, ticketing,* or any other method of link up." (Emphasis added.)

Both Pan American and TWA made reservations for *connecting flights* into or from Rhodesia on South African Airways, Air Rhodesia, or Air Malawi. In addition, *tickets* for these connecting flights were issued by Pan American and TWA. According to interviews with sources at Pan American, the airline did hold a *block of seats* on Air Rhodesia flights that it could sell up to four days before any particular flight. This arrangement was part of an *inter-line agreement* between Pan American and Air Rhodesia.[9] Thus, Pan American and the others were acting in violation of the specific provisions of Special Federal Aviation Regulation No. 21. Interviews also indicated that Air Rhodesia acted as Pan American's representative in Rhodesia; since no Pan American office is in operation there, Air Rhodesia provided tickets and reservations for Pan American flights, and represented Pan American in other transactions in Rhodesia.

Section 1(f) of Executive Order 11419 prohibits "transfer by any person subject to the jurisdiction of the United States *directly or indirectly* to any person or body in Southern Rhodesia of any funds or other financial or economic resources." (Emphasis added.)

Both Pan American and TWA received from the customer the full payment of the air fare from Washington to Salisbury and return, including payment for flights on other airlines. They then credited those payments to the connecting carriers. When the connecting carrier was Air Rhodesia, this would seem to have been at least an indirect "transfer of funds to a person or body in Southern Rhodesia."

Transfers of funds among international air carriers reportedly take place in one of two ways. The most common method is through the International Air Transport Association (IATA), an independent organization which, among other functions, serves as a clearinghouse through which international airlines settle accounts with each other. A letter from IATA dated July 16, 1973, confirmed that Air Rhodesia

[9] A source at TWA confirmed that it also had such an agreement with Air Rhodesia. In addition, reliable information indicates that eighteen other American carriers, together with sixty-five of their foreign competitors, were in a similar position. The foreign carriers are not bound, of course, by the Executive Order. The American airlines are Alaska, Allegheny, Aloha, American, Braniff, Continental, Delta, Eastern, Flying Tiger, Hawaiian, Hughes, National, Northeast, Ozark, Seaboard, Southern, United, and Western.

is not a member of IATA, and therefore cannot use IATA's services.

This leaves the second method of payment, a bilateral arrangement, as the means by which Pan American and TWA apparently transferred funds to Air Rhodesia. (It should be noted that neither Pan American nor TWA accepted payment for the hotels and rental cars for which it made reservations; the customer had to pay these directly. A "package" could be paid for by credit card, but the airlines received from the credit card company only that portion of the cost which represents the total air fare. The airlines still paid the connecting air carriers in these cases, however.)

According to an interview at Pan American, the amount credited to Air Rhodesia in 1972 was approximately $200,000, an increase of almost 200 percent from the previous year. This increase, we were told, could not be accounted for by higher costs and prices; the increase must, then, have represented an increase in the number of passengers purchasing tickets on Air Rhodesia flights through Pan American. According to a different official at the airline, these funds were not then transferred directly to Air Rhodesia. Rather, Air Rhodesia kept what it collected as Pan American's agent in Salisbury. The books were kept on a "net balance" basis, and no direct transfers are said to have taken place. In 1968, when such direct transfers ceased, Air Rhodesia was owed approximately $59,000. By the end of July, 1973, the credit balance in favor of Air Rhodesia had been reduced slightly, to $57,520. Pan American argues that since no money was actually transferred to Air Rhodesia, it was not in violation of Section 2(f) of the Order. But since Air Rhodesia could only keep the money it collected because of Pan Am's collections in the United States, an "indirect" transfer would appear to have taken place—and such transfers are specifically prohibited.

This raises questions, of course, about how the Executive Orders are implemented by the U.S. government. According to interviews with the airlines and with government officials concerned, there is some doubt about the meticulousness with which the government has monitored compliance by American air carriers with the Executive Order and the Federal Aviation Administration regulations. In interviews in 1973, some government officials recalled that checks had been made some years ago with Pan American and others. Other officials were not able to substantiate this, and one Pan American official who has some responsibility in this area could not recall such attention from the government. One FAA official, after reviewing his files, stated that no such contact with members of the airline industry had ever taken place before 1973.

The responsibility for monitoring compliance with the relevant sections of the Executive Order is delegated to the Secretaries of Transportation and the Treasury. Section 2(b) of the Order delegates "to the Secretary of Transportation, the function and responsibility of enforcement relating to the operation of air carriers and aircraft." Within the Department of Transportation, the Federal Aviation Administration has been given enforcement responsibility. According to interviews with FAA officials, no monitoring system existed to keep the agency informed of what the airlines were doing with regard to Rhodesian sanctions. Rather, the FAA relied on complaints about possible sanctions violations. According to FAA officials in 1973, no complaint had been received since the FAA's regulations went into effect in September, 1968.[10]

The FAA thus relied on the knowledge of the regulations by officials of American air carriers, and their willingness to comply with them. Yet twenty American carriers were apparently unaware of the regulations or consciously acting in violation of them.

Section 2(c) of Executive Order 11419 delegates to the Secretary of the Treasury, in effect, responsibility for enforce-

[10] One action the FAA has taken since that time has been to amend the 1968 regulations, to make it clear that American air carriers are allowed to cooperate with non-Rhodesian airlines that fly into Rhodesia. These would include South African Airways and Air Malawi. This change in the regulations was required because the regulations seemed to go beyond the Executive Order in this regard.

ment of Section 1(d), which governs the transfer of "financial or economic resources" to Rhodesia. If Pan American, TWA, and perhaps others were transferring funds to Air Rhodesia, their apparent violation of the Executive Order would fall within the Treasury Department's purview. Yet somehow the Treasury Department was apparently unaware of these and other transfers described elsewhere in this study.

In August, 1973, Stephen Park and I published a report under the auspices of the Carnegie Endowment, presenting these and many of the other facts reported in this chapter. As a result of our inquiries into the matter, the State Department asked the Treasury Department and FAA to investigate possible violations of the Executive Order by Pan American, TWA, and other American carriers. Despite what was apparently a number of requests for action by State and pressure on the FAA from a number of interested organizations, it was more than a year later—during the summer of 1974—before the FAA sent a letter to American air carriers calling on their assistance in "ensuring" that they were operating in full conformity with the FAA's regulations. Soon thereafter, Pan American stopped accepting requests for reservations on Air Rhodesia.

Treasury reportedly took the position that it was an FAA problem; if it had blocked any illegal activities by the airlines, the problem of indirect currency transfers would not have arisen.

There are a number of questions that must be asked in connection with the government's investigation of the matter:

—Were Pan American and TWA violating the law? For how long? Have they severed all their business relations with Air Rhodesia?

—What other American carriers have been doing business with Air Rhodesia?

—If there are others, have they done business with Air Rhodesia in knowledge of the law?

—Will they be prosecuted under the terms of the U. N. Participation Act?

—What were the financial arrangements between American airlines other than Pan Am and Air Rhodesia? For example, a TWA spokesman has said (in the *Washington Post* on August 26, 1973) that the airline had done $1,100 worth of business with Air Rhodesia in 1973. How were these funds transferred?

—How were such transfers of funds accomplished without the knowledge of the Treasury Department? How should that Department's procedures for monitoring such transfers be tightened?

—Should enforcement of the Executive Order and its own regulations by the FAA also be tightened, and some sort of monitoring procedures be instituted by that agency?

RENT-A-CAR IN RHODESIA

While American air carriers smoothed your way into Salisbury, Hertz and Avis offices in the United States were glad to reserve a Hertz or Avis car for your use while in Southern Rhodesia. In 1973, Park and I called the international reservations offices of both companies and within a few days such reservations arrived in the mail. Since neither Hertz nor Avis offices in the United States would accept payment for car rentals in Rhodesia, payment was to be made directly to the Rhodesian Hertz and Avis companies by the customer.

A letter from Avis dated August 2, 1973, stated that Avis in Southern Rhodesia is an independent company—an "independent sublicensee"—which has a sublicense to operate under Avis's name. The sublicense was granted by the Avis licensee in South Africa. This licensing arrangement came into being approximately eighteen months before, according to the letter from Avis. A subsequent letter, dated October 29, 1974, stated that the arrangement "had the approval of the United States Treasury Department." In a telephone interview, a Hertz official stated that Hertz had the same arrangement with a subsidiary in Rhodesia. The official did not indicate how long the licensee had been operating in Southern Rhodesia.

In 1974, Hertz closed its office in Salisbury, at least temporarily. Avis continued to accept reservations for cars at the Avis office in Salisbury.

Hertz and Avis may have been acting in violation of Section 1(d) of Executive Order 11419. As noted previously, this section prohibits the sale or supply of any commodities or products to any person or body in Southern Rhodesia, or to any person or body for the purposes of any business carried on in, or operated from, Southern Rhodesia. If one considers company names to be "commodities," then Avis and Hertz are clearly supplying commodities to Southern Rhodesian companies. One common definition of "commodity" is that it is something useful or valuable. Since their foreign licensees and sublicensees pay for the right to use the name of Avis and Hertz, those names are something useful or valuable.[11] And obviously, these names are used for business purposes in Southern Rhodesia.

Black's *Law Dictionary* defines "commodity" as follows: "In the most comprehensive sense, convenience, accommodation, profit, benefit, advantage, interest, and commodiousness. In the commercial sense, any movable or tangible thing that is produced or used as the subject of barter or sale." Why should the U.S. government adopt the most limited rather than this broader definition of this term?

Enforcement of this provision is the responsibility of the Commerce Department. The arrangement between Hertz and Avis and their namesakes in Rhodesia raises some questions which would appear worthy of further investigation by that Department.

—Are these companies illegally supplying commodities to businesses in Southern Rhodesia in selling the use of their names? If so, are any other American companies which have lent their names to independent Rhodesian subsidiaries since sanctions began also in violation of the law—for example, Holiday Inn, a subsidiary of which opened a new inn at Bulawayo in late 1973?

[11] The sublicensee in Rhodesia pays the company in the United States a percentage of its earnings in return for use of the name.

—Do other American car rental companies lease their names to independent Rhodesian firms and act as reservations agents for them here?

—If already existing arrangements of this kind cannot be terminated by the government, should future licenses be prevented?

VISIT SALISBURY, "GARDEN CAPITAL" OF RHODESIA

Until its operations were curtailed by the Treasury Department in May, 1974, a visitor to the office of Air Rhodesia and the Rhodesian National Tourist Board in New York could pick up travel brochures advertising package tours to Africa, including Southern Rhodesia, run by Bennet Tours,[12] Percival Tours, Merriman and Finnerty Associates, Orbitair International and United Touring Company. (All but the last are American-based companies. The United Touring Company is a Rhodesian concern.) Included in these brochures are invitations to visit the "garden capital" and Victoria Falls, "quite likely to be one of the great memories of your life. An indescribable experience. Words fail . . ." At Gona-re-zhou, "you may decide this is the ultimate experience and the peak of your trip." Or, take a cruise along the Zambezi River—"one of Africa's loveliest rivers."

There is no mention in these brochures, of course, of the fact that the Zambezi flows between territory held by the white minority regime in Southern Rhodesia and the African governments of the north; nor that there is a United Nations sanctions program against Southern Rhodesia; nor that Security Council Resolution 253 of May 29, 1968, stated: "All member states of the U.N. shall not make available to the illegal regime in Southern Rhodesia or to any commercial, industrial, or public utility undertaking, *including tourist enterprises,* in Southern Rhodesian any funds for investment or any other financial or economic resources and shall prevent their nationals and any persons within their territories from

[12] Bennet Tours reportedly dropped Rhodesia from its tours in 1974.

making available to the regime or to any such undertaking any such funds or resources." (Emphasis added.)

Although official statistics are not available, large numbers of tourists from the United States reportedly visit Southern Rhodesia every year. The American government makes little or no effort to discourage this travel, since it cannot legally invalidate their passports for travel there. The Treasury Department refuses to use financial controls to discourage travel to any embargoed area if passport controls do not apply. It therefore allows American tourists to spend money in Southern Rhodesia for living expenses, in violation of the U.N. resolution, but does not allow them to bring Rhodesian goods back with them to the United States.[13]

However, the activities of the American travel companies that include Southern Rhodesia in their tours of Africa raise other legal questions as well. According to travel company officials, the travel companies put together a packaged tour which can be looked upon as a "wholesale" product. Local travel agencies in the United States, through which the vast majority of dealings with potential tourists take place, act as "retailers." The retailer "sells" the wholesale product to the customer. Once the tour is sold, the "wholesaler"—the travel company—sets the tour up, including reservations for hotels, car rentals, and other services in the countries included in the trip. This is accomplished in many cases by acting through a ground operator—a tour company based in the foreign country. The ground agent in Southern Rhodesia for American travel companies is the United Touring Company. This ground agent does the actual scheduling in Southern Rhodesia, and conducts the tours for customers there.

[13] It should be noted that a letter from the British embassy indicates that the British are more strict about currency spent by their nationals in Southern Rhodesia. They are able to be so partly because they have generally stricter currency controls with regard to such foreign travel. The British government is reportedly unable to prevent, however, expenditures in Southern Rhodesia by British subjects of funds held outside the United Kingdom.

Most airline reservations are made by the local travel agency in the United States unless a "sponsor" airline is used by the travel company. The sponsor airline works in conjunction with the travel company, appears in advertising for the tour with a particular company, and is the air carrier for the tour. For example, Pan American has been the sponsor airline for Percival Tours.

Two sections of Executive Order 11419 appear applicable to the activities of these travel companies.

First, Section 1(f) forbids the transfer of funds to any person or body in Southern Rhodesia. A description of the financial arrangements made for these tours in Southern Rhodesia, based on interviews with officials of the travel companies, suggests that such transfers have, in fact, been made. Usually, the local travel agency in the United States receives full payment from the tourist for the African tour. The local agency then remits this money to the travel company minus a commission. If the local travel agent has made airline reservations, it is also responsible for paying the airline.

Once the travel company has the funds for the trip, it pays all the expenses to the Rhodesian firms. This is reportedly accomplished by direct payment, or else indirectly by paying the ground agent in Southern Rhodesia—who in turn pays the hotels, car rental companies, restaurants, etc. Either method of transfer is apparently a violation of the Executive Order. One tour company official said in an interview that Rhodesian enterprises will accept U.S. dollars and are paid by a check drawn on the company's U.S. bank account. Another company is said to have its bank—the Chemical Bank in New York City—make the foreign exchange transactions; the company then transfers Rhodesian currency to its agent in Southern Rhodesia.

Second, in addition to this apparent violation of Section 1(f), it could be argued that Section 1(d) has been violated. By publishing brochures and in other ways cooperating with local Rhodesian tourist agencies, these companies appear, in effect, to be supplying commodities to Southern Rhodesian businesses. And supplying copies of their brochures to the Rhodesian National Tourist Board in New York may have been a similar violation.

Authority for the enforcement of Section 1(f) is delegated to the Department of the Treasury. The Commerce Department is responsible for enforcement of Section 1(d).

The activities of these travel companies raise a number of questions which these departments should address:

—Have these companies been acting in violation of American law? Should they be prosecuted?

—Have their banks been meeting Treasury regulations in arranging currency transfers?

—What other American travel companies have been involved in Rhodesian tourism?

—Should the U.S. government try to do more to inform potential American tourists about the sanctions program against Southern Rhodesia and the specific U.N. injunction against tourist expenditures, through notices at travel agencies and U.S. passport offices? Should it say that it discourages such travel? (It now only makes efforts to inform them of restrictions on bringing Rhodesian goods into the United States. If asked, it informs potential tourists that "it is official policy to discourage such travel.")

—Should the Treasury Department tighten currency controls on tourist travel to Southern Rhodesia, since that would be the most effective way for the government to limit such travel?

CHARGE IT

When an American traveler to Southern Rhodesia has decided which tour company's itinerary is most appealing, which airlines to fly on, and whether to rent a car through Hertz or Avis, the question of payment remains.

Why not use an American credit card?

As noted previously, Pan American and TWA accepted major credit cards in payment for all the flights to and from Southern Rhodesia for which they made reservations—including flights on Air Rhodesia. According to Hertz's international reservations office, Hertz in Rhodesia accepted

American Express, Air Travel, Diners Club, Carte Blanche, and TWA credit cards. Avis worldwide reservations office states that Avis in Rhodesia accepts American Express, Mastercharge, Carte Blanche and Diners Club. And, it should be noted, other credit cards may be acceptable in payment for other goods and services in Rhodesia.[14]

Informed sources in that business say that funds are usually transferred from the credit card companies to the Southern Rhodesian enterprises in the following manner. The customer presents his credit card to the merchant in Southern Rhodesia, or to the Rhodesian's representative in America. The merchant or representative in turn presents the sales slip either to his own bank or to a member bank of an international association that serves as a clearinghouse for the credit card companies. This bank pays the merchant, and then either directly or through an international association presents the sales slip to the credit card company in the United States. The company bills the customer, and pays the merchant's bank.

Some of these transfers of funds to Southern Rhodesia may be considered legal by the U.S. government; as noted previously, tourists' expenses are allowed since the government says it is powerless to stop such tourism, despite Security Council Resolution 253. But even if it allows tourists to make these transfers, should it allow American credit card companies to facilitate them? And, in any case, other transfers of funds to Southern Rhodesia by the credit card companies would appear to violate Section 1(f) of Executive Order 11419, which prohibits fund transfers, with certain humanitarian, medical, or educational exceptions, whether they be direct or indirect. For example, any credit card fund transfers in payment of flights on Air Rhodesia would appear to have been clear violations. Enforcement of this section is the responsibility of the Treasury Department. As with the activities described previously in this report, there are serious questions here that deserve investigation by that Department.

[14] According to a letter dated August 8, 1973, from David Brancoli, a public information officer at the Bank of America, Bank Americard is not used in Rhodesia.

INVITATION TO INTERESTED INDUSTRIALISTS

On June 19, 1972, the *Journal of Commerce* of New York published a special sixteen-page supplement on Southern Rhodesia. In addition to articles describing Southern Rhodesia's economy, it contained advertisements for Rhodesian industries, banks, hotels, touring companies and other commercial enterprises. It was followed by similar articles and advertising thereafter.

While trade with Southern Rhodesia (with certain exceptions) and American investment there are prohibited, the *Journal's* readers have been treated to advertisements that ignore both prohibitions. In the first supplement on June 19, 1972, one found advertisements like these:

The Rhodesian Promotion Council . . . aims to promote knowledge of Rhodesia's economic development and potential. . . . please write to the Director who will be glad to supply you with the appropriate information and, if desired, to assist in travel arrangements and appropriate appointments.

Industrial Development Corporation of Southern Rhodesia, Ltd. . . . Interested industrialists are invited to contact us.

Whatever your product, the most profitable way to enter the Rhodesian market is via The Standard Bank. . . . Rhodesia exports, too.

Rhodesia's Information Office in Washington . . . knows a lot about the country—economics, trade, finance, raw materials and the people who count.

Bulawayo . . . a fine City for any industrialist to establish himself.

The Associated Chambers of Commerce of Rhodesia. . . . Rhodesian businessmen's belief in the country's future and the growth potential is such that foreign businessmen can make profitable investment in confidence.

In the February 5, 1973, issue, readers were invited to consider "Real Estate in Rhodesia"; "Transportation Consultants and Project Handlers" (a repeat from the June 19 issue); and "export experts, fully equipped to handle any shipment, large or small" (also a repeat).

On March 13, 1973, among other advertisements was one for "Hartley—The progressive town. . . . For Industrial Development." And on April 26, the reader was invited to "Invest in CABS—Rhodesia's Largest Building Society."

According to interviews with a number of those involved, the idea for the supplement came during conversations between members of the *Journal* staff and representatives of the Rhodesian Promotion Council. Who initiated the idea is not clear; most of those interviewed believe it was the Promotion Council. One source on the *Journal's* staff said, "It was not a perfunctory decision." But the *Journal* decided to go ahead for two reasons. First, it had traditionally supported trade among nations without regard to political differences. It was, for example, a leading advocate of increased East-West trade during the 1960s. Second, one of those making the decision at the *Journal* said in an interview that he believes that the Rhodesians "have something to say and do. If they are helped to do so, they may change their thinking, as they must, sooner or later."

One of the *Journal's* leading correspondents, Harold Horstmeyer, was sent to Rhodesia for three weeks and did most of the writing of the articles in the June, 1972, supplement. (Horstmeyer had covered trade possibilities in Eastern Europe for a number of years.) Horstmeyer has also written many of the articles in subsequent issues, and traveled to Rhodesia again in the late spring of 1973.

The advertisements were paid for by the Rhodesian companies through the Rhodesian Promotion Council. The transfer of funds reportedly took place through a "free" funds account at a bank in New York.[15] Rhodesian advertisers were charged the *Journal's* usual rates for advertising.

[15] According to the testimony of Barbara Rogers before the Africa subcommittee on May 15, 1973, such accounts are maintained at the Standard Bank and Barclay's Bank in New York. Interviews with government officials would seem to confirm this. As previously noted, these accounts contain funds accruing from humanitarian contributions by Americans to Rhodesians, as allowed under the U.N. Sanctions Program. According to an American government official, the banks are familiar with the regulations and do not allow illegal transfers through these accounts.

When the supplement first appeared, the reaction in London was quite intense, according both to the office of the *Journal of Commerce* there and to *Journal* officials in the United States. The *Journal* office there received critical telephone calls from British government officials and, with some frequency for a few weeks, from British journalists.

The articles and advertising from Rhodesia in the *Journal* also raise serious questions with regard to American law.

The supply of advertising space by the *Journal* to Rhodesian businesses may be a violation of Section 1(d) of Executive Order 11419. If the print and pages devoted to this advertising are considered "commodities," then the *Journal* is selling commodities to Rhodesian businesses.

In addition, Section 1(b) prohibits "any activities by any person subject to the authority of the United States which *promote or are calculated to promote* the export from Southern Rhodesia after May 29, 1968, of any commodities or any products originating in Southern Rhodesia." (Emphasis added.) *Black's Law Dictionary* gives the following definition of "promote": "to contribute to growth, enlargement, or prosperity of; to forward, to further; to encourage; to advance." Thus, it would seem clear that the *Journal* has violated the Executive Order. The intent and effect of the *articles* in the *Journal* may be ambiguous, and to argue that they run afoul of the Executive Order raises questions about freedom of the press under the First Amendment. But the *advertising* seems a simpler proposition. By definition, advertising has as its purpose the promotion of goods for sale.

The *Journal of Commerce,* in carrying this advertising, would seem potentially liable to serious legal charges. And a similar question can be raised about the Rhodesian Information Office. On June 26, 1972, it sent copies of the June 19 supplement on Rhodesia to hundreds of chambers of commerce throughout the United States. In a covering letter, Kenneth Towsey wrote, ". . . the enclosed supplement from the *Journal of Commerce* of June 19 is to let you know that Rhodesia is still around and entering a new era of development." According to our interviews, the Rhodesian Information Office feared that sending the supplement without an explanatory note might seem to be "promoting" trade. Towsey, therefore, stated in his letter that "with limited exceptions, trade between Rhodesia and the United States is forbidden by U.S. government regulations." But the letter later goes on to say, "Be that as it may, our [Rhodesia's] exports and imports last year each amounted to more than $400 million. *You will judge from this that sanctions are something less than water-tight.*" (Emphasis added.)

Thus, the RIO would seem to have joined the *Journal of Commerce* in promoting business with Southern Rhodesia. Why, then, has not the American government moved against the *Journal* and, perhaps, the RIO on this issue? According to testimony on May 17, 1973, before the Africa subcommittee by C. Clyde Ferguson, Jr., Deputy Assistant Secretary of State for African Affairs, the U.S. government has a different definition of "promote" or "calculated to promote" from those one will find in his dictionary or in everyday usage. (Nor, indeed, is it the definition used by the U.S. government when it describes what our commercial attachés do in promoting the sale of American goods abroad.) According to Ferguson, the term "promote or calculated to promote" was taken from the U.N. sanctions resolutions. As interpreted by the U.S. government, it does not "encompass general information dissemination, public relations activities or advertisements."

This interpretation of "promote" was reached within the American government after consultation with the British, who sponsored the U.N. resolutions on sanctions. Ferguson gave the following explanation:

These resolutions were in large part drafted by the United Kingdom and the United States government has sought, in respect to the interpretation, views of the United Kingdom both in its capacity as the principal drafter and also in its capacity as a lawful sovereign for Rhodesia.

After adoption of Resolution 232 the United Kingdom informed us that it interpreted the word "promotion" in the resolutions as relating to activities directly incidental to a prohibited commercial transaction. Hence (in utilizing the United Kingdom's interpretation of essentially their own language which appears in the Security Council resolution) to the extent that the activities are the general dissemination of information, public relations activities, and advertisements—they do not fall within the prohibited activities which are specified in other provisions of the resolution.

According to interviews with government officials concerned with the issue, the State Department consulted with the British about their definition of a number of terms in their draft resolution before the U.N. Security Council first ordered sanctions on December 16, 1966. The British definition of the term "promote or calculated to promote" was reportedly "vague." Therefore, after the resolution was passed and before the U.S. government issued Executive Order 11322 on January 5, 1967, the State Department again asked the British how they defined the term. Again, the British did not provide a specific definition. Instead, they listed a number of examples of how they had interpreted the term previously under their Orders in Council. These examples implied that they interpreted "promote" to mean an activity which was, to use the term of one American official interviewed, "transactionally related"—in other words, "promote" meant actually writing contracts or shipping orders.

Based on its interpretation of the consultations with the British government in late 1966, the American government apparently accepts a very limited definition of "promote or calculated to promote" in the context of the U.N. sanctions resolutions and the U.S. Executive Orders implementing them. No distinction is made, in the American definition, between promoting a sales contract and actually writing one.

To explore the subject further, Stephen Park wrote to the British embassy in Washington to ask their definition of the term, how it was reached, and when and how it conveyed this definition to the American government. After consulting with the Foreign and Commonwealth Office, the embassy responded in a letter dated July 19, 1973.

It drew attention to the distinction in British law between the prohibition of certain particular acts and the prohibition of "any act calculated to promote the exportation of any goods from Southern Rhodesia." "This provision," it stated, "and in particular the word promote, can only be authoritatively interpreted by the British courts. Prosecutions in the British courts for sanctions offenses have not so far involved the interpretation of 'promote.' We would expect it to be given its ordinary natural meaning, though its application to particular circumstances may not be easy to decide."

The relevant statutory instrument in British law is the Southern Rhodesia (U.N. Sanctions) (No. 2) Order 1968. It states that:

3.—(1) Except under the authority of a license granted by the Minister, no person shall export any goods from Southern Rhodesia.

    (2) Except under such authority as aforesaid, no person shall—

        (a) make or carry out any contract for the exportation of any goods from Southern Rhodesia after the commencement of this Order; or

        (b) make or carry out any contract for the sale of any goods which he intends or has reason to believe that another person intends to export from Southern Rhodesia after the commencement of this Order; or

        (c) *do any act calculated to promote the exportation of any goods from Southern Rhodesia.* [Emphasis added.]

Except under such authority as aforesaid, no person shall deal in any goods that have been exported from Southern Rhodesia in contravention of paragraph 1 of this article, that is to say by way of trade or otherwise for gain, acquire or dispose of such goods or of any property or interest in them or do any act calculated to promote any such acquisitions, disposal or processing by himself or any other person.

The "or" at the end of subparagraph (b) is important here. It makes clear that the British make a distinction between *carrying out* an activity and *promoting* an activity. Neither is allowed. In the American definition the one defines the other, and apparently both must be violated before the law applies.[16]

In light of this letter, a question naturally arises about the continuing validity of the American interpretation of the term "promote or calculated to promote" insofar as it is based on the British interpretation.

The American definition raises logical questions as well. One American government official concerned with the issue argued in an interview that while the *Journal of Commerce* supplement was misleading to its readers, no real harm was done because anyone applying for a license to carry out illegal trade or to make an investment in Southern Rhodesia would be denied. The implication is that since the government defines "promote or calculated to promote" as actually taking some part in such a transaction, by definition it is impossible to promote trade with Rhodesia without a license from the Treasury Department. This is rather like arguing that a drunken driver who is unable to damage property because of the restraining devices on the highway is not breaking the law.

In addition, in not distinguishing between "promote" and "calculated to promote," the American government's position apparently seems to require the assumption that the firms paying for the advertising had no immediate purpose in doing so. Indeed, unless the advertisements were placed out of a sense of patriotic duty to promote the image of Rhodesia as a whole (a theory the wording of the advertisements does not support), one can speculate about four possible motives.

First, they could be related to the importation into the United States of certain "strategic and critical materials" under the Byrd Amendment. Some of the firms which placed advertisements could be involved in this trade. Other advertisers,

---

[16] It should be noted that, according to the embassy's letter, advertisements have been published in British newspapers offering flight facilities to Rhodesia and on one or two occasions, tours. These advertisements did not, apparently, solicit trade or investment.

like "CABS—Rhodesia's Largest Building Society," clearly are not.

Second, they could be broadly designed to increase pressures within the United States for an end to sanctions—still a form of promoting trade.

Third, the advertisements could be designed to solicit future trade with, or investment in, their own firms after sanctions no longer exist. Since there seems little prospect of sanctions evaporating in the immediate future, the return on the advertising money expended for this contingency would not seem as large as the return on an investment in, say, CABS itself.

Fourth, the advertisements could be for the purpose of—or at least have the effect of—soliciting illegal trade or investment. And one can see how an American businessman could gain that impression. For example, on page 8 of the supplement of June 19, 1972, the *Journal's* reporter wrote:

> Given the present circumstances, the subject of foreign investment in Rhodesia has a cloak-and-dagger air about it, but there is little doubt that opportunities abound.
>
> Just who is going to take advantage of the prospects, and to what extent, remains a vital question here. *But where there's a will, there's a way.* [Emphasis added.]

The intriguing allusion in Towsey's letter to the less than "watertight" character of sanctions could also have the same effect on a reader.

Thus, the American definition of "promote or calculated to promote" appears to violate both logic and the dictionary meaning of the word "promote." And it does not seem in accord with the current British definition of the term—although U.S. government officials state that our definition was adopted as a result of consultations with the British. Either earlier consultations were misinterpreted by the Americans, or the British definition—as contained in the letter to us—has shifted. In either case, the American definition seems at variance with the British.

Despite its limiting definition, the American government did react to the supplement during the summer of 1972. At the request of the State Department, Treasury sent a letter of complaint to the editors of the *Journal*. It reportedly suggested that the *Journal* could be misleading its readers by not emphasizing the fact that, with certain exceptions, trade and investment in Southern Rhodesia are prohibited. The letter reportedly also asked about the channels through which the *Journal* had received payment for the advertisements.

According to a number of nongovernment sources, the *Journal* called the Rhodesian Information Office to solicit its advice about how payment should be made. (There is some disagreement among these sources as to whether the *Journal* had also been in contact with the Rhodesian Information Office to discuss the supplement before its publication.) When asked whether the RIO would pay for the advertising, Towsey reportedly informed the *Journal* that it would not. When asked what ideas he had on how payment should be made, Towsey reportedly said that he could not offer advice on that subject but could tell the *Journal* how the RIO itself received its funds. He then, it is said, described the "free" funds accounts and suggested that the *Journal* consult its lawyers and the Treasury Department. According to an official at the *Journal*, it had, in fact, received its first payments for the advertisements through a bank not authorized to make such a transfer. After some correspondence, the *Journal* returned this money and received payment properly, all within a few months of the supplement's publication.

Thus, the letter of complaint from the Treasury Department did apparently play a role in straightening out the channel for payment of the advertising. But the basic question of whether this advertising violates Executive Order 11419 remains unresolved. The Treasury Department's letter has not seemed to have had any inhibiting effect on the *Journal*, as it has continued to advertise the promise of the Rhodesian economy.

In the Africa subcommittee's hearings on May 17, 1973,

John M. Hennessy, Assistant Secretary of the Treasury for International Affairs, said with reference to the *Journal of Commerce* and the American definition of "promote or calculated to promote," "I think we would want to take another look at that." There do indeed seem to be some serious legal questions at which to look. Enforcement of the relevant sections of Executive Order 11419—Sections 1(d) and 1(b)—is the responsibility of the Commerce and Treasury Departments.

This chapter has suggested a number of ways in which American companies and others have been or may be acting in violation of U.S. law. In some cases, the legal issues appear clear—for example, with regard to the cooperation between American carriers and Air Rhodesia. In other cases, severely limited interpretations of the law have allowed the government to avoid acting. In other cases still, the U.N. sanctions resolutions are currently being violated, although U.S. law is not—for example, with regard to expenditures by American tourists in Southern Rhodesia. There are probably more questions to be raised about these activities than are noted here. There are certainly more answers to be found.

The record of the U.S. Executive Branch in implementing sanctions compares favorably with the performance of other members of the United Nations. Sanctions violators have been successfully prosecuted by the government in American courts. But interviews with officials of American companies doing business with Southern Rhodesia would seem to indicate that many American businessmen are unaware of what the sanctions against Southern Rhodesia mean, or do not care. Beyond the legal questions raised in this chapter, another point thus emerges. The government cannot rely so heavily on American companies' knowledge of the law and their willingness to comply. A better system for monitoring compliance seems required. One would have thought that after the embarrassment of the Byrd Amendment, which placed the United States in violation of its legal obligation to observe the sanctions fully, the Executive Branch of our government would have done all it could to implement the sanctions.[17] For whenever the American government does less than it can to meet its international legal obligation to observe the U.N. sanctions program, a final question is raised about American concern for international law as well as for the laws of our own society.

[17] Press reports in late 1975 of illegal recruitment in the United States of mercenaries to fight for the Smith regime provide still another field of investigation for the government.

6

The Byrd Amendment

The assorted lacunae of the American government described in the previous chapter are important, but they are minor compared to the damage done to the American sanctions program by the so-called Byrd Amendment. Signed by the President on November 17, 1971, this piece of legislation would authorize the importation into the United States of seventy-two "strategic and critical materials" from Rhodesia, the most important being chrome, ferrochrome, and nickel.

How could it have happened? How could the United States, whose own foreign policy for twenty-five years had been built on the same general concepts of collective security and international cooperation that were expressed in the Charter of the United Nations, have officially broken the only mandatory, comprehensive sanctions program ever voted under that Charter? No single explanation will suffice. The Byrd Amendment passed the Congress through a combination of factors, few of which reflect credit on the American system of making foreign policy when it comes to issues involving the United Nations and Africa. Corporate lobbying played a key role. So did the lack of public interest in the issue, and the early weaknesses of the lobbyists who opposed any American violation of sanctions. The ambivalent role of the administration must also be given major credit in this sad story. And, especially in the early stages of the legislative course of the Byrd Amendment, the parliamentary skill of its supporters was an essential ingredient.

It was not the first conservative effort within the Congress to shift the course of American policy toward Southern Rhodesia. Opposition to any kind of pressure against the Smith regime surfaced in the U.S. Congress soon after UDI. In 1966, Senator James O. Eastland (D.–Miss.) introduced a resolution çalling for an end to American economic measures against Southern Rhodesia. By 1967, several bills had been introduced in the House which condemned the U.N. response to UDI and urged the United States to end its observance of sanctions. None of these measures referred to or mentioned chrome. The Rhodesian issue lay dormant in the Congress in 1968, but in 1969 thirteen anti-sanctions resolutions were introduced in the House. By 1970 the arguments in the Congress had changed somewhat, although the sponsor of the Rhodesia-related resolution in the Senate—S. Res. 367—was once again Senator Eastland. The thrust of Eastland's measure was now twofold: to restore trading relations and to recognize the Ian Smith government. And a new argument was introduced: Sanctions had made the United States dependent on the Soviet Union for a strategic material, chrome ore. In the House, six resolutions were introduced in the autumn of 1970, all urging violation of the sanctions in some form. None of the measures received serious treatment on either floor of the Congress.

The year 1971 began in much the same fashion; ten conservative Congressmen introduced bills which urged violation of the sanctions, in one form or another. On February 22, a new formula was found. Representative James Collins (R.–Tex.) introduced H.R. 4712, "a bill to amend the United Nations Participation Act of 1945 to prevent the imposition thereunder of any prohibition on the importation into the United States of any metal bearing ore from any free world country for so long as the importation of like ore from any Communist country is not prohibited by law." On March 3, Collins introduced a different bill which deleted the phrase, "any metal bearing ore"; the bill now concerned any material determined to be "strategic and critical." Within weeks Sena-

tor Harry F. Byrd (Ind.–Va.) [1] introduced the similar S.
1404—the "Byrd Amendment."

With this new language, the traditional opponents of
sanctions against Rhodesia could argue that they were not
proposing to destroy American participation in the sanctions;
they were simply altering it to protect American national interests. More specifically, they said they were seeking to put an
end to an unhealthy American dependence on Soviet chrome
by allowing chrome from Rhodesia to flow, once again,
through American ports. *Chrome,* they said, was the issue. On
four different occasions in subsequent debate, Senator Byrd
flatly stated that the only commodity affected by S. 1404
would be chrome ore.[2] His opponents took him at his word,
and even the State Department assumed throughout the debate that only chrome was involved. Thus, Byrd and Collins
were able to win both ways with the language of their bills: It
was so broad that it did not seem on its face to be a direct
challenge to the United Nations or a special favor for American chrome importers, yet Byrd was able to steer the debate
away from consideration of what would, in fact, follow its
coming into force. The Amendment would actually allow the
importation of seventy-one other materials as well, thirteen of
which were produced in Rhodesia, a prospect which might
have given undecided Congressmen some pause.

There is some question about whether Byrd himself rea-
lized that the language of his bill would have such broad consequences. Interviews with members of the staffs of Congressmen on both sides of the issue suggest that he may well have
been more calculating than shortsighted. Most congressional
staffers who worked against the Amendment are convinced,
without evidence, that Byrd knew what it meant all along. The
remarks of three staffers who worked for passage of the

[1] For the sake of convenience, Senator Harry F. Byrd is sometimes referred to hereafter as simply Senator Byrd. Whenever reference is made to
Senator Robert Byrd of West Virginia, his first name will be included.

[2] He did so on June 16, July 22, September 10, and September 23,
1971.

Amendment are more revealing. When one was asked in an interview whether Senator Byrd knew his measure would cover more items than chrome, he replied, "The bill stated specifically that it would cover all strategic and critical materials. It was right there in print for everyone to read. I don't know what they said on the floor, but maybe they should have read the bill." Another stated flatly, "It was known all along." And the third said, "Anyone who read the bill should have known what it said. We can all read, can't we?"

The origins of the legislative language which became the Byrd Amendment are unclear. It was probably sometime late in 1970, somewhere in Washington, that a pen drafted the phrases that would allow the Congress to take the United States out of a key part of the U.N. sanctions program without mentioning either sanctions, the United Nations, or Southern Rhodesia. The offices of both Representative Collins and Senator Byrd claim original authorship of the language; one staff member stated that "several of the staff members may have gotten together" and discussed the question. It is widely believed among Capitol Hill opponents of the Byrd Amendment that lobbyists of Union Carbide and Foote Mineral thought up the magic phrases. This is heatedly denied by Byrd's and Collins's staffs. A source at Foote Mineral states that the Collins bill was not the result of any initiative by industry representatives, but that just before its introduction, John Donahey—the public relations director at Foote—was asked by the Congressman to come to Washington from Foote headquarters in Pennsylvania. Donahey reportedly did so, and supplied Collins with background information to support his case. Another theory is that the Byrd Amendment had its origins in Salisbury. At a press conference with forty-one visiting American newspaper editors on March 2, 1970, Ian Smith responded to a question by noting the American need for chrome from Rhodesia in terms similar to arguments made by supporters of the Byrd Amendment the following year. This indicates that chrome was gaining force as an issue in anti-sanctions circles in both Salisbury and the United States by 1970. It would not, however, appear to prove the assertion, as one observer has put it, that "the operation was planned from Salisbury . . ." [3]

In essence, Byrd faced three initial problems in pushing his bill through the Senate. First, he needed to develop information which would support substantive arguments in its favor. Second, he faced a rebuttal to these arguments, as they pertained to the need for Rhodesian chrome, in the form of a series of bills introduced by the administration which would have released chrome and other materials from the national stockpile. And, third, he had to devise a way to get his Amendment to the floor of the Senate despite the predictable hostility to it of the committee which had jurisdiction—the Foreign Relations Committee.

In the weeks before he introduced his measure at the end of March, Byrd reportedly received background information from Allegheny Ludlum Steel, Union Carbide and Foote. He was thus prepared to put his arguments about chrome forcefully and in some detail.

A week later, on April 7, the Subcommittee on National Stockpile and Naval Petroleum Reserves held hearings on the administration's bills, which authorized disposal of stockpile surpluses including approximately 1.3 million short dry tons of high-grade chromite. Administration witnesses supported release of this quantity of chrome from the stockpile, arguing that the government no longer needed to assume that it must keep enough reserves of each metal to tide it over for the period of time it would take to rebuild relevant plants in the unlikely event they were destroyed by sabotage or bomb attacks. Representatives of private industry then took over, and strenuously attacked the proposed stockpile releases. Senator Thurmond inserted into the record a telegram from the vice-president of Interlake Steel, Inc. L. G. Bliss, Foote's chief executive officer, then testified. He explicitly linked passage of

[3] Statement by Barbara Rogers at the hearings before the Subcommittee on Africa of the Committee on Foreign Affairs, House of Representatives, "Implications for U.S. International Legal Obligations of the Presence of the Rhodesian Information Office in the United States," May 15, 17, 1973.

Byrd's sanctions-busting measure and defeat of the stockpile disposal legislation. Bliss described the latter as only a "temporary expedient" to "hold world prices in line." But, he said, a solution to the chrome problem was at hand. "I refer to the bill, S. 1404, recently introduced by your distinguished colleague on the Armed Services Committee, Senator Harry F. Byrd, Jr., of Virginia." Were Byrd's bill to be passed, the Foote representative added, and "with some assurance that our stockpiles of critical chrome can be replenished at a future date, the objections to the release of a reasonable quantity of chromium ore are largely overcome."

The subcommittee decided to withhold approval of the administration's draft bill until the question of possible chrome imports from Rhodesia was settled. In a speech on April 29, the subcommittee chairman, Senator Howard Cannon (D.–Nev.) echoed Bliss's argument: "S. 773 [the administration bill] would serve a temporary expediency, but there can be no permanent relief until the importation of chrome ore from Rhodesia can be resumed." S. 1404 (Byrd's bill) would, however, "exempt chrome ore from the list of materials subject to the Rhodesian embargo and thus end our dependency upon the Soviet Union for this highly important commodity."

Senator Byrd had thus cleared his first two hurdles. He was on the offensive with regard to the issue itself, having defined it in terms of national security and economic advantage while downplaying the U.N. angle. And the administration's draft bill, which would have released chrome from the stockpile and thus undercut the argument that chrome from Rhodesia was needed, was blocked. This left the third of his important problems: getting his bill to the floor of the Senate.

There are few signs that liberals in the Senate were particularly concerned about Byrd's actions, even after Cannon's subcommittee had moved against the stockpile bill. After all, previous efforts by conservatives to take the United States out of the sanctions had failed in the Senate Foreign Relations Committee and the House Foreign Affairs Committee. And

Byrd's and Collins's measures had been referred to those committees. On June 13, 15, 17, 19, and 22, the House Subcommittee on International Organizations and Movements held
hearings on the issue. The Senate Subcommittee on African
Affairs followed suit on July 7 and 8. (A month and a half earlier, the administration had sent to the Foreign Relations
Committee its highly negative formal comments on Byrd's
bill.[4] But Byrd had pressed committee chairman Fulbright
(D.–Ark.) at least to hold hearings on it. At Fulbright's
request, Senator Gale McGee (D.–Wyo.), the chairman of the
African Subcommittee, granted Byrd his wish.) Assistant Secretary of State David Newsom and Representative Charles Diggs
(D.–Mich.) opposed the bill; Senator Byrd, Dean Acheson and
industry representatives supported it. At the close of the hearings, Senator McGee told reporters that he would recommend
that the full Foreign Relations Committee refuse to act on S.
1404. His recommendation was accepted without dissent in an
executive session of the committee on August 5, and S. 1404
died, as Representative Collins' bill died in the House Foreign
Affairs Committee.

But 1971 was to be different from previous years; Byrd
would not give up. As soon as he saw that McGee intended to
kill his bill, he began to make a new move. On July 14, Byrd
expressed on the floor of the Senate his belief that the United
States was dangerously dependent on Soviet chrome and that
it was "vital that the Senate have the opportunity to vote on
this important issue."

Very soon after the Foreign Relations Committee had
acted on August 5, Byrd caught the liberals totally by surprise
with a parliamentary masterstroke. The Senate Armed Services Committee was considering the Military Procurement
Act, which had already been passed by the House. Byrd, a
member of that committee, suddenly introduced most of the
language of S. 1404 as an amendment to the House bill. Sen-

[4] As discussed later, other signals from the administration were to give a
very different impression of its stance.

ate aides report that Byrd brought the Amendment up near
the end of the meeting, and it received little debate. Byrd had
deleted reference to the U.N. Participation Act, and, in the
words of one aide with knowledge of the committee's discussion, "it was discussed in 'national defense,' 'anti-Communism'
language." The committee attached Byrd's language to the
bill, as section 503, by a vote of 13 to 0. Senators Symington
(D.–Mo.), Hughes (D.–Iowa), and Jackson (D.–Wash.), all of
whom later opposed the Byrd Amendment, were not present.
According to their offices, Hughes and Symington had attended the session but left before Byrd pushed through Section 503. Senator McIntyre (D.–N.H.) voted for Section 503 in
committee, and later opposed it on the floor. According to his
staff, he thought it deserved that airing. There is some question, however, about how fully most members of the committee understood the implications of Byrd's measure.

In gaining the backing of the Armed Services Committee
for his Amendment, Byrd was doing more than simply finding a route for his measure to the floor. It now had the backing of a powerful committee, and it was attached to a bill
whose floor manager, Senator John Stennis (D.–Miss.), is, in
the words of a conservative legislative assistant, "a whale." Portraying the Senate as a sea filled with "whales" and "minnows,"
he points to the fact that while there were some of both on
each side of the argument over the Byrd Amendment, Byrd
was allied to an especially powerful group of leviathans—the
southern Senators who control some of the most important
committees in the Congress. The Military Procurement Bill
would clearly be passed, at least in amended form. And since
it contained authorization for a number of controversial defense projects, liberals would be more inclined to expend their
ammunition against new tanks and transport aircraft than
against the Byrd Amendment.

The burden had been on Byrd to force the issue. Now,
McGee had to act to find a way on the floor to delete Byrd's
language. On September 16, nine days after the Armed Ser-

vices Committee had reported the Military Procurement Bill
to the floor, McGee introduced an amendment deleting Section 503. Debate on his amendment followed a pattern which
has been evident in each of those few cases when southern African issues have come to the attention of the Congress: The
rhetoric, debating points, and facts and figures used by both
sides did not concern that region *per se* so much as they concentrated on "larger" issues. When the Congress debated the
quota allotted to South African sugar, supporters of the quota
were able to focus debate on questions of international sugar
supply. Its opponents found it difficult to force the Congress
to confront the idea that purchases of sugar from South
Africa represented a kind of aid to a society which practices
apartheid. Similarly, debate on McGee's amendment primarily
concerned chrome prices, the Soviet Union, "national security" and, to a lesser extent, the United Nations. The question
of American policy toward Southern Rhodesia was defined by
the positions taken on these other issues. And in this debate,
McGee and the supporters of his amendment were on the
defensive. They had to show that American security interests
were not threatened by the fact that the Soviet Union was a
major chrome supplier for American industry. As one assistant to a Congressman who opposed the Byrd Amendment
puts it, "If you introduce an element of 'national defense' and
'military procurement,' you become more effective. You can
adopt the 'can't take any chances with our national security'
type of stance. This is very hard to attack. When a liberal tries
to say, 'We really don't need this stuff,' he is in a very weak
position, one that is hard to defend."

Despite McGee's efforts to impress on other Senators that
approval of Section 503 would place the United States in violation of its obligations under the U.N. Charter and that the
surplus of chrome in the stockpile negated Byrd's national
defense arguments, Senate liberals reacted with more lethargy
than alarm. As McGee has put it, "A number of Senators felt
my amendment would prevail without difficulty and that neither their debating talents nor their actual votes were really

necessary." [5] On September 23, after cursory debate, McGee's amendment was defeated 36 to 46.

Immediately after the vote, supporters of the Byrd Amendment again demonstrated their parliamentary skill. Senator Stennis moved to reconsider the vote. Senator Cooper (R.–Ky.) asked for the yeas and nays on Stennis's motion, upon which Stennis quickly withdrew the motion, without objection. This minor flurry meant a major irritation for the Byrd Amendment's opponents, for it blocked liberal efforts to have the vote reconsidered. When Cooper asked if he could move to reconsider the vote which had defeated McGee's amendment, the presiding officer said he could not, because "only a Senator who voted with the prevailing side or who did not vote can move to reconsider."

The following day, Senator Fulbright tried to move reconsideration of the vote. He had missed the vote, despite the fact that one of McGee's major debating points had been the impropriety of the Armed Services Committee reporting to the floor a bill which Fulbright's committee had rejected. Fulbright was at a meeting of the Board of Foreign Scholarships, and just missed getting to the floor in time after a telephone call had alerted him to the imminence of the vote. (Some observers believe that Fulbright had thought that McGee's amendment would pass without him, and there was no point in offending his constituency by publicly breaking with his regional colleague on the issue.) Now, Fulbright asked for unanimous consent to his resolution that the vote he had missed be reconsidered, arguing that Stennis' motion to reconsider had never been voted on. Senator Robert Byrd (D.–W.Va.) challenged Fulbright's interpretation of the rules. The presiding officer agreed with Byrd, noting that there could be only *one* move to reconsider a vote, and, since Senator Stennis had no right to withdraw his motion on his own, he had done it by leave of the Senate. Senator Hansen (R.–Idaho) then formally objected to Fulbright's resolution, and it

[5] Gale W. McGee, "The U.S. Congress and the Rhodesian Chrome Issue," *Issue,* Summer 1972, p. 5.

was dead. Fulbright's frustration was demonstrated in the double-edged compliment he paid Robert Byrd as it became clear he had been outmaneuvered.

Mr. Fulbright: "The Senator from West Virginia is the only Member familiar with all the rules, and he knows them very well. Since the passing of the Senator from Georgia, the Senator from West Virginia inherited that mantle of knowledge of the rules."
Mr. Byrd of West Virginia: "The Senator pays me a great compliment, and it is not deserved."
Mr. Fulbright: "It is deserved. This is a very peculiar rule. If a Senator wants to object, he can; I would only say I think it is only an inconvenience for the Senate."

Fulbright's irritation had undoubtedly been heightened by Byrd's rather smug comment: "The rules are in the rule book, and there are only forty-four standing rules. Every Senator should know about that particular rule. There is a rule dealing only with reconsideration—rule XIII."

The "inconvenience" to which Fulbright referred was that opponents of the Byrd Amendment would now have to introduce a new amendment with language different from the McGee measure, which had called for simple deletion of Section 503. On September 27, Fulbright therefore introduced an amendment which would have given the President the power to refuse to implement the Byrd Amendment if "the national interest or a treaty obligation" required him to do so. Since the Byrd Amendment would violate an American treaty obligation under Article 25 of the U.N. Charter, the President would almost surely have been forced by Fulbright's amendment to refuse to implement it. The problem was that Fulbright's language gave Byrd and his supporters a new debating point. Byrd greeted Fulbright's amendment with the comment, "Mr. President, I am rather amused that the Senator from Arkansas [Mr. Fulbright], who has been perhaps the foremost advocate—at least I thought he was—of trying to have the Senate take back some of the power it has given to the President over the years, now presents an amendment, which, to use the Senator's words, leaves the options with the President on a vitally important matter . . ." Fulbright replied that he would have preferred a simple reconsideration of the McGee amendment. Byrd responded with the hope that Fulbright would vote against his own amendment. "The Senator from Arkansas is proposing an amendment to give additional power to the President. My goodness gracious, Mr. President. My goodness gracious. This is an interesting situation; almost as interesting, not quite but almost as interesting, as the Senator from Arkansas becoming the new quarterback for the administration in regard to a military procurement matter."

On September 30, Fulbright's amendment came to a vote. Substantive debate was similar to the debate over McGee's amendment a week before. And, once again, Fulbright was attacked for giving the President more power. In response, Fulbright offered to withdraw his amendment if his opponents would allow reconsideration of McGee's simpler formula. They would not, of course, let him off the hook. Senator Samuel J. Ervin (D.–N.C.) took the floor. "This is the most sorrowful moment I have ever experienced on the floor of the Senate. The distinguished Senator from Arkansas has led me in many fights demanding that Congress retain its powers, and not permit the executive to rob Congress of its power, and not abdicate its functions to the executive . . . I plead with my friend not to forsake the cause in which he and I have stood shoulder to shoulder and in which he has spoken with so much eloquence on the floor of the Senate in his valiant effort to preserve [its] powers."

At six P.M. on September 30, in what was apparently the final vote of the day, the Fulbright amendment was passed by a vote of 45 to 43. A number of liberals who had been absent on September 23 were now present to help nullify the Byrd Amendment. But immediately after the vote, Senators began drifting out of the Chamber, apparently in the belief that the day's work was done. The night's work was just beginning, however, and more conservatives than liberals remained. This was quickly apparent when the liberals were defeated by 36 to

40 in an effort to prevent reconsideration of the vote. A third vote was then held on a conservative motion to reconsider the vote; it was passed, 39 to 38. Fulbright then asked for a delay until the following day, since "a number of Senators . . . not anticipating the perseverance and determination of the Senators from Virginia and Mississippi, left the Chamber and left the Hill." He continued, "To force the Senate to a decision this late at night, under the misapprehension on the part of the absentees, it seems to me would be wrong and would be violating the spirit, I would say, of the Senate." [6] After more debate, Senator Hubert Humphrey (D.–Minn.) moved adjournment. His motion was defeated, 33 to 45.

Now, Senator Robert Byrd again demonstrated his parliamentary sophistication. The liberals suggested that there was not a quorum, and when the clerk called the roll, they did not answer to their names. A quorum was not present. But Byrd foiled this maneuver by moving for adjournment. Since, in the absence of a quorum, the only motion in order is a motion to adjourn, Byrd's motion could be the only motion pending. For the sake of appearances, Byrd then voted for his own motion, but his conservative allies all voted against it, and his motion was defeated by one vote. The session remained alive. More debate on adjournment and further votes followed. Several efforts to achieve unanimous consent to debate and vote on the issue at a later date were defeated by conservative objection. Finally, Robert Byrd suggested that the new vote on Fulbright's amendment be held a week later. The liberals agreed, the meeting was adjourned, and the following day the new

[6] Besides absenteeism, another factor which caused unpredictable shifts of one vote was the inexplicable pattern of Senator Lee Metcalf (D.–Mont.). On September 23, Metcalf voted with the Byrd forces; in the first vote on September 30, he voted in favor of the Fulbright amendment; he then switched again and voted against the McGee/Fulbright position on the first vote concerning reconsideration; on the second vote on reconsideration, however, he turned up once more with Fulbright and McGee, voting against the conservative move for reconsideration which he had just helped allow! He flopped back and forth in subsequent votes, but with less regularity.

vote was set for October 6. Despite passage of Fulbright's amendment, Section 503 was still alive.

Fulbright's measure was defeated in the October vote by 38 to 44, and the Byrd Amendment passed the Senate. Senator Lee Metcalf (D.–Mont.), who had voted for the Fullbright amendment on September 30, now voted against it. Senator William Roth (R.–Del.) also switched. Of the thirteen Senators not voting, seven were probable Byrd supporters and six (including presidential hopefuls Fred R. Harris (D.–Okla.), Henry M. Jackson (D.–Wash.), George McGovern (D.–S. Dak.), and Edmund S. Muskie (D.–Maine) were opponents of Section 503. The difference between the September 30 and October 6 votes lay in the Roth/Metcalf switches and the fact that the majority of those absent on September 30 but present on October 6 were conservatives.

Senator William Brock (R.–Tenn.), acting at the request of the White House with the concurrence of Senators Byrd and Stennis, then gained a unanimous vote for an amendment which delayed the application of Section 503 until January 1, 1972. The stated purpose of his amendment was to meet the concerns of Senators like McGee who had argued that passage of the Byrd Amendment would undercut the British, who were then in the process of negotiating the Home-Smith agreement. (The agreement was reached, the reader will recall, in November—and was subsequently rejected by the African population of Southern Rhodesia.) It is noteworthy that Brock was careful to raise the issue *after* the Fulbright amendment had been passed. To have given legitimacy to McGee's don't-weaken-the-British-hand argument before the vote on the Fulbright amendment might have persuaded wavering Senators to go along with McGee and Fulbright.

Senator Byrd's triumph was not yet complete; his amendment still had to survive a liberal attack in the House. But, through persistence and parliamentary skill, he had cleared the highest hurdle. The imprimatur of the Senate had been placed on Section 503, and this would carry great weight with the House. Let the reader suppose he or she is a Member of the House of Representatives. His or her constituency cares and knows little about Southern Rhodesia. Legislation concerning Southern Rhodesia has never before been debated at any length on the floor of the House. There is not time to study the issue. One inevitably risks being wrong on the substance of the argument. In political terms, is it more dangerous to be wrong by doing a disservice to the United Nations or by underestimating a Soviet threat? Especially once the relatively more liberal Senate has decided that there is something to Byrd's arguments, one's political inclination would probably be to go along with "national security" over the United Nations.

Section 503 had other factors working for it, as well, as it moved toward a vote in the House. As an addition in the Senate to a bill already passed by the House, it had to survive consideration in a Conference Committee, composed of representatives of both houses. The Conference Committee considering the military program bill was predominantly conservative, and the Byrd Amendment easily survived. Indeed, the conference report, filed on November 5, stated the arguments in favor of the Amendment in stark terms of a pressing national need for Rhodesian chrome. In addition to its support by the Conference Committee, the Byrd Amendment gained strength from the vote in the United Nations on October 25, 1971, when the People's Republic of China was admitted in place of Nationalist China. Photographs of African delegates leaping for joy after the vote did little to encourage conservative and moderate Congressmen to put the sanctity of American obligations at the United Nations over what they saw as the American national interest.

On November 10, when the conference report went to the floor of the House, Representative Donald Fraser, supported most notably by Representatives Diggs and Culver (D.–Iowa), offered an amendment to strike Section 503. It did not have a chance. With the memory of the U.N. vote on China still vivid, with the mantle of the Senate covering the

Byrd Amendment, with the fear that the military procurement bill might not be passed that year if Section 503 were deleted and the entire conference report lost, the House voted overwhelmingly to reject Fraser's plea. Section 503 was retained by a vote of 251 to 100, with 80 absent, after forty minutes of debate.

The Senate passed the conference report the following day. Senator Jacob Javits (R.–N.Y.) made one last effort, urging his colleagues to reject the whole bill because of Section 503. It was, he said, "a matter of basic principle in international law." But the conference report was agreed to by a vote of 65 to 19 with sixteen Senators not voting. Six days later, on November 17, 1971, President Nixon signed the Military Procurement Authorization Bill into law, without comment on Section 503.

That Section read as follows:

Sec. 503. The Strategic and Critical Materials Stock Piling Act (60 Stat. 596; 50 U.S.C. 98–98h) is amended (1) by re-designating section 10 as section 11, and (2) by inserting after section 9 a new section 10 as follows:

"Section 10. Notwithstanding any other provision of law, on and after January 1, 1972, the President may not prohibit or regulate the importation into the United States of any material determined to be strategic and critical pursuant to the provisions of this Act, if such material is the product of any foreign country or area not listed as a Communist-dominated country or area in general headnote 3(d) of the Tariff Schedules of the United States (19 U.S.C. 1202), for as long as the importation into the United States of material of that kind which is the product of such Communist-dominated countries or areas is not prohibited by any provision of law."

The next step was up to the administration. It faced a general choice and a specific technical question. The general choice was whether to try to find a way to avoid implementation of the Byrd Amendment. The technical question involved defining the "strategic and critical materials" affected by Section 503.

Had it been determined to avoid or delay placing the United States in official violation of sanctions, the administration could have found ways to do so. It could, for example, have prohibited imports of chrome and other relevant minerals from the Soviet Union and other Communist nations, thus blocking their import from Rhodesia as well, a difficult but not impossible step. Or it could have declared chrome and the other materials not to be "strategic and critical." There was some considerable discussion within the State Department about these and other methods of circumventing the Amendment, but the general conclusion was that they all raised technical questions and would also, if implemented, raise Congressional hackles. Thus challenged, Congress would probably reaffirm the Amendment in more specific terms. State therefore sent to the White House a memorandum listing the various options and the arguments pro and con, without suggesting a delay in implementation. Of course, even if it had argued for delay or evasion, it is doubtful that the White House would have agreed. On January 25, 1972, the Office of Foreign Assets Control at the Treasury Department issued a General License allowing the importation of Southern Rhodesian chrome, ferrochrome and "any other material of Southern Rhodesian origin, determined to be strategic and critical . . ." On February 18, the Office of Emergency Preparedness issued a list of "strategic and critical materials." It included seventy-two materials, among which were feathers and down as well as minerals like tungsten, copper and aluminum.

The flow of chromite to the United States soon began. The first shipment of 25,000 tons, consigned to the Foote Mineral Company, arrived in March at Burnside, Louisiana. Union Carbide received its first shipment in early April at Pointe a la Hache, Devant, Louisiana.

Thus, in early 1972, it was the congressional liberals who now were in opposition to the American sanctions policy, in its vastly weakened form. A list of the Congressmen introducing editorials and making short speeches on Rhodesia in early

1971 includes notably Senator James Allen (D.–Ala.), Representative Collins, Representative Harold Collier (R.–Ill.), Representative Samuel Devine (R.–Ohio), Senator Byrd (repeatedly), Representative John Rarick (D.–La.), Representative Richard Fulton (D.–Tenn.), etc.—conservatives all. In early 1972, the inserts into the *Congressional Record* were coming from liberals: Representative Diggs, Senator George McGovern, Representative John Conyers (D.–Mich.), Senator Humphrey, Representative Ronald Dellums (D.–Calif.), Representative William Clay (D.–Mo.), Senator Edward Kennedy (D.–Mass.), and Senator McGee. Senator Byrd and Representative Rarick were also active, but Rhodesia had now become a liberal rather than a conservative cause in the Congress.

Senator McGee was uncertain as to whether he should make a major attempt to repeal the Byrd Amendment, however, since any failure would simply dramatize again America's embarrassment at the United Nations. He decided to go ahead, he says, after receiving assurances of support from the White House. In mid-April, he succeeded in attaching to the USIA and Department of State Authorization Bill, then pending before the Foreign Relations Committee, an amendment repealing the Byrd Amendment. The bill moved to the floor in late April, with McGee's attachment. On April 25, Senator Byrd duly announced his intention to introduce an amendment to delete McGee's amendment. Subsequent floor debate on the bill covered the same issues as the debate of the previous fall. McGee, a devout believer in the United Nations, keyed his argument to American responsibility there. On May 31, the day of the vote, McGee admitted that the United Nations had been "in a low state for the past few months. But," he continued, "let us not be the one that gives up the last ray of hope for collective action through an organization of all of the nations, not just some of them. We have committed a great deal of that faith." Senator Byrd answered that Representatives from forty-two of the fifty American states had supported his Amendment and thus supported the position "that the U.S. Congress must not be subordinate to the U.N." [7] Senator Brock was still rankled by the China vote: "Look at the utter hypocrisy, the sheer, rank hypocrisy of the United Nations in the instance of Taiwan. They did not happen to like the country of Taiwan. They happened to decide they wanted to play the power game, so they chose a big guy over a little guy, and said, 'We are going to bring Red China into the United Nations, and at the same time we are going to throw them out.' What a bunch of garbage there is in that position. Consistency? It is not consistency, it is hypocrisy, pure and rank."

McGee could not impress on a majority of the Senate his view of the importance of the United Nations and international law, and the issue would again turn on "national security": a re-imposition of the embargo of Rhodesian chrome, Byrd and his allies argued, would place American industry at the mercy of Soviet chrome exporters. The Senate voted to delete the McGee amendment and thus save the Byrd Amendment, 40 to 36.

Representative Fraser was not deterred by Senator McGee's defeat. In June, he held two days of hearings on the issue before his International Organizations Subcommittee, and in July he persuaded the House Committee on Foreign Affairs to amend the foreign aid bill to include a section repealing the Byrd Amendment. It was reported to the full House, but was defeated by 253 to 140. The last effort in the Ninety-Second Congress to negate Senator Byrd's handiwork had failed.

OFFICIAL LOBBYING

While it is clear from this history that Byrd and his allies operated with greater skill than their opponents, especially in the early rounds of the fight, this is not a sufficient explana-

[7] For a general refutation of Byrd's effort to show that the impetus and support for his Amendment were not regional, see Raymond Arsenault, "White on Chrome: Southern Congressmen and Rhodesia 1962–1971," *Issue,* Winter 1972.

tion of what happened. The activities of industry lobbyists
and, perhaps more important still, the ambiguous role of the
administration played a central part. After the vote which defeated his amendment on May 31, a furious Senator McGee
rose to make an extraordinary statement. The White House,
he charged, had misled him. He had been told that it would
actively support him in 1972, as it had not in 1971.

> But, I now regret to report that the handling of the Rho-
> desian chrome ore question on the part of the Administration
> was no different than it was last time. This time I personally
> appealed to the White House for assistance. I asked that they
> make only five or six telephone calls to marginal Senators on
> the Administration side of the Senate aisle—several of whom
> had already told me a "call from the Administration would be
> necessary to change my vote." As it turned out, the White
> House would have had to make only three calls to turn the tide
> in our favor.
> My purpose in speaking at this time is to set the record
> completely straight. After all the high-sounding rhetoric and
> the pious pronouncements, the White House alone must bear
> the burden and responsibility for the defeat today.
> Let us keep one fact straight. It is not the Congress who
> can now be blamed for this defeat. It is not the Foreign Rela-
> tions Committee. It is not the steel companies or the steelwork-
> ers' unions. The White House, for whatever reasons, chose not
> to try to win.

Senator Byrd disingenuously responded, "But I as one
Senator feel that the Members of the Senate can make up
their own minds. I see no reason why the President should be
condemned because he does not pick up the telephone and try
to influence a Member of the Senate on a piece of legislation."
McGee, in turn, suggested that Byrd had "been here long
enough to know that when the President wants something, he
gets on the telephone. . . . We all know how the business
operates. And the conspicuous absence of it in this case suggested to me that there was less than devotion to the principle,
or an attempt to play both sides on that principle."

What McGee was objecting to was the startling difference between the State Department and the White House in their approach to the issue, both in their public statements and in their activities on Capitol Hill. State's representatives consistently opposed all the sanctions-busting measures introduced by Senator Byrd, Representative Collins and others. In letters of May 14 and June 17, 1971, David Abshire, the Assistant Secretary of State for Congressional Relations, sent to the Chairman of the House Foreign Affairs Committee the Department's strongly negative comments on the various anti-sanctions bills then before the House. State Department witnesses, including Assistant Secretary Newsom, testified in various hearings held by the Senate Foreign Relations and House Foreign Affairs Subcommittees, making arguments similar to those in Abshire's letter. In key periods between the passage of the Byrd Amendment in October, 1971, and the failure of the repeal effort on May 31, 1972, the State Department made its strongest statements of opposition to the Amendment. In his March report on American foreign policy, Secretary Rogers made clear his regret at the Congressional action. And on May 20, 1972, Senator McGee received (at his request) from John Irwin II, then Acting Secretary of State, a strong letter stating the administration's support for the Senator's repeal effort. Irwin argued, "Repeal now would serve to make us less vulnerable to unfavorable international reaction. As a result of the legislation now in force, our international interests have suffered in other respects. In Africa, where our position on Rhodesia has heretofore been seen as a test of our commitment to self-determination and racial equality, our credibility has suffered. The depth of African concern has been particularly strong in some nations where our interests far outweigh those in Rhodesia. In the United Nations, we lose face with each shipment of chrome or other commodity, and increased erosion of our position. While we have sought and continue to seek means of making the existing sanctions against Rhodesia more effective and less liable to circumvention by others, our ability to do so is seriously limited by the legislation now in effect."

In addition to these statements of opposition to the efforts of Byrd and his allies, the Department actively lobbied for its position. Michael Samuels, a young, competent member of the Office of Congressional Relations, was assigned to work full-time on the matter. He provided speaking materials, called Congressional offices, drafted letters to Senators who might cast swing votes, and worked at stimulating expressions of concern by higher-level administration officials. Senator McGee is said to have come to look on Samuels as practically a member of his own staff. Assistant Secretary Newsom was also very active, in the words of one official, "as active as the Congressional Relations Office allows any regional Assistant Secretary to be." And from New York, the chief American representative at the United Nations, Ambassador George Bush, also weighed in. He reportedly pressed several times for White House action.

But the White House was unwilling to show its hand on the issue, either in its statements or through the activities of the White House staff and their political allies. It was perfectly willing to let the State Department do what it could. The Office of Management and Budget—the President's budgetary arm—cleared Assistant Secretary Abshire's letters in the spring of 1971, as it does all of the State Department's comments on pending legislation. And according to a number of sources, the Irwin letter of May, 1972—the strongest attack by the administration on the Byrd Amendment—was cleared by the White House.

The White House also was willing to blame the Congress for passing the Byrd Amendment. In his Annual Report on American Foreign Policy of February 9, 1972, the President noted disapprovingly that the "Congress exempted strategic and critical materials, notably chrome, from the U.S. implementation of the mandatory U.N. sanctions on imports from Rhodesia."

But the White House carefully avoided calling on the Congress to reverse itself. On May 19, 1972, the day before Irwin's strong letter was sent to McGee (with behind-the-scenes White House approval), Jerry Warren, a presidential spokesman, had an uncomfortable minute with the press. The dialogue between Warren and confused reporters shows how carefully he was trying to express delicate opposition to the Amendment without committing the President to action on the issue:

Reporter: "Are you in a position to answer a question about Rhodesian chrome imports?"

Warren: "I hope so."

Reporter: "Does the White House have a position on Senator McGee's amendment to repeal the Byrd Amendment on Rhodesian chrome?"

Warren: "The White House feels it is appropriate for the Senate to seek conformity between our domestic laws and our international treaty obligations."

Reporter: "What does that mean, Jerry?"

Warren: "That means that the Senate has before it the issue and so the Senate should work it out."

Reporter: "But does that mean the White House thinks it should be repealed?"

Warren: "The Congress enacted the Byrd Amendment. And the Congress is now reviewing the legislation to seek conformity with the United States' international obligation. So it is up to the Congress."

Reporter: "Are you advocating the repeal of the Byrd Amendment?"

Warren: "We are advocating conformity between our domestic laws and our international treaty obligations."

Reporter: "What are our international treaty obligations in this respect?"

Warren: "I think you know as well as I do in this respect. It has to do with the United Nations. For details on that, you can get it from State."

Reporter: "The point is the Byrd Amendment takes our international obligations out of conformity with our domestic or the other way around, I should say."

Warren: "I am going to have to leave it where I left it before, George."

Reporter: "Didn't you or Ron [Ziegler] say just a day or two ago that the President was against that Amendment?"

Warren: "No, I don't believe so. I don't think this subject has come up recently . . . I am sure it has not."

As indicated by the exchange between McGee and Byrd previously cited, the Senator from Wyoming had expected that the White House would support him in his 1972 repeal effort, at least with calls to wavering Senators. In the autumn of 1971, the White House had been notably reticent in expressing a position. Indeed, according to Senator McGee, when a staff member of the Senate Foreign Relations Committee had asked a State Department representative to try to get the White House to go on the record with regard to the issue, he was warned that it might be better not to do so because the response from the White House might damage the anti-Byrd position! Now, eight months later, McGee thought he had a commitment from the White House that it would enter the lists. After receiving Irwin's letter of May 20, the Senator called the Congressional Relations Office of the White House, speaking with Tom Korologos, Deputy Assistant to the President for Legislative Affairs. McGee said that the Byrd Amendment could be repealed if the votes of only a few wavering Republican Senators could be gained. The President and Dr. Kissinger were then in Moscow; McGee asked if one of the senior White House officials still in the country—perhaps John Ehrlichman—could call Senators Schweiker (R.–Pa.), Weicker (R.–Conn.), Roth (R.–Del.), Saxbe (R.–Ohio) and Taft (R.–Ohio) to make it clear that the White House took the same position as Irwin, then the Acting Secretary of State. Korologos reportedly assured the Senator that he would see what could be done. The next day, just hours before the vote, McGee received a call from another White House official saying that it had done all it could do. None of the five Senators had received a call. McGee's effort failed by four votes; if three of the five had switched, he would have won.

"What could be done" by the White House had not been very much. White House lobbyists sat on their hands during the 1971 and 1972 maneuverings, and the position taken by high administration officials and the allies of the White House on Capitol Hill left little doubt that the President preferred to duck the issue. Rumors that Vice President Agnew was absent for key votes on Rhodesia because he wished to avoid having to decide any ties have not been substantiated. In general, his presence in the Senate was more noteworthy than his customary absence, and his staff denied in interviews that there was anything exceptional in his performance on the Byrd Amendment. But the rumors themselves played a part in defining his position. In addition, corporate lobbyists working for passage of the Byrd Amendment were occasionally seen conferring with Walter Mote of the Vice President's Congressional staff. According to Mote, who is a personal friend of Union Carbide's chief lobbyist on the issue, he was "just gathering information" from the corporate representatives. Mote says that he and the others in his office made it a practice to take head counts in advance of major votes, in order to inform the Vice President of ties that might arise, and he and the lobbyists were simply comparing notes. Mote states that the Vice President's office was "neutral" on the Byrd Amendment. But taking him at his word, neutrality was not the official position of the administration. And exchanging information with corporate lobbyists in reception rooms off the floor of the Senate could be, and was, interpreted by others as implying a position of something less than neutrality. It certainly did not convey support for the position being urged by the State Department.

It was also noticeable that Secretary Rogers did little lobbying to drive home the message being carried to Capitol Hill by his subordinates. Senator McGee puts the blame for this on the White House: "Even the Department of State was content to let its interest be conveyed only by a relatively low-ranking, albeit highly capable, civil servant in the Office of Congressional Relations. To our knowledge, no official of greater rank than the Assistant Secretary of State made more than a token effort to support the Fulbright-McGee amendment. And this bureaucratic inertia—although inexcusable in itself—seemed directly traceable to the White House attitude." [8]

Another reflection of the White House position could be found in the activities of Senator Robert Dole (R.–Kans.), then Chairman of the Republican National Committee. During the 1971 votes on the McGee-Fullbright amendments to delete Section 503, Dole consistently voted in favor of the Byrd Amendment. Informed sources state that Dole had come under pressure from Union Carbide and Foote Mineral representatives. When he asked the White House staff what he should do, he was reportedly given the word that the White House was sitting it out. Other sources indicate that Dole informed fellow Republicans that the administration was actually neutral, and that they were on their own.

The Republican leadership in the Senate hardly went down fighting for the administration's "official" position. Senator Hugh Scott (R.–Pa.), the Minority Leader, voted with both the Byrd and anti-Byrd forces during the long night of September 30. On the key substantive votes on September 23 and September 30, Scott recorded his vote with the anti-Byrd Amendment forces, but in each case canceled it by giving a live pair to an absent Senator supporting the Byrd Amendment. Senator Robert Griffin (R.–Mich.), the Minority Whip, voted with Fulbright and McGee on those two votes, and then switched back and forth on subsequent votes during the evening of September 30; on two of these votes, he voted for the position of the McGee-Fulbright forces but gave a live pair to one of their absent opponents. He also negated his vote against the Byrd Amendment on May 31, 1972, by giving Senator Howard Baker (R.–Tenn.) a live pair.

The position of the White House reflected both internal politics on the President's staff and various calculations of political and legislative advantage. The National Security Council staff generally supported the State Department's efforts, and

[8] McGee, "Rhodesian Chrome Issue," p. 5.

would have had no objection to explicit White House opposition to the Byrd Amendment. Its position reflected a general
concern with the foreign policy implications—the problems at
the United Nations and with the Africans. But any real concern seems to have been felt only at the lower levels of the
staff. Dr. Kissinger's office did not, reportedly, become much
involved, and the NSC staff never made an issue of the White
House's silence. (Marshall Wright, later to become Assistant
Secretary of State for Congressional Relations, was now the
pivotal figure on the staff on African affairs. Roger Morris
had resigned in mid-1970.) Indeed, the final draft of press
spokesman Warren's remarkably restrained comments on the
issue were drafted by the NSC staff.

The foreign policy experts in the White House did urge
that the President's staff act behind the scenes on one aspect
of the affair, however, and were successful. In the fall of 1971,
British officials indicated their concern that implementation of
the Byrd Amendment might threaten what seemed to be an
imminent agreement with Smith; the NSC staff therefore suggested that the White House try to delay the date on which the
Amendment would come into force. Representatives of the
White House reportedly asked Senators Peter H. Dominick
(R.–Colo.) and William E. Brock (R.–Tenn.) to introduce an
amendment which would delay the active date of the Byrd
Amendment. Brock then took the lead in introducing the
amendment which carried out the wishes of the White House.

Some observers have placed great weight on the role
played by Presidential Adviser Peter Flanigan. First as the
President's liaison man with the business community and later
as Chairman of the Council on International Economic Policy,
it would have been natural for Flanigan to argue for the position of Union Carbide and Foote Mineral. But reliable officials
in a position to know state that there is little evidence that
Flanigan was deeply involved. They indicate that Flanigan
may have recommended to the Congressional Relations Office
a low posture on or even quiet support for the Byrd Amendment, but state that if he did so, it was informally, without insistence, and only in the most general of terms. It seems most

likely that the White House took the position it did not out of
primary concern for Union Carbide and Foote, although some
such concern was present, but as part of an attempt to achieve
other political goals.

The Congressional Relations Office usually sets the priorities for White House lobbying on Capitol Hill. Foreign policy
issues received less attention in that office than in the President's Oval Office; and among foreign policy issues, Southern
Rhodesia loomed hardly at all. Battling congressional liberals
over Southeast Asia and NATO, the White House lobbyists
were loath to waste any ammunition on so peripheral a concern, by their reckoning, as southern Africa. In addition, the
Congressional Relations Office and the political strategists in
the White House wished to avoid offending Senator Byrd, who
had been elected as an Independent in the 1970 elections. It
was in the interest of the administration, of course, and especially of those who were arguing for a Southern strategy, that
Byrd be encouraged to define "Independent" in as Republican
terms as possible. White House officials say that for this and
other reasons, Patrick Buchanan and Chief of Staff Robert
Haldeman opposed NSC arguments against breaking sanctions. According to two of them, Haldeman would stop NSC
memoranda before they reached the President, solicit Buchanan's written views or those of another of the particularly
conservative staff members, and cover the NSC document
with a memorandum pointing to the alternative expression of
opinion.

But the White House faced something of a dilemma.
While the political benefits of pleasing Byrd were clear, the
White House did not wish to antagonize McGee. It needed
McGee's continued support on Southeast Asia and security assistance appropriations. This was especially true during his
repeal effort in May, 1972—a period of American escalation
in Indochina. In addition, it was clear by then that Senator
Byrd was not going to line up officially with the Republicans
in the Senate, or, indeed, vote with the administration on
foreign policy matters as consistently as McGee.

The way out of the dilemma seemed to be to make

friendly private noises to McGee while avoiding any activity which could offend Byrd and his allies. The strategy failed because McGee asked for more than the White House was willing to give; he was understandably dismayed to discover that its sympathetic tone did not imply supportive action. To anyone concerned with the Rhodesian issue, the performance of the White House would seem to indicate cynical and covert support for the Byrd Amendment. This misses the point. In fact, the White House was mostly indifferent about the issue, and decided to duck it for reasons unrelated to events in southern Africa. As an official at Foote Mineral puts it, "I don't think the White House cared one way or the other—they just didn't want to be forced to take a stand."

PRIVATE LOBBYING

The ambivalence of the administration helped insure Byrd's victory. The ambivalence was important in itself; and more, it allowed the corporate lobbyists who supported Byrd's efforts to be the most potent outside force influencing the Congress—as Senator Humphrey has put it, in "twisting public policy for private interest." [9]

In December 1971, a Christmas party was given by the Rhodesian Information Office in Washington to celebrate the successful passage of Section 503. A song was written for the occasion. As printed in an article by journalist Bruce Oudes in the *Washington Post,* the song provides a "Who's Who" of the anti-sanctions lobbying effort. Sung to the tune of "O Tannenbaum," the "503 Club Marching Song" went like this:

1

(*To be sung with great joy*)
Oh, 503, oh, 503
We gave our very best for thee;
Oh, 503, oh, 503

[9] Hearing before the Subcommittee on African Affairs of the Committee on Foreign Relations, United States Senate, "Importation of Rhodesian Chrome," September 6, 1973, p. 88.

We celebrate our victory.
To Harry Byrd, we'll drink a toast
And sing his praise from coast to coast;
Jim Collins, too, we'll honor thee
And hang you on our Christmas tree.

2

(To be sung mournfully)
Oh, 503, oh, 503
You nearly were the death of me;
Oh, 503, oh, 503
The roll call votes were agony.
We very nearly lost our wits;
Fulbright and Fraser gave us fits.
We frown upon you, Gale McGee,
And dimly view Ted Kennedy.

3

(To be sung with great sincerity)
Oh, 503, oh, 503
Rhodesia's future rode with thee.
Oh, Fulton Lewis Number Three,
We honor your tenacity.
We love the people we are with,
And raise a glass for Ian Smith.
Congratulations, we assume
Are due Lord Goodman, Alec Home.

4

(To be sung with wistful melancholy)
Oh, 503, oh, 503
We faced a mighty enemy;
Oh, 503, oh, 503
The State Department thwarted thee.
We ran afoul of David Newsom,
Culver and Diggs—an awesome twosome;
The U.N. fought you mightily
And Harold Wilson censured thee.

5

(To be sung lovingly)
Oh, 503, we'll blow a kiss
To Margaret S. and Tony Bliss.
And Andy Andrews, you're true blue—
John Donahey, we hail you too.
Hey, Howard Cannon, you're a hit,
Sam Ervin—bless you for your wit;
Bill Brock, we greet you gratefully—
Defender of the 503.

6

(To be sung bravely, if hoarsely)
Oh, noble House, your Members there
Nailed down the victory with a flair.
Let songs of joy ring through the air;
We won the battle fair and square.
And so, tonight let's have some fun;
It's better to have fought and won!
And you'll go down in history,
Our dear, beloved 503.

7

(To be sung diplomatically)
Oh, Kenneth T., oh, Kenneth T.,
Ambassador one day you'll be.
And may John Hooper follow thee
To posts of great authority;
Next winter may it be your lot
To spend your Christmas where it's hot.
Please raise a toast in Salisbury
In memory of 503.

The first reference to the Rhodesian and chrome lobbies comes in the third stanza where Fulton Lewis III is honored for his "tenacity." Lewis worked with the Rhodesian Information Office, spoke out on radio against sanctions, and worked on a number of members of Congress and officials in the Executive branch. More than a year before Senator Byrd and

Representative Collins introduced their bills, Lewis was arguing in his news broadcasts that the United States was becoming
dangerously dependent on the Soviet Union for its imports of
raw materials, especially chrome and nickel.

Lewis asserted in an interview that he did not lobby for
the Byrd Amendment during 1971 and 1972. But he did take
an active interest: "At dinner or on the street if I'd run into a
Congressman, as a newsman I would ask what's happening
with Byrd . . . but I didn't initiate any calls or solicit any
votes." Even if we accept Lewis' description of his actions at
face value, it is clear that they were still influential in a number
of ways. His persistence kept the issue before the Congressmen who would be most likely to support the Amendment.
And for the waverers, the prospect of being denounced in
Lewis' broadcasts could only help discourage them from supporting Senator McGee. Numerous sources indicate that Lewis
discussed with at least six Congressmen, including representatives from Ohio, Pennsylvania, and Michigan, "the political
problems" (to use the phrase used by Lewis himself in an interview) which they would have if they voted against the Byrd
Amendment. "I report all of this, of course," Lewis has said in
an interview, "but I didn't threaten." To the Congressmen,
however, the threatening implication was clear. One said in an
interview, "I'd like to go against the Byrd Amendment, and
just might. But God, Lewis is going to give me hell in my district." Finally, supporters of the Byrd Amendment found that
Lewis' broadcasts made useful handouts when they received
inquiries about their position. One assistant in the office of
Senator Cannon constantly referred in an interview to one of
these broadcasts, and finally handed the handout to the inter-
viewer saying that Lewis is "a radio commentator who knows a
lot about Africa. This article [sic] is pretty good. I think it will
answer most of your questions."

On February 21, 1973, Lewis' credibility may have suffered, however, when he first denied, then admitted before a
joint hearing of the House Subcommittees on Africa and In-

ternational Organizations and Movements that in 1972 he had accepted $1,000 from the Rhodesian Information Office to help meet his expenses for a trip to Southern Rhodesia.

It is the fifth stanza of the "503 Club Marching Song" that most neatly summarizes the lobby at work on the Byrd Amendment. "We'll blow a kiss to Margaret S. and Tony Bliss" refers to Margaret Cox-Sullivan, a consultant to the Union Carbide Corporation who was active in late 1970, and to L. G. "Tony" Bliss, the former chairman of the board of the Foote Mineral Company, who began lobbying against the sanctions program almost before it started. Bliss started coming to Washington in early 1967, asking that Foote be allowed to import chrome that had been mined by its Rhodesian subsidiaries before mandatory sanctions took effect. Bliss also put pressure on representatives from ferroalloy districts to introduce sanctions-busting legislation from 1967 onward. The same stanza of the song mentions Foote's John Donahey, who also did a great deal of effective lobbying on the Amendment. On May 31, 1972, Senator McGee paid bitter tribute to the effectiveness of Foote's and Union Carbide's lobbying: "It is, indeed, a sad day when the U.S. Senate falls victim to a ploy as reprehensible as this and allows foreign policy considerations to be determined by two corporations who have significant holdings in Rhodesia."

Stanza 5 thanks "Andy Andrews" as well—E. F. Andrews, a vice-president for purchases at Allegheny Ludlum Industries—who was another major lobbyist for Section 503. Andrews, as a representative of the stainless steel industry, appeared before congressional hearings and met with many Congressmen on the issue. His lobbying and that of other stainless steel companies was coordinated and directed by the Washington law firm of Collier, Shannon, Rill and Edwards. In fact, interviews indicate that it was this law firm, representing the Tool and Stainless Steel Industry Committee, that did most of the lobbying on the Byrd Amendment. According to an interview with one of the firm's senior partners, Thomas Shannon, he himself introduced the idea of the Amendment to Senator Byrd in late 1970. The firm researched the issue thoroughly, sent people to Rhodesia and assigned two lawyers to the effort. In addition, they had all their member companies—like Allegheny Ludlum—lobby representatives in their own districts.

Not mentioned in the song were several others involved in the lobbying effort. For instance, another Carbide staffer, Washington lobbyist Jerry Kenney, said in an interview that telegrams were sent to Congressmen from states in which Carbide had ferroalloy plants. Although Kenney told us he did no other "official" lobbying on the Byrd Amendment, Union Carbide was heavily involved. A *New York Times* article reported that, "Shortly before the vote, a Union Carbide lobbyist gleefully told a member of the Senate Foreign Relations Committee staff, 'We've got the votes.'"

Still another corporate group lobbying for the Byrd Amendment was the American Iron and Steel Institute (AISI), the trade association for the nation's carbon steel manufacturers. James Collins, the AISI regional vice-president in Washington, said in an interview that he wrote letters to Congressmen and encouraged member companies to write letters to visit their representatives. But in his view, it was Shannon and the Tool and Stainless Steel Industry Committee that "carried the ball" on the Byrd Amendment.

Arrayed against this lobbying effort was a disorganized coalition of groups, including black leaders, the American Committee on Africa, labor unions, churches, Democratic politicians, and the Americans for Democratic Action. Too often, as the Byrd Amendment wound its way through the Congress in 1971 and 1972, these groups got there last with the least.

Congressman Charles C. Diggs, Jr., the chairman of the Subcommittee on Africa, was, together with Congressman Fraser, the most persistent opponent of the Byrd Amendment in the House of Representatives. He testified against it, circulated his views in writing to other members of Congress, and even resigned as a member of the American delegation at the United Nations in late 1971, in part because of the administration's policies toward Rhodesia. Diggs also was instrumental in the position on the Byrd Amendment adopted by the Congressional Black Caucus. On September 29, 1971, the Caucus sent a letter to Secretary Rogers and a telegram to the President asking that they take a public stand in support of the Fulbright amendment repealing Section 503. This effort was dismissed, it appears, out of hand. And Diggs's activism was not emulated by the other members of the Black Caucus, who devoted far less attention to the struggle. An aide to one black Congressman says, "Most of our work was through the Caucus. The issue came up pretty rapidly and sort of caught us by surprise. And it was not a terribly important issue."

Outside the Congress, various black groups demonstrated against the Byrd Amendment after it came into force in early 1972. But the difficulty in translating a slowly awakening black American concern with African issues into effective political pressure was illustrated by an event in late May, 1972. As Ross K. Baker has noted in an interesting article on the constituency for black Africa in the United States, a "May 1972 conference at Howard University and the African Liberation Day demonstrations that followed it in Washington mounted an impressive attack on current policies. But in the crucial area of legislative action there was no parallel effort. Even as the African Liberation Day demonstrators were meeting at the State Department, the Senate was debating the legislation sponsored by Senator McGee which was fostered by the State Department and which would have reinstated the ban on Rhodesian chrome. Yet the proponents of the bill received virtually no support or encouragement from the demonstrators." [10]

The American Committee on Africa was less active and less influential than Representative Diggs and the Black Caucus. But it did what it could, sending letters and calling congressional staffers who might be able to use its assistance. Its efforts were sadly flawed, however, by its tardiness in becom-

[10] "Towards a New Constituency for a More Active American Foreign Policy for Africa," *Issue,* Spring 1973, p. 18.

ing engaged. In mid-September, after the Armed Services Committee had reported Senator Byrd's Amendment to the floor, the New York headquarters of the ACOA had not even heard of its existence. The head of ACOA's Washington office had gone on vacation after his unsuccessful fight that summer to defeat the American sugar quota for South Africa.

As a result, the church groups which support the ACOA and rely on it to keep them informed of legislation of interest to them, were also generally caught by surprise. While the leaders of various American Protestant churches called on the administration in early 1972 to maintain the embargo despite the Byrd Amendment, and church representatives in Washington supported McGee's repeal effort that spring, the churches were not an important factor when the Byrd Amendment was passed in 1971.

Labor union lobbyists were more effective, especially the United Steel Workers of America. In September, 1971, they provided research materials to Congressmen who opposed the Amendment, and sent letters stating their position to all Congressmen. The force of the union's efforts was vitiated, however, by the actions of William A. Hart, a local union leader from western Pennsylvania. On September 22, Senator Stennis inserted into the record a telegram from Hart urging passage of the Byrd Amendment. Hart warned that if it failed, "there [would] be no specialty steel industry in Pennsylvania or the United States." A week later, Senator McGee inserted a letter from I. W. Abel, the president of the United Steel Workers, opposing the Byrd Amendment and stating that Hart's telegram was neither endorsed by the executive board nor reflected the position of the union. Abel argued that the problems of the specialty steel industry and the ferralloy industry could be solved by import quotas and "not by breaking the Rhodesian embargo on chrome ore." "We hope," he said, "that this untimely and socially indefensible provision of H.R. 8687 will be dropped either in conference or by further action by the Senate. The price of human dignity should not be measured in terms of the cost of chromite in the United States

market." [11] Senator Byrd responded, on September 30, that
Abel's letter should be discounted: "Another union official has
sent a letter in a different tone. That merely shows that there
is a difference of opinion among the union leaders, just as
there is among the members of the U.S. Senate." In equating
Abel with Hart, Byrd failed, of course, to note that Abel was
the president of the union whereas Hart was reportedly an
employee of a Pennsylvania company with financial interests
in Rhodesia.

Labor opposition to the Byrd Amendment was also reflected in a number of incidents in 1972 in which longshore-
men refused to unload Rhodesian nickel and other minerals.
But these local actions did not seriously impede the ability of
American importers to get their goods.

Democratic politicians also made occasional statements of
ritual support for sanctions and opposition to the Byrd
Amendment, as the 1972 campaign got underway. Senators
McGovern, Muskie, and Humphrey, as well as Mayor John
Lindsay and Senator Eugene McCarthy, stated these views and
opposition to the Home-Smith agreement in December, 1971,
and early 1972. At the same time, the Americans for Democratic Action sent a cable to the White House from such liberals as Cyrus Vance, Ramsey Clark, and Nicholas Katzenbach, opposing the agreement and calling for executive action
to prevent imports from Rhodesia. But this plea, like the statements of the candidates, came after the Byrd Amendment had
been passed, not during the crucial days in September. And
occasional statements from liberal quarters could never stir
the White House.

The most serious challenge to implementation of the
Byrd Amendment came in April, 1972, when Congressman
Diggs, other members of the Black Caucus, the ACOA, and
others [12] filed a complaint in the U.S. District Court for the

[11] Hearing before the Subcommittee on African Affairs of the Committee
on Foreign Relations, United States Senate, "Importation of Rhodesian
Chrome," September 6, 1973, p. 52.

[12] Council for Christian Social Action of the United Church of Christ,
Episcopal Churchmen for South Africa, IFCO-Action, Southern Africa

District of Columbia against the Secretary of the Treasury, other government officials, Foote, and Union Carbide. The plaintiffs sought "preliminary and permanent injunctive relief to prevent the importation from Southern Rhodesia of metallurgical chromite and other materials"; a court order "directing government officials having authority to seize and impound goods imported into the United States in violation of law, to proceed forthwith to impound metallurgical chromite and other materials which may have been imported into the United States" in violation of the U.N. sanctions resolutions and the Executive Orders implementing them; and "a declaratory judgment that the General License issued by the Office of Foreign Assets Control of the United States Treasury Department" authorizing imports of chrome and other materials from Southern Rhodesia was null and void—"and/or the Byrd Amendment if construed to authorize the General License is itself null and void."

In essence, the case was decided on two issues: the standing of the plaintiffs (i.e., their ability to show that they had a valid interest in the case and were damaged by the Byrd Amendment), and the legality of the Byrd Amendment itself. The plaintiffs lost the first round of the battle in a lower court in June, 1972, when the court held that they did not have standing. Diggs and his co-plaintiffs then moved to appeal the decision. In November, the U.S. Court of Appeals in Washington reversed the lower court's opinion and found that most of the plaintiffs did have standing—but that the Byrd Amendment was legal. The court was persuaded by the plaintiffs' arguments that the Byrd Amendment violated an American treaty commitment, and shared their dismay. Its opinion clearly stated that the Byrd Amendment showed "blatant disregard of our treaty undertakings" as a member of the United Nations. But under the Constitution, the court said, Congress

---

Committee, Southern Christian Leadership Conference, Zimbabwe African National Union; and, as "concerned individuals," Thomas M. Franck, Edward Weisband, Bert Lockwood, Shelly Fenchel, Joel Carlson, Robert Goldschmidt, Robert Janosik, Nigel Rodley, Diane Flaherty, and Antoine Van Dongen.

has the power to "set treaty obligations at naught," and it had exercised this power in passing the Byrd Amendment.

The plaintiffs were trapped in a paradoxical position. They were arguing that Congress had not specifically stated that its intent was to abrogate an American treaty obligation, and that therefore it was not exercising its constitutional power to do so—in which case the treaty obligation remained. But the legislative history showed that Senator McGee and others had made a major point of the fact that the Byrd Amendment would indeed place the United States in violation of its obligation at the United Nations. The plaintiffs had to try to dismiss this legislative history as not germane. The only way to do so was to show that the Amendment was clear on its face, since it is only when a piece of legislation is unclear that a court turns to the legislative history. They were thus trapped in a contradictory argument: on the one hand, they were trying to show that the Byrd Amendment was unclear with regard to its intent to abrogate a treaty obligation, but on the other hand demonstrate that it was clear enough that the legislative history did not count. They could not have it both ways. In fact, the Congress seemed to have acted consciously if unconscionably in passing the Amendment and placing the United States in violation of its obligations at the United Nations.

On April 16, 1973, the Supreme Court declined to review the decision of the Court of Appeals. The Byrd Amendment had survived this challenge in the courts—although the plaintiffs won a partial victory in being judged to have standing to bring the suit, a decision which could be important in future litigation on southern Africa.

The failures of the anti-Byrd Amendment lobbyists to prevent its passage and of the White House to intervene with wavering Congressmen were compounded by the near silence of foreign governments. Most American officials interviewed for this study could not recall a single instance of an African ambassador in Washington forcefully asking the State Department or White House to work more strenuously against the

Byrd Amendment in 1971 or 1972. Only an exceptional government would instruct its representatives in Washington to raise an issue of indirect interest which could damage its economic relations with the United States. American embassies in Africa did receive some pressure from their host governments, particularly in Kenya and Nigeria, but not enough to persuade the White House that the Africans cared very deeply about the issue. Nor can the Africans have received the impression that the Executive branch was particularly interested in their views. For example, later, after the Amendment had been passed, the Sudanese foreign minister is said to have raised the issue with Secretary Rogers, arguing for a new effort to repeal the Amendment. Rogers is said by sources familiar with the incident to have cut the foreign minister off with an expression of irritation at the continuing criticism of the Byrd Amendment by African representatives at the United Nations.

The British did intervene to request a delay in the effective date of the Amendment, as previously noted. And Lord Home is said to have raised the issue with Secretary Rogers on one or two occasions. But officials both in London and in Washington state that Her Majesty's government appeared almost indifferent as to whether or not the Amendment passed. The only issue for them seemed to be timing. British officials at the working level were reportedly horrified at passage of the Amendment, but their horror was not, apparently, shared by their superiors.

The recitation in this chapter of legislative maneuvers and special interest pressures is, in a way, misleading. It conveys a picture of corporate lobbyists blitzing an interested Congress. The fact is that the Byrd Amendment intruded little into the consciousness of most members of Congress. Public indifference (broken only by some letter-writing campaigns and occasional editorials on both sides of the issue) allowed most Congressmen and the White House to treat the Byrd Amendment as a minor issue deserving of little study and the expenditure of less political capital. As the next chapter shows, under such circumstances, the substantive arguments made by supporters of the Byrd Amendment were more likely to appeal to busy and distracted legislators than the less dramatic pleas of its opponents.

7

Irony in Chrome
The Consequences of the
Byrd Amendment

The substance of the debate over the Byrd Amendment seemed to many members of Congress reasonably simple. Should the United States bar Rhodesian chrome and let the Soviets control our supply of this "strategic and critical" material? Should we let Moscow raise its price for chrome, damaging the position of the American ferrochrome industry and costing American workers their jobs? Does the American obligation to observe the United Nations sanctions against Rhodesia justify allowing the Soviets such a position? Indeed, is it a legal obligation? To majorities in both Houses, the answers were apparently as simple as the questions: In order, they were, "No," "No," "No," and either "No" or "It doesn't matter." A number of legislators on both sides of these questions debated them in sophisticated detail. But to most of our busy lawmakers, the Rhodesian sanctions are not even a secondary issue. There was neither time nor inclination to see the complexities in these simple questions.

Three years after passage of the Byrd Amendment, it is possible to take a harder look at these questions and the assumptions behind them, by examining the Amendment's actual consequences. Such an examination reveals a series of ironies. First, there are the larger ironies of the position into which the United States was placed by the passage of Section 503:

—The United States, whose record in enforcing sanctions had been about as good or better than that of any other nation, is now one of only four nations in the world which violate sanctions as a matter of official policy. One, Switzerland, is not a member of the United Nations, and so is not bound by the Security Council's action. The two others have been South Africa and Portugal.

—The United States, which played a leading role in the birth of the United Nations and which has sacrificed so much in support of the concept of collective security, is now undercutting the only effort ever made by the United Nations to use mandatory economic sanctions to enforce the will of the international community. And the same United States which has so often proclaimed its devotion to international law is now acting in violation of it.

—Finally, the United States, which has so much to lose here at home from any large-scale racial conflict between black and white abroad, has given heart to the white politicians in Southern Rhodesia who are most opposed to the peaceful sharing of political power with the black majority there.

To these ironies must be added the further irony of the unintended impact of the Byrd Amendment on the American ferrochrome industry, which processes raw chrome ore with iron into an alloy called ferrochrome. (This material is then used in the production of stainless, tool and alloy steels.) The industry's lobbyists on Capitol Hill were successful in 1971 and 1972, but their success had unintended results.

Far from saving jobs and increasing production in an already faltering industry, the Amendment has instead accelerated the industry's decline; by the end of 1973, two of the four major domestic producers had decided to go out of the ferrochrome business. Many of the ferrochrome industry's lobbyists for Section 503 seem to have been unaware of the potential disaster they were inviting by their actions. The Amendment was broadly worded, at least partly as a tactical legislative device. It seems clear now that the Foote Mineral Company had no idea that this wording would permit the import not just of Rhodesian chrome, but also of a competitive flood of low-cost ferrochrome itself. Apparently, only the Union Carbide Corporation, a huge multinational concern with both chrome mines *and* a ferrochrome processing plant in Southern Rhodesia, understood the full implications of the Amendment.

An analysis of the implications of the Amendment can be presented most clearly by listing separately the arguments made at the time by its opponents and its supporters, and then examining each in the light of subsequent experience.

THE ARGUMENTS

First, let us look at the line of argument presented by those who opposed the Byrd Amendment in 1971 and worked unsuccessfully for its repeal in 1972. Most of their effort was devoted to rebuttal of the points made by supporters of the Amendment. But they also predicted certain unhappy consequences of its passage.

In summary form, these predictive arguments against Section 503 were as follows:

—It would violate an international treaty obligation. This would harm our reputation for reliability and would have a deleterious effect on the observation by others of international law itself. The growth of international law is in the American interest.

—It would damage the U.S. reputation in predominantly black Africa.

—It would hurt the U.S. position at the United Nations, and harm the United Nations itself.

—It would undermine the British negotiating position in the talks that led to the Home-Smith agreement.

—It would give both psychological and economic relief to the illegal Rhodesian regime and support development of an apartheid system there; thus, it would adversely affect the well-being of the black population and the future of Southern Rhodesia.

None of these points touched many sensitive nerves in Congress. The arguments, predictions and warnings presented by supporters of the Byrd Amendment stood in sharp contrast. They were slick, well-presented, and emphasized two issues of direct concern: the American economy and national security. And all of these arguments were cleverly intertwined so that the Byrd Amendment came to be seen as the solution to two general problems: the needs of the American ferrochrome industry and our national security requirements for an assured supply of chrome. The major points they made were both descriptive and predictive. They claimed that the embargo against Rhodesian chrome was having damaging effects in the United States and also implied that certain benefits would therefore accrue if the ban on chrome were lifted.

The arguments that convinced Congress to pass the Byrd Amendment were as follows:

—The sanctions against Rhodesian chrome made the United States dependent on the Soviet Union for a "strategic and critical material," endangering our national security.

—The price of metallurgical-grade chrome had risen substantially since the embargo, and the Russians particularly were able to inflate their prices because Rhodesian chrome was not available to U.S. buyers.

—Other nations were violating the sanctions and thus gaining an economic advantage over the United States in two ways. First, sanctions-violating countries like Japan and West Germany were using cheap Rhodesian chrome to make their own cheap ferrochrome and stainless steel for export to the United States. Second, the Russians themselves were secretly buying Rhodesian chrome and transshipping it to the United States at hugely inflated prices.

—The United States ferrochrome industry was therefore being threatened by the sanctions. Rhodesian chrome was needed to make the industry competitive, and continuing the sanctions would mean the loss of American jobs in the ferrochrome and steel industries.

—It is in the best interests of the United States to support free trade everywhere.

—Neither the United Nations nor the United States should, or legally could, meddle in the internal affairs of another "state." The basis for the Security Council's imposition of mandatory sanctions—the finding that there was a "threat to the peace" in Southern Rhodesia—was not valid in fact. And, in any case, since the Congress never voted in favor of the American sanctions program, the Executive lacked the authority to maintain it.

The contrast between the two sets of arguments is clear. Assume, as many members of Congress apparently did, that both have some validity. It was clear which side had greater political weight: Considerations of "national security" and the "economy" were more compelling politically to most Congressmen than the broader, less immediate claims of "international law" and "diplomatic" advantage. But which of the arguments on both sides best predicted the future? We turn now to a scorecard on the Byrd Amendment.

THE SCORECARD

Original Prediction by Those Opposed

The predictions of the opposition to the Amendment were for the most part accurate. But the consequences of those events for the United States did not seem all that dire to American political leaders.

Consider first the prediction that passage of the Byrd Amendment would place the United States in violation of an international treaty obligation. Indeed, this is what has happened.

In brief, there have been three arguments about the legality of American participation in the sanctions: the legality of the sanctions themselves; the obligation of the United States to observe them; and the authority of the President to order their implementation by the United States without specific congressional approval.

First, the sanctions *are* legal. Some have argued that they violate article 2, paragraph 7 of the U.N. Charter, which states: "Nothing contained in the present Charter shall authorize the United Nations to intervene in matters which are essentially within the domestic jurisdiction of any state . . ." Yet the paragraph later continues: ". . . but this principle shall not prejudice the application of enforcement measures under Chapter VII"—the chapter under which the sanctions were ordered. Nor, indeed, is Rhodesia a "state." Legally, it remains under British sovereignty.[1]

In addition, the Security Council had the legal authority to determine that a "threat to the peace" existed in the Rhodesian situation. Equally important, whether or not such a threat existed—whether or not the Security Council was right, something which can never be proved or disproved—the fact is that it did make such a finding, legally, and the sanctions were ordered, legally. *Ex post facto* disagreement with this action does not negate the fact that it happened and that a legal obligation for all members states was thus created.

This brings us to the second question: Was the United States legally bound by the sanctions? As noted previously, Article 25 of the Charter does so bind all states. As a Permanent Member of the Security Council, the United States could have vetoed the sanctions resolutions and thus avoided the obligation. It did not. In fact, it supported and voted for them.

The third question concerns the President's power to implement the sanctions. Did his Executive Orders implementing the sanctions not violate the constitutional powers of the Congress to regulate foreign trade? In fact, in passing the U.N. Participation Act of 1945, the Congress gave the President express authority to implement sanctions. That was one of the purposes of the Act. Section 5(a) of the Act authorized the President, "through any agency which he may designate," to "investigate, regulate, or prohibit, in whole or in part, economic relations . . ." when the Security Council called on the United States to apply mandatory sanctions.

Thus, since passage of Section 503, the United States has been in violation of a legal international obligation. The American observation of sanctions is not, as some occasionally assert, a case of unilateral American meddling with another nation's economy. It is a part of a legal international effort.

[1] See chapter 3 for a fuller discussion of these legal arguments.

But what have been the actual adverse consequences for the United States of our violation? In truth, few can be shown, without extraordinary feats of extended causal argumentation, in gross U.S. economic statistics or national security calculations. The consequences are broader and indirect. When the United States brushes aside considerations of international law, the law itself suffers. And that hurts the United States, for how can we insist that others abide by treaty commitments and respect the rights of other states when we have failed to meet our own legal obligations?

Thus, the paradox faced by opponents of the Byrd Amendment: While their invocation of international law did raise one of the most basic issues of American national interest, they could not demonstrate how this violation of a treaty obligation would directly damage the national interest in the short run. And too often, in heated and superficial debate, it is the short run that offers the best debating points.

Similarly, there was indeed the predicted hostile reaction at the United Nations, but without direct, short-term consequences for the United States. Part of the damage would come in the future; if the American action helped turn the sanctions program into a total failure, an important instrument of U.N. action would be damaged, if not destroyed. And the United States could have a stake in sanctions, the most powerful weapon provided the United Nations, short of force, on other issues. Another part of the damage has been more direct: condemnation of, and hostility toward, the United States would inevitably harm our bargaining position with other delegations, particularly those from Africa. As George Bush, then our representative to the United Nations, pointed out in March, 1972, when describing his trip to Africa: "There are forty-two votes in the United Nations there; forty-two votes out of one hundred thirty-two, and it is terribly important to us from just a plain political standpoint . . ." [2] Bush's point

[2] "United Nations and Africa," Joint Hearing before the Subcommittee on Africa and the Subcommittee on International Organizations and Movements of the House Committee on Foreign Affairs, March 1, 1972, p. 13.

was subsequently confirmed when some African delegates told observers that they had voted against the United States on a key resolution on terrorism because of their dislike for the Byrd Amendment.

On November 8, 1971, a month after the Amendment's passage, the African group at the United Nations issued a statement attacking the Amendment. On November 16, the General Assembly appealed to the U.S. government not to implement it. On December 3, the U.N. Sanctions Committee recommended that the Security Council call on all states not to pass or implement legislation which would allow the import of prohibited goods. The Security Council did so, in effect, in resolutions of February 28, July 28, and September 29, 1972. And on May 22, 1973, it requested "states with legislation permitting importation of minerals and other products from Southern Rhodesia to repeal it immediately."

It is little wonder that John Scali, our ambassador to the United Nations, stated in a speech on June 7, 1973: "I have respectfully invited the Congress of the United States to reconsider the Amendment to the Defense Appropriation Act which two years ago placed the United States in open violation of international law. At that time the Congress voted legislation making it impossible for the Executive Branch to prevent imports of chrome and other strategic commodities from Rhodesia as required by the Security Council, a decision which the United States voted and which is legally binding on the United States. The evidence is mounting that this Amendment not only damages America's image and reputation as a law-abiding nation, but that it has net economic disadvantages as well."

Of course, the American delegation did little to dissipate African hostility by taking the line of defense that "others violate sanctions, too." This might have been a good debating point; it did not help other delegates understand how the same State Department which had opposed the Byrd Amendment in the Congress could now defend it in the United Nations.

Predictions of hostility among Africans were also accurate. In a letter of June 12, 1973, Assistant Secretary of State for African Affairs David Newsom stated: "In my four years as Assistant Secretary the exemption on Rhodesian sanctions has been the most serious blow to the credibility of our African policy. While you and I in our travels may not encounter strong expressions on this subject, our Ambassadors in certain key countries emphasize the importance of this issue in the basic attitudes of these countries toward us. The fact that we have in African eyes chosen to go counter to a mandatory Security Council resolution and have for our own purposes weakened sanctions suggests to the Africans that we do not attach importance to the institutions and issues of significance to them." The OAU has called upon the United States to end its "flagrant violation of sanctions."

Yet, despite the strength of their words, there is little sign that the leaders of African governments are prepared therefore to penalize the United States—for example, by limiting American investment opportunities in their nations—if such measures would prejudice their own economic plans. (And, as earlier noted, what real choice do they have?) So, although the United States is in no way helped by the hostility of African politicians and editorialists on the issue, and a majority government in Zimbabwe might someday penalize America for our violation of sanctions, here again opponents of the Byrd Amendment, while right about predicted events, have difficulty demonstrating immediate, quantifiable damage to the American position.

A fourth prediction, that the Amendment would undercut Britain's negotiating position with the Smith regime, is more difficult to judge. On the one hand, there is evidence that this was a matter of some concern to some individual members of Parliament. On the other hand, the British government itself brought little pressure on the White House to do more to prevent the passage of Section 503. As previously noted, the British did reportedly ask the administration to try to gain a delay in the effective date of the Amendment, so that it would not come into force before the negotiations with

Smith were completed. But one would suppose that if British negotiators thought their ability to achieve a solution to London's agonizing Rhodesian problem was being seriously undermined by an imminent American breach of sanctions, the British would have been willing to press very strongly, perhaps even publicly, for White House intervention against the Amendment itself. That they apparently did not do so indicates at the least that the British were not terribly concerned about the effect of Section 503 on their negotiations—even if, in the spring of 1973, Foreign Secretary Home stated that he had made representations to the United States on the issue.

Finally, there are the predicted consequences for the situation within Southern Rhodesia. The claim was that an American breach of sanctions would lend support to Smith and therefore do damage to the aspirations of the black majority. Some supporters of the Byrd Amendment argued that, on the contrary, sanctions hurt the black population.

One way to judge the accuracy of these claims and counterclaims is to listen to the statements of those involved. Rhodesian mining circles were "jubilant," according to the Chamber of Mines Journal in February, 1972. And the jubilation was probably not solely because of anticipated profits from the Amendment itself. The Johannesburg *Star* in South Africa described its larger impact: It was a "devastating blow to American—and indeed international policy on Rhodesia." On the other hand, the reaction of Bishop Abel Muzorewa, leader of the African National Council and the primary spokesman for the majority during this period, was one of dismay: The Amendment, he said, was "the worst blow we have suffered from any quarter."

Trade statistics provide another way of looking at the accuracy of the predicted consequences for Southern Rhodesia. According to State Department figures, as a result of the Byrd Amendment the United States provided the Rhodesian regime with $13.3 million in badly needed foreign exchange in 1972. In the first nine months of 1973, more than $17 million was added. This is particularly important because most analysts of the sanctions agree that their most telling pinch has been on Rhodesia's foreign exchange reserves.

Thus, the relief given the Smith regime by the Byrd Amendment has, as predicted, been important—both physically and psychologically. Still the future of Southern Rhodesia and its people is far away from the day-to-day concerns of more than a very few Americans. What seemed to matter in the debates on the Byrd Amendment were arguments about national security and our domestic economy. We turn now to them.

Original Prediction of Those in Favor

Two of the arguments made in favor of the Amendment placed little reliance on predictions, and need no detailed consideration here. The legal argument—essentially that the United Nations cannot legally intervene in the affairs of a sovereign nation—was discussed earlier in this chapter. Its weaknesses are apparent. The "free trade" argument was seldom made, perhaps because the ferrochrome industry had previously sought restrictions on ferrochrome imports. It also faced a problem of priorities—in a crusade for free trade, surely there are many unilateral trade barriers to be torn down before turning to one erected by the international community.

For many members of Congress, perhaps the most persuasive argument used in behalf of the Byrd Amendment was the "national security" argument. It was persuasive largely because it did not require detailed statistical evidence. And here, a major irony arises. The claim was that sanctions had made the United States "dependent" on the Soviet Union for a material—chrome—which was necessary to our defense. In a crisis, they might cut us off. The implication was that removal of the sanctions would remove that danger to the national security. Ironically, if anything, the reverse has happened.

Before considering what happened after the Amendment was passed, a look at the history of imports of chrome before the sanctions began will help put the "dependency" argument

in the proper perspective. The Soviet Union reentered the
world metallurgical-grade chrome [3] market in the early 1960s.
It quickly became a major supplier of chrome ore to the
United States, even *before* Rhodesia declared its "independence." In 1964 and 1965, it supplied 42 percent and 36 percent of the metallurgical-grade chrome imported into the
United States. So, to the extent we actually have been
dangerously "dependent" on the Soviet Union for chrome—a
difficult line of argument in any case, especially when the
President's policies are emphasizing détente and trade—the
"dependency" predates the imposition of sanctions, and no
one should have expected their relaxation to alter the basic situation.

Now, what actually happened? In 1972 and 1973 the Soviet Union lowered its chrome prices and therefore gained a
larger share of the U.S. market. Thus, ironically, since passage
of Section 503 we have become more, not less, "dependent"
on the Soviets for chrome ore. According to the State Department, in 1971, 45 percent of American imports of metallurgical-grade chrome came from the Soviet Union, compared to
3.6 percent from Rhodesia. In 1972, with the Byrd Amendment in force, the Soviet share had risen to 60.2 percent,
against 9.3 percent for Rhodesia. In the first six months of
1973, 53.6 percent was from the Soviet Union and only 2 percent from Rhodesia!

Another aspect of the "national security" argument
should also be examined here: the degree to which chrome is
vital to the national defense. In fact, only 10 percent (or less)
of the metallurgical-grade chromite used in the United States
(and about the same percentage of our chrome imports) goes
to direct defense needs, according to the Defense Department.
And although a large part of the remainder does go into essential services, such as industry, transportation and construc-
tion, even these needs could be met in a crisis by the huge

---

[3] Metallurgical- or high-grade chromite—having a chromic oxide content
of 46 percent or higher—is the type consumed almost exclusively by the
alloy steel industry.

oversupply of chrome in the U.S. strategic stockpile. On July 20, 1973, Deputy Secretary of Defense W. P. Clements, Jr., wrote Representative Fraser, "According to an estimate prepared in 1973 by OEP, the metallurgical-grade chromite needed by industry to support the Defense Department's steel requirement during the first year of the war amounts to 128,300 short tons, or 2.3% of the quantity held in the inventory as of 31 December 1972. Thus, it can be seen that the Defense requirement for metallurgical-grade chromite is relatively small, and that the bulk of the stockpile inventory would be used by the non-defense industry in the event of an emergency."

A letter from presidential adviser Peter Flanigan, chairman of the Council on International Economic Policy, to Congressmen Donald Fraser and Charles Diggs, dated June 26, 1973, summed it up: "Access to Rhodesian chrome and other minerals is not, however, an important element in U.S. security or in our overall foreign economic policy given: 1) the substantial excess of our stockpile resources and 2) the comparatively minor amounts we actually import from Rhodesia."

A second, and more sophisticated, argument seems in retrospect to have had some validity. This "prices argument" included intertwined economic and anti-Communist appeals. The argument held that the price of chrome ore had risen substantially since the embargo, and that this was due to the sanctions. More specifically, it was argued that the Russians, as a major supplier of metallurgical-grade chromite to the United States, had taken advantage of the situation to double and, in some cases, even to triple their chrome prices to American buyers. The implication here was that the best way to achieve lower chrome ore prices was to remove the embargo.[4]

[4] For example, in the Senate debate of September 23, 1971, on the Byrd Amendment, Senator Harry Byrd claimed: "Yet the United States is pursuing a policy which gives Soviet Russia virtually a monopoly on the sale to us of a vital defense material and the cost of that material has increased from $25 a ton to $72 per ton. Here is an opportunity for the Senate, for Congress, to help fight inflation and to help protect jobs of American workers."

There are several points to be examined here. First, the causal link between the rise in the price of chrome, including the Soviet ore, and the Rhodesian sanctions is not clear. While sanctions were undeniably one factor in the price rise of metallurgical-grade chromite in the 1966–1971 period, it is important to remember that during this time the price of minerals was rising worldwide.[5] And, with specific regard to Soviet chrome, it should be noted that the price of chrome sold by other major suppliers of U.S. chrome markets was rising with the Russian prices. In fact, according to Assistant Secretary of State Newsom, Iran, not the Soviet Union, was the first country to raise its chrome ore prices. And because Russian ore is of a generally higher chromic oxide content than either Rhodesian, South African or Turkish ore, it merits a somewhat higher price per ton. Similarly, because South Africa's metallurgical-grade chromite is generally of lower quality, it is priced lower than that of our other major foreign suppliers.

Second, the price pattern in the first half of 1973 shows how little effect the level of imports of Rhodesian chrome has on the price of Soviet chrome. As the level of these imports from Rhodesia fell in that period, the price of Soviet chrome should have risen, according to the line of reasoning of proponents of the Byrd Amendment. In fact, the Soviet price fell. Obviously, the Soviets do not make their chrome-pricing decisions on the basis of the availability of Rhodesian chrome to the American market.

A third point to bear in mind is that the major problem for some American chrome importers during sanctions was not just prices, but access. Some American companies, like Union Carbide and Foote Mineral, had never or rarely bought chrome from the Soviet Union. When sanctions cut off access to their own Rhodesian mining subsidiaries, they had difficulty switching to Soviet chrome and were forced to pay premium prices for it. For example, a spokesman for Union

[5] As noted in a letter of June 12, 1973, from Assistant Secretary of State David Newsom to Representative Guy Vander Jagt.

Carbide, which was cut off from its own source of cheap chrome ore from its Rhodesian mines when the sanctions went into effect, claims it was paying $55.50 a ton for Soviet metallurgical-grade chrome ore in 1971, when the Byrd Amendment was introduced. AIRCO Alloys, on the other hand, the largest ferrochrome producer in the United States and a long-time buyer of Russian ore, had none of these problems. Since AIRCO had long-term contracts with the Soviet Union, the company never voiced any complaints about the price of Russian ore. So it seems not so much a question of the Russians generally gouging American customers, but rather that companies which had no long-standing trading relationships with the Soviet Union were charged higher rates. And, at the same time that Union Carbide was reportedly paying $55.50 a ton for Russian ore, Turkish chrome ore was also selling for about $55. Even the price of lower quality, lower priced South African ore had risen almost 20 percent between 1970 and 1971.

Finally, it is important to note that although the quoted price of a country's metallurgical-grade chromite may be held up as proof of a significant price increase, the only true measure is the actual price paid. And in this period, the actual increases in prices paid were less than the changes in quoted prices.[6]

Yet while sanctions thus were not the sole or perhaps even the prime culprit in the rise of chrome prices during 1965–1971, it does appear that the prices were somewhat inflated. In fact, prices charged by all of the major U.S. suppliers of metallurgical-grade chromite—and not just those of the Soviet Union—dropped after the enactment of the Byrd Amendment.[7] The implied prediction that the Russians (and

[6] For example, the Bureau of Mines estimated Russian ore prices at $55–$70 per ton during 1970. But if one divides value of chromite imports by tons of imports (using Bureau of Mines data), Russian ore actually cost an average of $31.30 per ton during 1970.

[7] For example, although the Turkish quoted price of $55–$56 per long ton delivered in 1971 remained the same in 1972 (post-Byrd Amendment) quotations, the actual selling price dropped to $43–$47, according to John

others) would lower their prices if Southern Rhodesia were again permitted to sell its chrome ore to the United States was reflected in events. What is very unclear is the causal relationship between the Amendment and the price drop. Nor can it be inferred from recent price reductions that the price rises from 1965 to 1971 were primarily due to sanctions, since the prices charged today by the USSR are still substantially higher than the 1965 and 1966 prices. Additionally, the prices charged by the Rhodesians following passage of the Byrd Amendment were also significantly higher than the pre-sanctions prices. Thus, since no country's prices for chrome ore have returned to their 1965, pre-sanctions level, inflation must be acknowledged as a significant factor in the price rise of the 1966–1971 period.

And, of course, the cut in Russian prices had the unpre-

Morning, a physical supervisory scientist with the U.S. Bureau of Mines. Similarly, the quoted price of South African chrome ore dropped from $27 per long ton delivered in 1971 and the first quarter of 1972, to $24–$27 for the remainder of 1972. The drop in the quoted price of Soviet chrome ore was from $51.50–$55 per metric ton undelivered in 1971 to $45–$46.50 per metric ton undelivered in 1972.

The reader should be aware, however, of the difficulty of precisely comparing the Soviet chrome ore prices before and after 1971. First of all, the quoted price has been changed from a "delivered price" (including transportation charges) used up to 1971, to a "shipping point price" (where transportation costs are not included in the quotation) starting in 1971. Secondly, the guaranteed chromic oxide content of the ore had been altered in the 1965–1971 period. For example, in 1965 the USSR price was for 55 percent chromic oxide ore; in 1971, however, the guaranteed chromic oxide content was only 48 percent. Consequently, no accurate comparison can be made of Russian quoted prices without taking these significant differences into account; but a general comparison is possible. In 1965, the quoted price for Soviet chrome ore—55 percent chromic oxide and delivered to U.S. Atlantic ports—was $30.50–$33 per long ton. In 1971, that price was $51.50–$55 per ton with the important differences that: 1) The tons were not metric; 2) the chrome ore was only guaranteed 48 percent chromic oxide, and 3) the price did not include shipping costs. According to Morning, the 1971 Russian price would have been about $70 per long ton if calculated in 1965 terms. Similarly, the 1972 quoted prices, which decreased to $45–$46.50 per ton, would be about $60 per ton in 1965 terms.

dicted effect mentioned above—expansion of the Soviet share of the American chrome market. As noted previously, this consequence of the Amendment should have been predictable in the light of the "prices argument." But the lobbyists for the Amendment conveniently stopped short of saying that, since it would have destroyed their useful "national security" debating point.

A related argument concerned unfair competition from covert sanctions violators—the "Uncle Sucker" argument. There were widespread violations of sanctions, it was said, and there always would be, because the commercial interests of nations and individuals will always be stronger than moral and political impulses. Thus, others were buying Rhodesian chrome on the sly while the United States unrealistically penalized itself.

There is no doubt that the Rhodesians have been producing great quantities of chrome since sanctions were imposed. Although exact figures are a Rhodesian state secret, the U.S. Bureau of Mines has estimated Rhodesian production as follows:

Year	Tons
1966	550,000
1967	350,000
1968	420,000
1969	400,000
1970	400,000
1971	400,000

And few doubt that very large amounts of this chrome have been sold to foreign buyers.

So the claim made during the Byrd Amendment debates that other governments were looking the other way while their nationals traded with Southern Rhodesia was apparently true. However, the implication that this clandestine trade was a key factor in permitting our industrial competitors, like companies in Japan and West Germany, to undersell U.S. producers of both ferrochrome and steel has not been substantiated. Secret sanctions violations by foreign companies may, perhaps, be seen as one factor making other nations more competitive in these basic industrial materials. While that has not been proved, it cannot be disproved. But the evidence—most notably import statistics for the several years preceding the implementation of sanctions—shows that the reason for U.S. industries' generally losing ground to foreign competition can be summarized in two words: higher costs. And that includes higher costs for labor, power, pollution controls, transportation and, in many cases, lack of access to particular raw materials. Union Carbide itself admitted these difficulties in its July, 1971, testimony to the Senate's Africa Subcommittee. Fred C. Kroft, Jr., president of the Ferroalloys Division, said: "Labor rates, power costs and the costs of pollution control have been rising more swiftly here than in other parts of the world where ferrochrome is produced and the U.S. industry has been placed at an increasing disadvantage." [8]

The "Uncle Sucker" argument had another facet that seemed still more galling. This was that one nation in particular—the Soviet Union—was allegedly violating sanctions by buying Rhodesian chrome and then selling it at inflated prices to the United States. This was, however, never more than a rumor—based on questionable tests—circulated by one of the companies with a vested interest in the passage of the Byrd Amendment. In fact, it was the Washington representative of Colt Industries, the parent company of a major stainless steel producer, Crucible Stainless Steel, that first injected this dark thought into the Byrd Amendment debate. At the June, 1971, House hearings held by Representative Fraser's Subcommittee on International Organizations and Movements, Mr. Blair Bolles, a vice-president of Colt Industries and Crucible Steel, stated that Colt scientists had performed a test which implied

[8] While these competitive difficulties made more pressing their desire for cheap chrome ore, they also made domestic ferrochrome producers more vulnerable to competition from foreign ferrochrome. And, as shown below, the domestic ferrochrome producers have in fact suffered from these imports.

that the samples of Russian ore examined contained Rhodesian ore. However, the credibility of this test was destroyed by scientists of the U.S. Geological Survey, who presumably had no particular interest in either side of the question. They concluded that the similar titanium contents were merely coincidental. In their own tests of the Russian ore, they found that its chromium oxide content was far below that of the Rhodesian ore sold on the world market. Thus, although this claim has been repeated often, it apparently has no basis in fact. (This does not rule out, however, the possibility that the Soviets might have bought and used Rhodesian chrome ore while selling us their own.)

There was a further implication in the argument about unfair, illegal foreign use of Rhodesian chrome: Since foreign companies, and particularly our chief industrial competitors, were violating sanctions, was there not good reason for the United States to violate sanctions as well? However, the logical implication of the argument is quite different. If one is sincerely concerned about leaks in the boycott, one would logically argue for a strengthening, not a weakening, of the U.N. sanctions against Rhodesia—for example, by pressing the American government to protest more vigorously such violations by companies registered in allied and other nations.

All these arguments were significant; they had a persuasive cumulative effect, particularly insofar as they were related to national security. But the most important substantial argument, and the one which was obviously of greatest concern to the impressive array of corporate lobbyists on the side of the Byrd Amendment, had to do with the effects of sanctions on American industry and American jobs. The argument dealt with the U.S. ferrochrome industry directly and, indirectly, with the domestic specialty steel industry, which is the major user of ferrochrome. It had a simple yet sophisticated message: 1) The United States ferrochrome industry was being hurt by the sanctions, since Rhodesian chrome could not be imported by U.S. producers. 2) The industry's ability to compete with foreign ferrochrome producers depended on access to low-cost Rhodesian chrome ore. 3) Therefore, if the sanctions were not relaxed, American steelworker and ferrochrome-worker jobs would be imperiled. Before considering the irony of the last prediction, we should take a moment to look at the argument itself.

First, how correct was the assumption that the American ferrochrome industry was being hurt by sanctions?

This industry, which until recently consisted of four major and two minor producers, has been in decline since the early 1960s—before UDI and before U.N. sanctions against Southern Rhodesia. It has been hard hit by imports and rising labor and power costs, as well as by requirements to install costly pollution control devices to meet stiff new federal air quality standards.

In 1961, there were eleven companies producing ferrochrome in eighteen furnaces in ten different American states. By 1965—*before* UDI—that number had fallen to six companies operating eleven plants in only six states. Paralleling this marked decline was an equally conspicuous increase in ferrochrome imports into the United States. In 1964, significant quantities of low-priced South African ferrochrome moved into the American market; by 1965, imports of low-carbon ferrochrome were the highest ever.[9] In 1966, due to a combination of factors—high demand for chrome alloys and reduced output of one of the major American producers because of a lengthy strike—total ferrochrome imports rose to their highest level in seven years. The imports returned to their 1965 level for several years but by 1971—when the Byrd Amendment was introduced—the situation had substantially worsened again.

While it is true that the loss of access to Rhodesian

[9] Until recently the stainless steel industry had consumed primarily low-carbon ferrochrome. However, a new argon-oxygen decarburation process (AOD) has resulted in a shift to lower priced, high carbon or "charge" ferrochrome, since more carbon can be removed in the steelmaking process itself with AOD. Industry officials estimate that low-carbon ferrochrome will be used less and less in the future.

chrome ore in late 1966 may have served to make a bad situation worse, there is no responsible way of attributing the industry's competitive problems to this one factor.

What, then, of the implicit prediction that passage of the Amendment would allow the industry new access to Rhodesian chrome and thus enable it to compete once again? Experience shows that the effect has been the opposite. The legislation has probably hurt more than helped the competitiveness of a basically noncompetitive industry. Instead of preventing the loss of American jobs—as the Amendment's proponents claimed passage would do—the legislation has in fact contributed to the loss of American jobs. And the irony is that some of the supporters of the Byrd Amendment were damaged by their own tactical skill. The broad wording of the Amendment, which never mentioned chrome but simply referred to "strategic and critical materials," made passage easier. The "national security" argument seemed stronger that way; the impression that special interests might be at work was less obvious. But when, pursuant to Section 503, the licenses were issued by the Treasury Department in January, 1972, they included seventy-two materials. So the Byrd Amendment has allowed not just chrome, but huge amounts of nickel, and more important, processed ferrochrome to be imported into the United States from Southern Rhodesia. In actual fact, it is the startling jump in *ferrochrome* imports into the United States between 1971 (pre-Byrd) and 1972 and the first part of 1973 (post-Byrd) that was held a prime reason for the decision of Foote Mineral and Ohio Ferroalloys, the number three and number four domestic ferrochrome producers, to cease production of this material.

In the first year after Section 503 was passed, 1972, total U.S. imports of ferrochrome almost doubled over the preceding year. The greater part of that increase was due to massive shipments from both South Africa and Southern Rhodesia.

And in the first few months of 1973, the effect was even more startling: For the first quarter of 1973, Rhodesia provided 16,000 tons—or nearly 45 percent—of the 36,000 tons of high-carbon ferrochrome brought into the United States. In addition, high-carbon ferrochrome imports were running in 1973 at a rate about 20 percent higher than even the record rate of 1972. In 1973 as a whole, Rhodesia supplied some 41 percent of these record imports.

For contrast, consider the import statistics since the Byrd Amendment for chrome ore itself. The results here are equally surprising and nearly as ironic. The Byrd Amendment did not produce the quantities of Rhodesian chrome many expected. The statistics for 1972 and 1973 show, in fact, that relatively little Rhodesian chrome ore was imported. In 1972, only 93,000 tons of a total of 792,000 tons, or less than 12 percent, of chrome imported into the United States was from Southern Rhodesia. And, as indicated previously, only 9.3 percent of the metallurgical-grade chrome imported into the United States that year was from Rhodesia. On the other hand, 21,500 tons of ferrochrome came from Rhodesia, of a total of almost 150,000 tons from all countries,[10] more than 14 percent. In 1973, imports of Rhodesian metallurgical chromite fell to only 43,000 tons. In dollar terms, in the same period, the United States imported $7.7 million worth of Rhodesian ferrochrome and only $68,000 worth of chrome ore.

This surge of low-cost imports of ferrochrome from Rhodesia has done more harm to American industry than any of the chrome ore-related hardships—real and imagined—that occurred during the period of sanctions. In September, 1972—nine months after the Byrd Amendment went into effect—America's fourth largest producer of ferrochrome, Ohio Ferroalloys, cited severe price erosion and loss of profits in its decision to suspend ferrochrome operations "until such time as the market price on this product might return to a reasonable level that would allow a profit." By year's end the temporary suspension had become a permanent decision; Ohio Ferroalloys announced it would produce materials "more

[10] Figures include imports of high and low-carbon ferrochrome and chromium silicon.

profitable than ferrochrome" at its Brilliant, Ohio, plant. In the words of the company president, R. L. Cunningham, "We are closing down because we could not compete with prices quoted by the South African and Rhodesian exporters." [11]

Following closely on the heels of the Ohio Ferroalloys shutdown came the announcement by the Foote Mineral Company—one of the prominent lobbyists for the passage of the Byrd Amendment—that it too could no longer compete with imports and was going out of the ferrochrome business. In explaining its decision to close its Steubenville ferrochrome plant as well as two non-chrome-related facilities, Foote attributed the Steubenville decision to low-cost foreign ferrochrome imports as well as the necessity of investing several million dollars in pollution-control devices. Competitive imports were not the only factor in this decision. But they were an essential part of it. As Foote's former public relations director John Donahey explained in an interview, the pressing demand for Foote to make heavy capital investment in pollution controls necessitated a decision about the short- and long-term profitability of its ferrochrome operations. In the end, according to Donahey, the import situation and other factors convinced the company that "it just wasn't worth it."

Together, the Foote and Ohio Ferroalloys actions meant the loss of about 750 American jobs.

Thus, twenty months after the Byrd Amendment went into effect, the American ferrochrome industry had lost two of its four principal producers. And the Ferroalloys Association was gloomily predicting:

Unless aid is forthcoming soon it will only be a matter of time until almost all domestic production of ferrochrome and chromium metal will cease and the bulk of our country's requirements will be supplied from and dependent on foreign production. [12]

[11] Letter of April 17, 1973.
[12] "Statement for Relief from Excessive Import," Ferroalloys Association, Washington, D.C., May, 1973.

Of the top two U.S. ferrochrome producers, AIRCO Alloys, a division of Air Reduction Corporation, is the leader. It has never had an investment in Rhodesian chrome mines. Instead, it has been a major customer of the Soviet Union since the USSR re-entered the world chrome market in the early 1960s. AIRCO did not lobby for the Byrd Amendment. And the Satraloy Corporation has taken over and modernized the Steubenville plant abandoned by Foote. Like AIRCO, it buys its chrome ore from sources other than Rhodesia.

Union Carbide was in better shape than Foote: It owns not only chrome mines in Rhodesia, but also a large ferrochrome-processing operation there called Union Carbide Rhomet. In addition, the company has reportedly been exploring possibilities of investing in South African ferrochrome facilities. Although the company points out that the operations of its Rhodesian subsidiaries, including Union Carbide Rhomet, are under Rhodesian government control and that no profits have been remitted, it is acknowledged that Union Carbide Rhomet's capacity has been tremendously expanded in the past few years. And Carbide officials regularly visit the Rhodesian facilities. Carbide's eventual hope must be a total end to sanctions, so that it can legally get at Rhomet's ferrochrome profits.

It seems probable that Union Carbide was well aware of the implications for ferrochrome of the broad and general wording of the Byrd Amendment. And while the Amendment can be seen as having backfired on Foote, which lobbied for its passage only to find itself drowned by Rhodesian ferrochrome imports, the Union Carbide Corporation benefited doubly: It gained access to its own Rhodesian chrome for use in its domestic ferrochrome facilities and, at the same time, became free to send its own cheap Rhodesian ferrochrome into the United States to compete with the other domestic producers here.

It is important to remember in all this just why Rhodesian and South African ferrcochrome is so much cheaper. Cheap power, the lack of pollution controls and the proximity to the raw material—chrome—are all important in keeping costs low in southern Africa. There is also the fact that labor unions are almost unheard of and the mostly African labor forces in both countries are paid very low wages for their work in the mines and the ferrochrome-processing plants. Apartheid and cheap-labor systems in South Africa and Southern Rhodesia help allow companies like Union Carbide to produce ferrochrome relatively cheaply in southern Africa. The letter written to Congressman Diggs by Carbide's chairman of the board in February, 1973, describing their operations in southern Africa, put it in terse terms: "Labor difficulties and work stoppages: none."

Union Carbide officials are quick to point out the fact that "only" 10 percent of the direct costs in producing chrome are labor costs (with 10 percent for power and 80 percent for raw materials). But important marginal savings are still allowed when labor costs are cut. And there is no doubt that Union Carbide's black employees in Rhodesia are exploited, when their situation is compared to that of its white employees. Consider the fact that, as of 1970, Union Carbide's chrome affiliates there paid its African workers $46 to $130 per month, while its white employees received from $122.50 to $750 a month.

If companies like Foote Mineral and Ohio Ferroalloys were oblivious to the potential impact of the amendment, the Rhodesian regime could not have been. From their perspective, it is much more attractive to sell ferrochrome to the American market than raw chrome ore: the return on ferrochrome is about five times that for chrome ore. For instance, according to the U.S. Treasury Department, the United States imported about 92,000 tons of chrome ore worth $2,822,930 from Southern Rhodesia from January 24, 1972, to January 12, 1973. At the same time we imported just over 18,000 tons of finished high-carbon ferrochrome from Rhodesia worth almost exactly the same amount—$2,990,713.

THE FINAL SCORE

In sum, then, our scorecard on the actual effects of the Byrd Amendment shows:

—that it damaged both the American interest in international law, and our diplomatic position at the United Nations and in Africa;

—that it damaged the United Nations itself;

—that it probably set back the chances of a peaceful settlement of the Rhodesian problem, by encouraging the Smith regime in its present course;

—that while it actually did not make much difference, in view of the size of our chrome stockpiles, it made the United States relatively more than less "dependent" on imports of Soviet chrome;

—that it probably had some effect in reducing the price of Soviet chrome; but

—that whatever its effect on the price of chrome, by allowing imports of cheap ferrochrome from Rhodesia, it damaged rather than helped the domestic American ferrochrome industry and contributed to the loss of jobs here.

These conclusions are based on what happened after the Byrd Amendment became law. To test the issue further, we should look at the effects if the Amendment were not in force. What would happen if the Byrd Amendment were repealed and the United States returned to compliance with its international legal obligations? What would be the negative consequences to American industry? What would be the positive contributions of such a reversal?

THE CONSEQUENCES OF REPEAL

First, how would repeal of the Byrd Amendment affect our national security? If the view that the Amendment had a bearing on our national security ever had validity, it has now been overcome by events. Since the passage of the Byrd Amendment, the United States has moved toward establishment of extensive trading relations with the Soviet Union. In light of these developments, the argument that repeal of the Byrd Amendment would place us at the mercy of an "enemy" loses much of its force—if it ever had any. Even more importantly, that argument is mooted by the administration's recent assessment, in calling for disposal of most of the nation's strategic materials stockpile, that these materials are needed only in quantities sufficient for a one-year national emergency. In introducing its new Stockpile Disposal Bill in 1973, the White House said that "the quantities of materials required for the national security are much lower than previously calculated." The new objectives would require that less than 500,000 tons of metallurgical-grade chromite be kept and that almost no ferrochrome be saved. Since our direct defense needs are only a tiny proportion of annual consumption (one official in the OEP has stated that direct military requirements for metallurgical-grade chromite were about 6,536 short tons in 1971, equal to only about 0.9 percent of that year's consumption),[13] there is no doubt—at least in the minds of those in our government who decide about our emergency planning—that large amounts of chrome are not necessary and our own stockpile, even with the proposed reductions, will be enough to meet foreseeable needs.

The next question concerns adequate supplies for all U.S. needs of chrome ore, and now ferrochrome as well, if Rhodesia were once more cut off as a supplier to U.S. markets.

As far as chrome itself goes, it would be difficult to sustain an argument that we would be denied an important source if the Byrd Amendment were repealed. For it has been shown that U.S. imports of Rhodesian chrome have become almost insignificant. The minor amount of chrome now coming in from Rhodesia could easily be obtained from other sources, including Turkey and Iran.

In addition, with passage of a new stockpile disposal bill

[13] Letter from William A. Lawrence of the OEP to Charles C. Diggs, Jr., chairman of the House Subcommittee on Africa, May 2, 1973. This figure is for direct military usage of chrome; it does not include indirect usage through military consumption of stainless steel.

more than two million tons of metallurgical-grade chrome ore can be freed for use by American consumers, principally the ferrochrome industry. Although some companies claim that not all of this chrome is "usable," what they are really saying is that it does not perfectly meet their requirements. The bulk of this chrome is in fact usable in American industry.

By 1973 and 1974, however, the argument over the Byrd Amendment was shifting from the earlier emphasis on the need for chrome to a new emphasis on the need for ferrochrome. A parallel shift had taken place in the nature of the lobbying: While the passage of the Byrd Amendment was pushed originally by the American ferrochrome industry with the assistance of the stainless steel manufacturers, the Amendment's most vociferous supporters were now the stainless steelmakers themselves—for they are the ones who want Rhodesian ferrochrome.

A stainless steel industry spokesman claimed in an interview that the Byrd Amendment had been the major factor in the industry's turnaround in 1972 and 1973. Cheap chrome and ferrochrome from Southern Rhodesia helped U.S. stainless steel companies to compete with foreign producers. In 1972, stainless steel imports fell to their lowest level in eight years, from 21.9 percent of the domestic market in 1971 to 12.1 percent in 1972. There is no doubt that this was a significant and important development. However, it is highly doubtful that the Byrd Amendment can legitimately be given primary credit for this upturn in the competitiveness of the American specialty steel industry. Two other events played a major role. First, a new set of voluntary restraint agreements was negotiated in 1971. While the 1968 voluntary agreements had only limited steel in terms of tonnage and had thus caused foreign producers to shift to stainless exports, because of the higher value per ton, the 1971 agreements included specific tonnage limitations on specialty steel as well. So this was one factor operative in the 1972 import drop. Another was the late 1971 devaluation of the dollar, which made foreign steel more expensive. It is clearly impossible to separate out the effects of the new voluntary agreements, the dollar devaluation and the Byrd Amendment in determining the causes of the stainless steel industry's recovery. Nor does the recovery necessarily depend on continued supplies of Rhodesian ferrochrome. As with chrome, stockpile disposals can obviate the need for such ferrochrome.

In addition, even in unusual situations like the 1973 high-demand, boom-level period of steel production, if American producers were unable completely to fill the demand, there are many other ferrochrome-exporting countries which can and will sell to U.S. markets. For example, the 1973 statistics show major purchases of high-carbon ferrochrome from Brazil, which had not previously exported significant amounts of ferrochrome to the United States.

Taking all this into account, there is no reason to believe that the Byrd Amendment is necessary to our current or predicted national chrome and ferrochrome requirements. Stockpile releases can maintain supply. And, if the price of ferrochrome released from the stockpile is about the same as the price of current ferrochrome imports from Rhodesia, there is every reason to believe that the domestic American ferrochrome industry would be in a better competitive position without the Byrd Amendment, while the stainless steel industry would not suffer significant damage.

There is one more question that must responsibly be asked regarding the consequences of any repeal of the Byrd Amendment. *If* the price of chrome and ferrochrome were to rise as the supply of both from Rhodesia was cut off, and there were insufficient stockpile releases, what would happen to costs in the steel industry and prices therefore charged to American consumers? In short, would repeal of the Byrd Amendment have inflationary effects?

The argument in support of maintaining the Amendment is that since Rhodesia is now a major factor in the world (high-carbon) ferrochrome market, cutting off such a significant source could have the effect of raising prices, assuming demand remains constant. Since specialty steel manufacturers would have to pay more for ferrochrome (both imported and domestic), they would be forced to raise their own prices to their customers, who would, of course, pass them on to consumers of stainless steel goods.

This is a legitimate concern that must logically be acknowledged by those who oppose the Amendment. There is no way now, however, to calculate exactly what these price increases would be. Howard Beaver, president of Carpenter Technology Corporation, has estimated an increase of 1.4 percent in its production costs if the embargo were resumed. E. F. Andrews, vice-president of Allegheny Ludlum, estimated the cost to the stainless steel industry at $80–$200 million. But both based their calculations of a rise in chrome and ferrochrome prices on the assumption that it would match the rises that took place while the embargo on Rhodesian materials was in effect. As noted previously, the causal relationship between the embargo and those prices has not been established. What can be said in this regard is that, historically, the price of both chrome and ferrochrome on world markets has been related as much or more to the demand for both commodities as to the supply; the price of ferrochrome has fluctuated quite widely according to demand in the steel industry. Thus, important price increases will probably be tied more significantly to steel industry booms and recessions than to any decision about Rhodesian sanctions.

Most important, if the excess ferrochrome and chrome in the stockpile is released, the effect should be to restrain—at least temporarily—rises in price resulting from a cut-off of Rhodesian chrome and ferrochrome. If it is not, there is a possibility of some rise in costs, as yet undetermined and of unknown significance, in the stainless steel industry.

Thus, a final embarrassment of the Byrd Amendment emerges. For seen in the light of experience since it came into effect, it is clear that a stark choice is presented so long as the Amendment remains law. When false issues like the "national security" argument are stripped away, we are left with two basic alternatives. On the one hand, there is an international legal obligation. Whatever one thinks of the wisdom of our as-suming it in 1966 and 1968, the obligation exists. We could have vetoed the sanctions measures. We voted for them. Our violation of this obligation is carefully noted at the United Na-tions, by the people of Southern Rhodesia and by govern-ments throughout Africa. On the other hand, if the Byrd Amendment were not in force, we could face the prospect of some upward pressure on prices in the stainless steel industry. This pressure cannot be calculated exactly, and would be ame-liorated by releases of chrome and ferrochrome from the stockpile—but it is a possibility.

The final embarrassment is that we and others through-out the world can thus judge what price the United States puts on its word.

8
To Repeal a Policy

P artly as a result of the unpredicted economic as well as the predictable diplomatic damage done by the Byrd Amendment, a new effort during 1973–1974 came very close to gaining its repeal. This effort provides further background to a look at the future of American policy toward Southern Rhodesia.

ALMOST REPEAL

"It's about time we got organized," said a congressional staffer at a meeting of anti-Byrd Amendment groups on May 25, 1973. Some forty representatives of various unions, including the Steelworkers and the United Auto Workers (UAW), the Washington Office on Africa, and more than twenty-five other interested organizations had come together to discuss strategy in support of repeal bills introduced in the Senate and House three days previously. Twenty-three Senators had cosponsored a bill introduced by Senator Hubert Humphrey that would kill the Amendment and return the United States to official observation of the U.N. sanctions program. Fifty-three Congressmen were sponsoring similar legislation in the House.

The meeting went well. Notes were compared on potential swing votes, and targets for lobbying efforts were chosen. It was announced that funds were available to hire a full-time staff member at the Washington Office on Africa who could help coordinate the lobbying drive. The group concluded that, with a sustained push, victory was quite possible in the new Senate that had been elected the previous fall. The House would be another matter. These predictions were, as it turned out, all too accurate.

The issue had been raised from time to time in the preceding year. The 1972 Democratic Party platform stated that "U.N. sanctions against the illegal racist regime in Southern Rhodesia should be supported vigorously, especially as they apply to chrome imports." An ill-advised trip to Rhodesia in December, 1972, by Clark MacGregor, formerly President Nixon's chief congressional lobbyist and the chairman of his re-election committee, had provided new ammunition for those favoring repeal. In a newspaper interview there, MacGregor predicted an end to sanctions and a change in the American policy of nonrecognition of the Smith regime. This seemed outrageous to the editorialists in the United States who quickly blasted his statement. They would have been less puzzled, if no less outraged, if they had known of the similar line of thought contained in the "tar baby" option of the White House three years before. (See chapter 4.) In February, 1973, the House subcommittees on Africa and International Organizations and Movements had held hearings at which pro-sanctions testimony was given. But little public or congressional attention was paid to this plank of the Democratic platform or to the hearings.

During the winter and early spring, the Washington Office on Africa had been analyzing the new Congress and laying plans. Now, in May, a push would begin. The congressional staffer who had called for better organization was encouraged: "This is the first time we have had an organized lobbying effort. We're all working together now. . . ."

UAW President Leonard Woodcock had issued a strong statement on May 23 supporting the new repeal legislation. On May 29, the Steelworkers followed with letters to Congressmen, arguing that repeal would not threaten steelworkers' jobs.

Lobbying continued through the summer and fall, including notably resolutions supporting repeal by the American

Bar Association and by the Oil, Chemical and Atomic Workers, which represents many of Union Carbide's employees. Twenty-eight interested groups issued a joint statement taking the same position.

Meanwhile, the administration—including representatives of the White House—began to take a much firmer line against the Byrd Amendment.

On June 7, 1973, Ambassador John Scali, the United States representative to the United Nations, concluded a U.N. Day speech by calling on the Congress to repeal the amendment, arguing its economic as well as diplomatic disadvantages. Shortly before, the United States had been placed in an embarrassing position. It had abstained on U.N. Security Council Resolution 333, which called for various measures to strengthen the sanctions program. In explaining the abstention, Scali had stated, "What is required is to act now to make the present sanctions more effective rather than to expand or widen their scope." The resolution passed by a vote of 12 to 0, with three abstentions. It requested states with legislation permitting the importation of Rhodesian goods to repeal it immediately. If, as Scali suggested, the need was to "make the present sanctions more effective," repeal of the Byrd Amendment was the place for Washington to start.

On June 12, Assistant Secretary of State Newsom made the case for repeal in a well-argued letter to Representative Guy Vander Jagt. Despite Secretary of State Rogers' apparent lack of interest—he told an African representative in mid-June that the repeal effort would lose and he didn't want to discuss the subject—Newsom's letter was followed, on June 26, by the supportive letter from Peter Flanigan in the White House to Congressman Fraser cited in chapter 7.

The Senate Foreign Relations Committee met at the end of July to consider the repeal legislation. At Senator Hugh Scott's insistence, the committee agreed to defer action until its Africa subcommittee held hearings on the matter. Senator Humphrey, who had replaced Senator McGee as chairman of the subcommittee, held the hearings on September 6, 1973.

Senator Edward M. Kennedy, Ambassador Scali, Assistant Secretary Newsom, and a United Steelworkers representative supported repeal. Officials of Union Carbide and Allegheny Ludlum testified in opposition. Foote Mineral was notably absent. Humphrey clearly enjoyed the few hours of sparring he carried on with the industry spokesmen.

The next day, at the hearings on his nomination to be Secretary of State, Henry Kissinger was asked if the administration favored repeal. Still speaking as a White House official, he said that it did. While in later appearances on Capitol Hill Kissinger betrayed a very limited knowledge of the issue, the fact remained that the anti-Byrd Amendment forces finally had the White House formally committed to their cause. On October 3, Kissinger sent a letter to Representative Diggs confirming his position. A letter from William Timmons of the White House Congressional Office on October 27 stated the President's own support for full compliance with the sanctions.

On September 18, the full Senate Foreign Relations Committee favorably reported Humphrey's bill to the floor, by voice vote and without dissent.

The question now became one of bringing the issue to a vote. Behind the scenes, Senatory Harry F. Byrd, with the support of Senator Robert Byrd, the Democratic Whip, began what amounted to a silent filibuster, persuading the Democratic leadership that the anti-sanctions forces would tie up Senate business by an open filibuster on Humphrey's measure should it be taken up on the floor. In mid-November, under strong pressure from Senator McGee, Senate Majority Leader Mike Mansfield finally agreed to schedule debate, but on a double-track system which would allow discussion of the issue without blocking the other business of the Senate. (This system has been used for some time to limit the damage of filibusters, but it also makes them easier to maintain. One liberal aide who opposes this system argues that it would be better to return to the old days, when Majority Leader Lyndon B. Johnson "would have made them stay up and talk all night.")

Debate began on November 20, 1973, with a long statement
by Senator Humphrey. Senator Byrd's tactic then became evident. On the following day, and each time the issue came up
thereafter, he simply refused to agree to set a time limit on
debate. This necessitated a cloture motion. On November 23,
1973, Senator Mansfield publicly admitted his doubt that the
necessary two-thirds vote for cloture could be gained.

McGee and Humphrey refused to abandon the effort,
however, and a cloture vote was taken on December 11. The
repeal forces fell short, gaining only 59 votes for cloture to 35
opposed. A second effort, two days later, barely failed. Senator Fulbright, who voted the first time against cloture, "took a
long walk," according to an aide, and missed the vote. Strong
editorials by the *New York Times* (on December 12) and the
Washington Post (on December 13) may have helped the repeal
forces but not enough.

At this point, Humphrey himself reportedly began to get
discouraged, but McGee urged another try. A lobbying effort
by the White House and State Department, telegrams from
constituents, and Humphrey's and McGee's new appeals produced, at last, the required votes on December 18, 1973. Cloture was voted by 63 to 26 and Humphrey's bill was passed.
The Senate had repealed the Byrd Amendment. Conservative
columnist James J. Kilpatrick was furious. "At this moment,"
he wrote, "the Senate may have touched bottom."

But the law would not be changed until the House voted
to repeal as well. And there, it was a different story.

The repeal effort in the House looked fairly encouraging
in the autumn of 1973. At hearings held by the Fraser subcommittee on October 17, Representative John Buchanan of
Alabama, previously a supporter of the Byrd Amendment,
read a thoughtful statement announcing that he had come to
support repeal. A month as a member of the American delegation at the United Nations had helped change his mind.

But the House Foreign Affairs Committee did not move
quickly, and it was not until August, 1974, that the issue was

scheduled for action on the floor, following the committee's approval (by twenty-five to nine) of the repeal legislation.

The issue was never joined, however. On a number of occasions in August, and again in December, debate and a vote were said by the bill's sponsors to be only twenty-four hours away. But each time, a last-minute head count indicated an even—or slightly less than even—chance of passage. And each time, the sponsors decided to wait. In August, they agreed to a suggestion by White House lobbyists that the issue be deferred until more work could be done, after the Labor Day recess, to follow up on a statement of August 20 by Jerry terHorst, the President's press spokesman, that President Ford favored repeal. His statement came at the same time as editorials supporting sanctions by, among others, the *Los Angeles Times,* the *Baltimore Sun,* and the *New York Times.*

In December, despite further lobbying by the White House, the prospects had, if anything, worsened. New events in Rhodesia—release of Sithole and Nkomo, a semicease-fire, the prospect of serious negotiations between black and white Rhodesians—produced a new argument used by those who were against repeal. If the Rhodesian issue was soon going to be settled, why force American companies to cancel contracts now, requiring them to compete for new contracts when sanctions were lifted?

On December 19, minutes before the repeal bill was to be taken up by the House, it was withdrawn. The Democratic leadership and the administration agreed that risking defeat was asking for too great a diplomatic embarrassment. It would be better to wait for the next Congress. Elected in the Democratic landslide of 1974, new liberal muscle in the House would presumably force repeal. But with a new Congress, the process would have to begin again. The strategy, as designed in early 1975, would be to push repeal through the House first, and then move it again through the Senate.[1]

[1] The optimism, as it turned out, was misplaced. On September 25, 1975, the House rejected repeal by a vote of 187 to 209.

A TIME FOR CHANGE

Just as the prospects for repeal of the Byrd Amendment, sooner or later, seemed good in early 1975, so the tide of events was running against the Smith regime (chapter 1). In addition, President Ford, in favoring repeal of the Amendment despite his support of it as a Congressman, showed more flexibility on the issue than many had expected. A new situation in southern Africa, a new American President, national elections coming in 1976—surely these provide an opportunity for a fresh look at the concepts behind the American approach to the region, in the light of the experience of the five years of "communication" since "option two" was adopted.

The option was based on a questionable set of assumptions, as stated in the interagency response to NSSM 39:

Premise:

The whites are here to stay and the only way that constructive change can come about is through them. There is no hope for the blacks to gain the political rights they seek through violence, which will only lead to chaos and increased opportunities for the communists. We can, by selective relaxation of our stance toward the white regimes, encourage some modification of their current racial and colonial policies and through more substantial economic assistance to the black states (a total of about $5 million annually in technical assistance to the black states) help to draw the two groups together and exert some influence on both for peaceful change. Our tangible interests form a basis for our contacts in the region, and these can be maintained at an acceptable political cost.

Now, five years later, the fallacies of this approach are still more clear than when they were pointed out by "tar baby's" State Department opponents in 1969.

First, the whites in the Portuguese territories were not "here to stay," at least in positions of authority. The future of the whites in Rhodesia is severely threatened. And the white government in South Africa thus faces the prospect of becoming the only one of its kind on the continent.

As a result of this miscalculation about the staying power of the Portuguese in Africa, the American government simply ended up on the wrong side. Since 1969, American diplomats in Africa had, on orders, shied away from contacts with representatives of such liberation groups as FRELIMO (the Front for the Liberation of Mozambique). Their sporadic efforts in 1974 and 1975 to establish friendly relations with the future rulers of Mozambique were complicated by this previous coolness.

At present, the calculation of some Congressmen that repeal of the Byrd Amendment would penalize American businessmen in competition for contracts after a Rhodesian settlement is similarly shortsighted. Especially at a time when the fortunes of the African nationalists are waxing, one would have thought that all interested Americans would recognize the importance of future relations with Zimbabwe no less than any short-term benefits of current relations with Rhodesia. As Assistant Secretary of State for African Affairs Donald Easum testified before the House Foreign Affairs Committee in December, 1974, it was a "psychologically important moment . . . to return the United States to full compliance with United Nations resolutions, to encourage continued progress toward a peaceful solution in Rhodesia, and to help insure long-range availability of Rhodesian minerals."

The second assumption behind option two—that the blacks could not gain political rights through violence—is also challenged by events. The drain on Portugal created by the activities of liberation forces in its African territories was a key to the coup in Lisbon. In that sense, the Africans did gain their rights through armed violence. And, with the advent of African rule in Mozambique, the tide is running in favor of the black guerrillas operating in Rhodesia.

This does not mean that the United States should necessarily support violence in southern Africa. It does mean that an effort at friendly persuasion of the Smith regime to modify its racial policies is irrelevant to the real forces at work in the area. Black leaders in Southern Rhodesia do not want mere amelioration of the conditions of white rule. They want majority rule. Ian Smith and his lieutenants cannot be *talked* into so fundamental a concession by the United States. External pressure might do so—especially the pressure from the South African government and the threat of a deteriorating security situation, with its attendant economic and psychological problems. In such circumstances, constructive American influence—marginal, at best, in any case—can best be enhanced by a return to strict observation of sanctions.

Third, insofar as Rhodesia is concerned, the statement that "our tangible interests form a basis for our contacts in the region" obviously flies in the face of our legal obligation to observe the U.N. resolutions establishing sanctions. The kindest view would be that the framers of option two had South Africa in mind in stating this assumption, and simply forgot to note that access to "tangible" American economic interests in Southern Rhodesia was legally blocked by the sanctions. This is another illustration of the point that the concept of "communication" could make sense, even in theoretical terms, only for South Africa. It could not have been, and is not, a valid basis for policy toward Southern Rhodesia.[2]

[2] Nor, indeed, has it been a sufficient guide to American policy toward South Africa itself. There will always be "communications" between the United States and South Africa. The question is what kind of message the United States should be sending. If the dialogue is to be used to promote the erosion of apartheid, every American statement and action must be judged in that light. Due to either the inattention or the proclivities of top American policymakers since "tar baby" was adopted, the policy has instead become simply a thin rationalization for closer cooperation with the South African government. While American support for South Africa's pressure on Rhodesian whites and perhaps for its efforts to achieve détente with neighboring black states makes sense, the message of recent years—an impending return to normalcy in our relations—goes much too far, since it implies a growing acceptance of apartheid within South Africa.

The key point was made by the State Department as it fought against the White House's policy shift in 1970: We must recognize the limits of our influence. It was the Portuguese coup, not our stance, that forced the new South African diplomatic approach to Rhodesia.

We should set clear limits on the scope of our official relations with South

Even when it was adopted in early 1970, the "tar baby" option made no sense with regard to Rhodesia. Only a general inclination to give comfort to Smith in return for some illegal Rhodesian chrome and other materials could explain allowing the theory of "communication" to shape Washington's approach to Salisbury as well as Pretoria. In short, as had been the case with American policy toward the Portuguese territories, by early 1975 it seemed all the more clear that our stance was only placing us on the losing side in Southern Rhodesia, while continuing to put us in violation of international law and in jeopardy with African opinion.

A new approach is needed. Most obviously, repeal of the Byrd Amendment has been increasingly desirable each day since the Amendment was passed. Beyond the direct value of repeal, it would offer the administration a chance to state, in strong terms, its determination to see the sanctions meticulously enforced so long as they remain in force. Strong answers to the question listed in chapter 5 about possible American violations would help turn such rhetoric into observable action. As suggested below, a better system of coordinating the sanctions program should also be devised. Diplomatically, the United States should continue to encourage South African pressure on Smith to concede majority rule, while avoiding official actions that support apartheid within South Africa or Pretoria's control of Namibia. And, to make sure that we can do what we say we will, Washington should maintain at the United Nations a stance of opposition to truly unenforceable sanction measures; such a stance would be more credible once the Byrd Amendment were repealed.

These moves make sense both in substance, I believe, and

Africa until it becomes clear, probably many years hence, that one way or another her blacks have gained the rights they are now denied.

A distant policy of this sort would not try to force change; we cannot do so. But it would serve us well in the event of a racial crisis in South Africa or if black African nations should someday force us to choose between cooperation with them or with Pretoria. And it would better respond to the views of concerned blacks in America.

in terms of the processes of American decision-making on African issues.

The basic point to bear in mind in this regard is one that is painful to most Africanists, but true nonetheless: southern African problems are seldom considered and rarely of real concern at the top levels of the American government. Unless a disaster befalls the African continent—for example, through a full-scale race war in southern Africa—this indifference is unlikely to change. Any American policy toward Southern Rhodesia, and toward southern Africa as a whole, must therefore be manageable by the bureaucracy without constant, high-level supervision. This means that the policy must be clearly stated and easily understood. It cannot be a policy, like "tar baby," of seeking to influence events in southern Africa through complex or subtle diplomatic strategies. In addition to its conceptual drawbacks, option two has been a practical failure because it required initial secrecy and thus left the bureaucracy, which would have to implement it, in the dark; it required careful management when only sporadic high-level attention was available; and it thus called for an ill-advised, ill-coordinated but increasing American involvement in the Rhodesian affair when our capacity for doing harm there exceeded our ability to help, and when prudence would in any case suggest keeping at least an arm's length away. The extraordinary secrecy, sloppiness, and either cynicism or naiveté so apparent in the White House approach to the issue of the consulate in Salisbury (see chapter 4) provides perhaps the best illustration of the dangers involved in attempting to maintain an essentially interventionist, unilateral policy toward Southern Rhodesia when international law and national interest require the opposite: clear observance of the United Nations sanctions and a distant stance from the Smith regime in other respects.

The history of American policymaking on Rhodesia also suggests more than a change in that policy. It indicates that the American position on questions involving international law and the United Nations must not be treated as separable from our other foreign policies. The decision of the Western powers to dump the Rhodesian problem on the United Nations in the mid-1960s as a means of evading more difficult national choices, without giving the world body sufficient power to make the sanctions work, damaged the United Nations by making less credible future sanction efforts. It also trapped the United States and others into an international legal commitment which it has been embarrassingly inconsistent (like others) in observing. It may be, because of the complexities cited in chapter 3, that asking the United Nations to carry out sanctions while avoiding confrontation with South Africa made sense in policy terms. But, at the least, the United States should have made sure that its own actions would be absolutely consistent with the terms of the limited sanctions program for which it voted.

To insure American compliance with the sanctions program, a small office might have been established in the White House which could have overseen and coordinated the activities of the various government agencies involved in enforcing the Executive Orders. Such an office still could be established. The State Department has failed to manage the program effectively, as chapter 5 shows, despite the efforts of concerned officers in the bureaus of International Organization Affairs, and African Affairs and the Legal Adviser's office. The White House staff has the authority to move officials in Treasury or Commerce to speedy action in the face of countervailing institutional impulses (e.g., export promotion drives by Commerce). Such an office might have played a useful role in supporting administration lobbying with the Congress against the Byrd Amendment. And it would have provided a useful point of contact with citizens' groups or individuals who wished to bring apparent violations of sanctions to the attention of the government.

Implicit in this suggestion, of course, is the assumption that the White House which created such an office would like to see the sanctions carefully observed. This was not the case in the first few years after the 1969–70 shift in policy. It can only be hoped that it will be the case now, when the penalties of American violations of sanctions so clearly outweigh the advantages, both in principle and in practice.

The stance of the White House, and future administrations, will be determined in part by the pressures brought to bear by interested people outside the government. The Congress has received most of their attention because of the battles over the Byrd Amendment. But American policy toward southern Africa consists, and will continue to consist, far more of actions and statements decided by the Executive branch without formal reference to the legislature.

Unlike American policy toward South Africa, about which U.S. corporations have had little complaint, policy toward Southern Rhodesia has been argued and sometimes strongly influenced by businesses which have a stake in relaxation of the sanctions. In addition to the Byrd Amendment, which Senator Humphrey called a case of "twisting public policy for private interest," recall, for example, the case of the Union Carbide exception (chapter 4). Yet "idealist" groups have traditionally concentrated on South Africa in approaching the administration; Southern Rhodesia has been relatively neglected. How can these groups, which opposed business interests in the struggle for repeal of the Byrd Amendment, most effectively now make their case to the government? Eight basic ways come to mind.

1. *In order to press its case effectively, a pressure group must seek to demonstrate political power.* In arguing with government officials, the potential votes of one's constituency are often more important than the intellectual force of one's arguments. Hence, the potential importance of the black community; hence also the weight the labor unions had in lobbying for repeal of the Byrd Amendment.

2. *Especially when a group lacks political power in its own right, it should try to make its concerns a political issue.* Anti-apartheid groups like the American Committee on Africa (ACOA) have been unable to create widespread concern in the United States about southern Africa. Nor have they yet made a sustained ef-

fort to get candidates for public office to take a clear position on southern Africa. Especially at a time when Americans seem so fatigued by foreign affairs, the former would be very difficult. The latter would not be so hard to accomplish, and would have some marginal impact, at least, on public opinion.

3. *Groups which lack political power should attract and maintain allied efforts by more powerful groups* in approaching the Executive branch. These larger groups—e.g., labor, the League of Women Voters, Common Cause—bring more to such an alliance than their political clout. Their involvement may persuade senior government officials that if established groups with general interests have decided that this issue is worth their attention, it may be worth their own. The Washington Office on Africa did well in encouraging such groups to be active with the Congress. A similar effort would be useful with the administration.

4. *Reliable sources of information should be developed within the bureaucracy and the Congress to provide early word of emerging issues.* This has been a major failure of anti-apartheid groups in the United States. They have rarely anticipated and tried to affect policy decisions within the government. For example, there seems to have been very little outside knowledge of the major review of southern Africa policy during late 1969. And the Byrd Amendment caught the ACOA by surprise in 1971. Information-gathering about events on Capitol Hill has improved; similar information about events within the Executive branch is more difficult to obtain, but equally important, since that is where most of our southern African policy is made.

5. *Reliable information should also be developed to identify decision levels and potential allies within the bureaucracy. Allies should then be given support through pressure on their bureaucratic opponents, rather than the sermons they more usually receive.* It is officials in the State Department who are most berated by anti-apartheid, pro-sanctions groups, despite the fact that they are the ones within the bureaucracy who advocate the strongest line against white rule in southern Africa. Their frustration at this is easily understood.

Rather then taking *ex post facto* and sporadic complaints to
the African Bureau in the State Department, concerned citizens would do better to let officials in Defense, Commerce,
and the White House hear from them at least as often. Not
that they will bring all officials there to their own point of
view, but they will thus provide support to the officials in the
State Department who most nearly share their views.

6. *Predictability on the issues should be avoided.* If one has a
general point of view, it must naturally shape one's positions
on specific issues. But it would not hurt if pro-sanctions
groups gave occasional credit to the government when it did
something with which they agreed. Future criticism would
then be less easily ignored as the sort of automatic reaction
which bureaucrats expect of "idealists."

7. *In arguing for a desired action, pressure groups should emphasize the degree to which it would be safe, easy, and in the "American
interest."* Unhappily, moral appeals which are unaccompanied
by arguments couched in the form and language officials understand best—calm demonstrations of national as well as
larger interests—generally have the effect of forcing official
withdrawal into a defensive shell. Most officials act on the
belief, reinforced by their training and working culture, that
their job is to serve the national interest, not notions of greater
international good, even if the two are often synonymous.
They tend to react with defensive hostility when outsiders
argue that the official has a personal responsibility to look
beyond definitions of national interest. And, in any case, on
Southern Rhodesia, careful observance of sanctions and a
stance generally distant from the Smith regime is in the American interest. This implies that there is a very high return
when African embassies in Washington take an active interest
in southern African issues. When African ambassadors complain about the Byrd Amendment, for example, they are by
definition making the argument in terms of the American national interest, since what their governments think about the
United States must have at least a potential effect on American interests in their countries.

8. *A group should follow up every major policy decision with some comment, both in public and privately to the officials concerned.* While it is useless to make publicity for its own sake, it is worthwhile to let officials know that their actions are being watched. And policy decisions—even irreversible ones—make useful subjects for discussion to educate the public. The failure to make the policy shift in 1969–70 a public issue, even when it was revealed in 1970 and 1971, or to react strongly to the Union Carbide exception did more than undercut the State Department officials who opposed these measures. Such failures also reinforced the comfortable confidence of the officials involved that they would not be pressed publicly on the wisdom of their decisions.

In the long run, in the absence of dramatic events in southern Africa which force a policy change, the direction U.S. policy takes will depend heavily on the black community here. It is the only American group with both the inherent motive and the political means of forcing such a shift. The development of black consciousness about African issues will be a key in deciding the pace of pressure on the government.

This is fitting, since the most important consequences of American policy toward southern Africa are not for that area, but for America itself. The character of those policies will be seen by a growing number of Americans, especially black Americans, as a statement about the character of America and its approach to international law. Southern Africa will certainly not become so profound an issue for America as Vietnam. But it might achieve a strong symbolic importance, at least for black Americans and their friends, beyond their basic concern with domestic American issues. The United States would then have a new stake in abandoning its traditional policies of straddle and ambiguity. In the meantime, a concern for justice and international law should be reason enough to abandon "option two" and release the tar baby's hold.

Appendix 1

UNITED NATIONS RESOLUTIONS ON RHODESIA

Text of Resolution 232 [1966]

The Security Council,

Reaffirming its resolutions 216 [1965] of November 12, 1965, 217 [1965] of November 20, 1965, and 221 [1966] of April 9, 1966, and in particular its appeal to all States to do their utmost in order to break off economic relations with Southern Rhodesia.

Deeply concerned that the Council's efforts so far and the measures taken by the administering Power have failed to bring the rebellion in Southern Rhodesia to an end.

Reaffirming that to the extent not superseded in this resolution, the measures provided for in resolution 217 [1965] of November 20, 1965, as well as those initiated by Member States in implementation of that resolution, shall continue in effect.

Acting in accordance with Articles 39 and 41 of the United Nations Charter,

1. *Determines* that the present situation in Southern Rhodesia constitutes a threat to international peace and security;

2. *Decides* that all States Members of the United Nations shall prevent:

[a] the import into their territories of asbestos, iron ore, chrome, pig-iron, sugar, tobacco, copper, meat and meat products and hides, skins and leather originating in Southern Rhodesia and exported therefrom after the date of this resolution;

[b] any activities by their nationals or in their territories which promote or are calculated to promote the export of these commodities from Southern Rhodesia and any dealings by their nationals or in their territories in any of these commodities originating in Southern Rhodesia and exported therefrom after the date of this resolu-

tion, including in particular any transfer of funds to Southern Rhodesia for the purposes of such activities or dealings;

[c] shipment in vessels or aircraft of their registration of any of these commodities originating in Southern Rhodesia and exported therefrom after the date of this resolution;

[d] any activities by their nationals or in their territories which promote or are calculated to promote the sale or shipment to Southern Rhodesia of arms, ammunition of all types, military aircraft, military vehicles, and equipment and materials for the manufacture and maintenance of arms and ammunition in Southern Rhodesia;

[e] any activities by their nationals or in their territories which promote or are calculated to promote the supply to Southern Rhodesia of all other aircraft and motor vehicles and of equipment and materials for the manufacture, assembly or maintenance of aircraft and motor vehicles in Southern Rhodesia: the shipment in vessels and aircraft of their registration of any such goods destined for Southern Rhodesia: and any activities by their nationals or in their territories which promote or are calculated to promote the manufacture or assembly of aircraft or motor vehicles in Southern Rhodesia;

[f] participation in their territories or territories under their administration or in land or air transport facilities or by their nationals or vessels of their registration in the supply of oil or oil products in Southern Rhodesia; notwithstanding any contracts entered into or licenses granted before the date of this resolution;

3. *Reminds* Member States that the failure or refusal by any of them to implement the present resolution shall constitute a violation of Article 25 of the Charter;

4. *Reaffirms* the inalienable rights of the people of Southern Rhodesia to freedom and independence in accordance with the Declaration on the Granting of Independence to Colonial Countries and Peoples contained in General Assembly resolution 1514 [XV]; and recognizes the legitimacy of their struggle to secure the enjoyment of their rights as set forth in the Charter of the United Nations;

5. *Calls upon* all States not to render financial or other economic aid to the illegal racist régime in Southern Rhodesia;

6. *Calls upon* all States Members of the United Nations to carry out this decision of the Security Council in accordance with Article 25 of the United Nations Charter;

7. *Urges,* having regard to the principles stated in Article 2 of the United Nations Charter, States not Members of the United Na-

tions to act in accordance with the provisions of paragraph 2 of the present resolution;

8. *Calls upon* States Members of the United Nations or of the specialized agencies to report to the Secretary-General the measures each has taken in accordance with the provision of paragraph 2 of the present resolution;

9. *Requests* the Secretary-General to report to the Council on the progress of the implementation of the present resolution, the first report to be submitted not later than March 1, 1967;

10. *Decides* to keep this item on its agenda for further action as appropriate in the light of developments.

Text of Resolution 253 [1968]

The Security Council,

Recalling and reaffirming its resolutions 216 [1965] of 12 November 1965, 217 [1965] of 20 November 1965, 221 [1966] of 9 April 1966, and 232 [1966] of 16 December 1966,

Taking note of resolution 2262 [XXII] adopted by the General Assembly on 3 November 1967,

Noting with great concern that the measures taken so far have failed to bring the rebellion in Southern Rhodesia to an end,

Reaffirming that, to the extent not superseded in this resolution, the measures provided for in resolutions 217 [1965] of 20 November 1965, and 232 [1966] of 16 December 1966, as well as those initiated by Member States in implementation of those resolutions, shall continue in effect,

Gravely concerned that the measures taken by the Security Council have not been complied with by all States and that some States, contrary to resolution 232 [1966] of the Security Council and to their obligations under Article 25 of the Charter, have failed to prevent trade with the illegal regime in Southern Rhodesia,

Condemning the recent inhuman executions carried out by the illegal regime in Southern Rhodesia which have flagrantly affronted the conscience of mankind and have been universally condemned.

Affirming the primary responsibility of the Government of the United Kingdom to enable the people of Southern Rhodesia to achieve self-determination and independence, and in particular their responsibility for dealing with the prevailing situation,

Recognizing the legitimacy of the struggle of the people of Southern Rhodesia to secure the enjoyment of their rights as set forth in the Charter of the United Nations and in conformity with the objectives of General Assembly resolution 1514 [XV],

Reaffirming its determination that the present situation in Southern Rhodesia constitutes a threat to international peace and security,

Acting under Chapter VII of the United Nations Charter,

1. *Condemns* all measures of political repression, including arrests, detentions, trials and executions which violate fundamental freedoms and rights of the people of Southern Rhodesia, and calls upon the Government of the United Kingdom to take all possible measures to put an end to such actions;

2. *Calls upon* the United Kingdom as the administering Power in the discharge of its responsibility to take urgently all effective measures to bring to an end the rebellion in Southern Rhodesia, and enable the people to secure the enjoyment of their rights as set forth in the Charter of the United Nations and in conformity with the objectives of General Assembly resolution 1514 [XV];

3. *Decides* that, in furtherance of the objective of ending the rebellion, all States Members of the United Nations shall prevent:

[*a*] The import into their territories of all commodities and products originating in Southern Rhodesia and exported therefrom after the date of this resolution (whether or not the commodities or products are for consumption or processing in their territories, whether or not they are imported in bond and whether or not any special legal status with respect to the import of goods is enjoyed by the port or other place where they are imported or stored);

[*b*] Any activities by their nationals or in their territories which would promote or are calculated to promote the export of any commodities or products from Southern Rhodesia; and any dealings by their nationals or in their territories in any commodities or products originating in Southern Rhodesia and exported therefrom after the date of this resolution, including in particular any transfer of funds to Southern Rhodesia for the purposes of such activities or dealings;

[*c*] The shipment in vessels or aircraft of their registration or under charter to their nationals, or the carriage (whether or not in bond) by land transport facilities across their territories of any commodities or products originating in Southern Rhodesia and exported therefrom after the date of this resolution;

[*d*] The sale or supply by their nationals or from their territories of any commodities or products (whether or not originating in their territories, but not including supplies intended strictly for medical

purposes, educational equipment and material for use in schools and other educational institutions, publications, news material and, in special humanitarian circumstances, food-stuffs) to any person or body in Southern Rhodesia or to any other person or body for the purposes of any business carried on in or operated from Southern Rhodesia, and any activities which promote or are calculated to promote such sale or supply;

[e] The shipment in vessels or aircraft of their registration, or under charter to their nationals or the carriage (whether or not in bond) by land transport facilities across their territories of any such commodities or products which are consigned to any person or body in Southern Rhodesia, or to any other person or body for the purposes of any business carried on in or operated from Southern Rhodesia;

4. *Decides* that all States Members of the United Nations shall not make available to the illegal regime in Southern Rhodesia or to any commercial, industrial or public utility undertaking, including tourist enterprises, in Southern Rhodesia any funds for investment or any other financial or economic resources and shall prevent their nationals and any persons within their territories from making available to the regime or to any such undertaking any such funds or resources and from remitting any other funds to persons or bodies within Southern Rhodesia except payments exclusively for pensions or for strictly medical, humanitarian or educational purposes or for the provision of news material and in special humanitarian circumstances, food-stuffs;

5. *Decides* that all States Members of the United Nations shall:

[a] Prevent the entry into their territories, save on exceptional humanitarian grounds, of any person travelling on a Southern Rhodesian passport, regardless of its date of issue, or on a purported passport issued by or on behalf of the illegal regime in Southern Rhodesia; and

[b] Take all possible measures to prevent the entry into their territories of persons whom they have reason to believe to be ordinarily resident in Southern Rhodesia and whom they have reason to believe to have furthered or encouraged, or to be likely to further or encourage, the unlawful actions of the illegal regime in Southern Rhodesia or any activities which are calculated to evade any measure decided upon in this resolution or resolution 232 [1966] of 16 December 1966;

6. *Decides* that all States Members of the United Nations shall prevent airline companies constituted in their territories and aircraft of their registration or under charter to their nationals from operating to or from Southern Rhodesia and from linking up with any airline company constituted or aircraft registered in Southern Rhodesia;

7. *Decides* that all States Members of the United Nations shall give effect to the decisions set out in operative paragraphs 3, 4, 5, and 6 of this resolution notwithstanding any contract entered into or license granted before the date of this resolution;

8. *Calls upon* all States Members of the United Nations or of the specialized agencies to take all possible measures to prevent activities by their nationals and persons in their territories promoting, assisting or encouraging emigration to Southern Rhodesia, with a view to stopping such emigration;

9. *Requests* all States Members of the United Nations or of the specialized agencies to take all possible further action under Article 41 of the Charter to deal with the situation in Southern Rhodesia, not excluding any of the measures provided in that Article;

10. *Emphasizes* the need for the withdrawal of all consular and trade representation in Southern Rhodesia, in addition to the provisions of operative paragraph 6 of resolution 217 [1965];

11. *Calls upon* all States Members of the United Nations to carry out these decisions of the Security Council in accordance with Article 25 of the United Nations Charter and reminds them that failure or refusal by any one of them to do so would constitute a violation of that Article;

12. *Deplores* the attitude of States that have not complied with their obligations under Article 25 of the Charter, and censures in particular those States which have persisted in trading with the illegal regime in defiance of the resolutions of the Security Council, and which have given active assistance to the regime;

13. *Urges* all States Members of the United Nations to render moral and material assistance to the people of Southern Rhodesia in their struggle to achieve their freedom and independence;

14. *Urges,* having regard to the principles stated in Article 2 of the United Nations Charter, States not Members of the United Nations to act in accordance with the provisions of the present resolution;

15. *Requests* States Members of the United Nations, the United

Nations Organization, the specialized agencies, and other international organizations in the United Nations system to extend assistance to Zambia as a matter of priority with a view to helping her solve such special economic problems as she may be confronted with arising from the carrying out of these decisions of the Security Council;

16. *Calls upon* all States Members of the United Nations, and in particular those with primary responsibility under the Charter for the maintenance of international peace and security, to assist effectively in the implementation of the measures called for by the present resolution;

17. *Considers* that the United Kingdom as the administering Power should ensure that no settlement is reached without taking into account the views of the people of Southern Rhodesia, and in particular the political parties favouring majority rule, and that it is acceptable to the people of Southern Rhodesia as a whole;

18. *Calls upon* all States Members of the United Nations or of the specialized agencies to report to the Secretary-General by 1 August 1968 on measures taken to implement the present resolution;

19. *Requests* the Secretary-General to report to the Security Council on the progress of the implementation of this resolution, the first report to be made not later than 1 September 1968;

20. *Decides* to establish, in accordance with rule 28 of the provisional rules of procedure of the Security Council, a committee of the Security Council to undertake the following tasks and to report to it with its observations;

[*a*] To examine such reports on the implementation of the present resolution as are submitted by the Secretary-General;

[*b*] To seek from any States Members of the United Nations or of the specialized agencies such further information regarding the trade of that State (including information regarding the commodities and products exempted from the prohibition contained in operative paragraph 3[d] above) or regarding any activities by any nationals of that State or in its territories that may constitute an evasion of the measures decided upon in this resolution as it may consider necessary for the proper discharge of its duty to report to the Security Council;

21. *Requests* the United Kingdom, as the administering Power, to give maximum assistance to the committee, and to provide the

committee with any information which it may receive in order that the measures envisaged in this resolution and resolution 232 [1966] may be rendered fully effective;

22. *Calls upon* all States Members of the United Nations, or of the specialized agencies, as well as the specialized agencies themselves, to supply such further information as may be sought by the Committee in pursuance of this resolution;

23. *Decides* to maintain this item on its agenda for further action as appropriate in the light of developments.

Appendix 2

EXECUTIVE ORDER 11322

Relating to Trade and Other Transactions
Involving Southern Rhodesia

By virtue of the authority vested in me by the Constitution and laws of the United States, including section 5 of the United Nations Participation Act of 1945 [59 Stat. 620], as amended [22 U.S.C. 287c], and section 301 of Title 3 of the United States Code, and as President of the United States, and considering the measures which the Security Council of the United Nations, by Security Council Resolution No. 232 adopted December 16, 1966, has decided upon pursuant to article 41 of the Charter of the United Nations, and which it has called upon all members of the United Nations, including the United States, to apply, it is hereby ordered:

Section 1. The following are prohibited effective immediately, notwithstanding any contracts entered into or licenses granted before the date of this Order:

[a] The importation into the United States of asbestos, iron ore, chrome, pig-iron, sugar, tobacco, copper, meat and meat products, and hides, skins and leather originating in Southern Rhodesia and exported therefrom after December 16, 1966, or products made therefrom in Southern Rhodesia or elsewhere.

[b] Any activities by any person subject to the jurisdiction of the United States, which promote or are calculated to promote the export from Southern Rhodesia after December 16, 1966, of any of the commodities specified in subsection [a] of this section originating in Southern Rhodesia, and any dealings by any such person in any such commodities or in products made therefrom in Southern Rhodesia or elsewhere, including in particular any transfer of funds to Southern Rhodesia for the purposes of such activities or dealings:

Provided, however, that the prohibition against the dealing in commodities exported from Southern Rhodesia or products made therefrom shall not apply to any commodities or products which, prior to the date of this Order, had been imported into the United States.

[c] Shipment in vessels or aircraft of United States registration of any of the commodities specified in subsection [a] of this section originating in Southern Rhodesia and exported therefrom after December 16, 1966, or products made therefrom in Southern Rhodesia or elsewhere.

[d] Any activities by any person subject to the jurisdiction of the United States, which promote or are calculated to promote the sale or shipment to Southern Rhodesia of arms, ammunition of all types, military aircraft, military vehicles and equipment and materials for the manufacture and maintenance of arms and ammunition in Southern Rhodesia.

[e] Any activities by any person subject to the jurisdiction of the United States, which promote or are calculated to promote the supply to Southern Rhodesia of all other aircraft and motor vehicles, and of equipment and materials for the manufacture, assembly, or maintenance of aircraft or motor vehicles in Southern Rhodesia; the shipment in vessels or aircraft of United States registration of any such goods destined for Southern Rhodesia; and any activities by any persons subject to the jurisdiction of the United States, which promote or are calculated to promote the manufacture or assembly of aircraft or motor vehicles in Southern Rhodesia.

[f] Any participation in the supply of oil or oil products to Southern Rhodesia [i] by any person subject to the jurisdiction of the United States, or [ii] by vessels or aircraft of United States registration, or [iii] by the use of any land or air transport facility located in the United States.

Sec. 2. The functions and responsibilities for the enforcement of the foregoing prohibitions are delegated as follows:

[a] To the Secretary of State, the function and responsibility of enforcement relating to the importation into, or exportation from the United States of articles, including technical data, the control of the importation or exportation of which is provided for in section 414 of the Mutual Security Act of 1954 [68 Stat. 848], as amended [22 U.S.C. 1934], and has been delegated to the Secretary of State by section 101 of Executive Order No. 10973 of September 3, 1961.

[b] To the Secretary of Commerce, the function and responsibility of enforcement relating to—

[i] the exportation from the United States of articles other than the articles, including technical data, referred to in subsection [a] of this section; and

[ii] the transportation in vessels or aircraft of United States registration of any commodities the transportation of which is prohibited by section 1 of this Order.

[c] To the Secretary of the Treasury, the function and responsibility of enforcement to the extent not delegated under subsections [a] or [b] of this section.

Sec. 3. The Secretary of State, the Secretary of the Treasury, and the Secretary of Commerce shall exercise any authority which such officer may have apart from the United Nations Participation Act of 1945 or this Order so as to give full effect to this Order and Security Council Resolution No. 232.

Sec. 4. [a] In carrying out their respective functions and responsibilities under this Order, the Secretary of the Treasury and the Secretary of Commerce shall consult with the Secretary of State. Each such Secretary shall consult, as appropriate, with other government agencies and private persons.

[b] Each such Secretary shall issue such regulations, licenses, or other authorizations as he considers necessary to carry out the purposes of this Order and Security Council Resolution No. 232.

Sec. 5. [a] The term "United States", as used in this Order in a geographical sense, means all territory subject to the jurisdiction of the United States.

[b] The term "person" means an individual, partnership, association, or other unincorporated body of individuals, or corporation.

The White House,
January 5, 1967.
[F. R. Doc. 67-241; Filed, Jan. 5, 1967; 1:23 p.m.]

Appendix 3

EXECUTIVE ORDER 11419

*Relating to Trade and Other Transactions
Involving Southern Rhodesia*

By virtue of the authority vested in me by the Constitution and laws of the United States, including section 5 of the United Nations Participation Act of 1945 [59 Stat. 620], as amended [22 U.S.C. 287c], and section 301 of Title 3 of the United States Code, and as President of the United States, and considering the measures which the Security Council of the United Nations by Security Council Resolution No. 253 adopted May 29, 1968, has decided upon pursuant to article 41 of the Charter of the United Nations, and which it has called upon all members of the United Nations, including the United States, to apply, it is hereby ordered:

Section 1. In addition to the prohibitions of section 1 of Executive Order No. 11322 of January 5, 1967, the following are prohibited effective immediately, not withstanding any contracts entered into or licenses granted before the date of this Order:

[a] Importation into the United States of any commodities or products originating in Southern Rhodesia and exported therefrom after May 29, 1968.

[b] Any activities by any person subject to the jurisdiction of the United States which promote or are calculated to promote the export from Southern Rhodesia after May 29, 1968, of any commodities or products originating in Southern Rhodesia, and any dealings by any such person in any such commodities or products, including in particular any transfer of funds to Southern Rhodesia for the purposes of such activities or dealings; *Provided,* however, that the prohibition against the dealing in commodities or products exported from Southern Rhodesia shall not apply to any such commodities or

products which, prior to the date of this Order, had been lawfully imported into the United States.

[c] Carriage in vessels or aircraft of United States registration or under charter to any person subject to the jurisdiction of the United States of any commodities or products originating in Southern Rhodesia and exported therefrom after May 29, 1968.

[d] Sale or supply by any person subject to the jurisdiction of the United States, or any other activities by any such person which promote or are calculated to promote the sale or supply, to any person or body in Southern Rhodesia or to any person or body for the purposes of any business carried on in or operated from Southern Rhodesia of any commodities or products. Such activities, including carriage in vessels or aircraft, may be authorized with respect to supplies intended strictly for medical purposes, educational equipment and material for use in schools and other educational institutions, publications, news material, and foodstuffs required by special humanitarian circumstances.

[e] Carriage in vessels or aircraft of United States registration or under charter to any person subject to the jurisdiction of the United States of any commodities or products consigned to any person or body in Southern Rhodesia, or to any person or body for the purposes of any business carried on in or operated from Southern Rhodesia.

[f] Transfer by any person subject to the jurisdiction of the United States directly or indirectly to any person or body in Southern Rhodesia of any funds or other financial or economic resources. Payments exclusively for pensions, for strictly medical, humanitarian or educational purposes, for the provision of news material or for foodstuffs required by special humanitarian circumstances may be authorized.

[g] Operation of any United States air carrier or aircraft owned or chartered by any person subject to the jurisdiction of the United States or of United States registration [i] to or from Southern Rhodesia or [ii] in coordination with any airline company constituted or aircraft registered in Southern Rhodesia.

Sec. 2. The functions and responsibilities for the enforcement of the foregoing prohibitions, and of those prohibitions of the Executive Order No. 11322 of January 5, 1967 specified below, are delegated as follows:

[a] To the Secretary of Commerce, the function and responsibility of enforcement relating to—

[i] the exportation from the United States of commodities and products other than those articles referred to in section 2[a] of Executive Order No. 11322 of January 5, 1967; and

[ii] the carriage in vessels of any commodities or products the carriage of which is prohibited by section 1 of this Order or by section 1 of Executive Order No. 11322 of January 5, 1967.

[b] To the Secretary of Transportation, the function and responsibility of enforcement relating to the operation of air carriers and aircraft and the carriage in aircraft of any commodities or products the carriage of which is prohibited by section 1 of this Order or by section 1 of Executive Order No. 11322 of January 5, 1967.

[c] To the Secretary of the Treasury, the function and responsibility of enforcement to the extent not previously delegated in section 2 of Executive Order No. 11322 of January 5, 1967, and not delegated under subsections [a] and [b] of this section.

Sec. 3. The Secretary of the Treasury, the Secretary of Commerce, and the Secretary of Transportation shall exercise any authority which such officer may have apart from the United Nations Participation Act of 1945 or this Order so as to give full effect to this Order and Security Council Resolution No. 253.

Sec. 4. [a] In carrying out their respective functions and responsibilities under this Order, the Secretary of the Treasury, the Secretary of Commerce, and the Secretary of Transportation shall consult with the Secretary of State. Each such Secretary shall consult, as appropriate, with other government agencies and private persons.

[b] Each such Secretary shall issue such regulations, licenses or other authorizations as he considers necessary to carry out the purposes of this Order and Security Council Resolution No. 253.

Sec. 5. [a] The term "United States", as used in this Order in a geographical sense, means all territory subject to the jurisdiction of the United States.

[b] The term "person" means an individual, partnership, association or other unincorporated body of individuals, or corporation.

Sec. 6. Executive Order No. 11322 of January 5, 1967, implementing United Nations Security Council Resolution No. 232 of December 16, 1966, shall continue in effect as modified by sections 2, 3, and 4 of this Order.

The White House,

July 29, 1968.

[F. R. Doc. 68-9212; Filed, July 29, 1968; 4:04 p.m.]

Bibliographical Notes

1. SOUTHERN RHODESIA: TWO NATIONS IN SEARCH OF A STATE

Most of the facts on the Rhodesian economy are drawn from reports by the United Nations Sanctions Committee; articles in *The Economist, Africa,* the *Journal of Commerce of New York,* and the *New York Times;* and summaries of Rhodesian and South African press reports published in *Africa Diary,* in newsletters published in London by the African Bureau, and in *X-Ray,* published by the Justice for Rhodesia Campaign (also in London). *Token Sanctions or Total Economic Warfare?,* by Alan Baldwin of the Africa Bureau, was also useful, as was the *Economic Survey of Rhodesia: 1971,* published by the Government Printer in Salisbury.

Descriptions of anti-African legislation passed since 1959 were based on United Nations documents, news reports in the *New York Times* and the *Washington Post, Newsbrief Rhodesia,* and *Southern Rhodesia: Background to Crisis,* by Jane Symonds.

I found the most useful histories of Rhodesia (written from differing points of view) to be Patrick Keatley's *The Politics of Partnership: The Federation of Rhodesia and Nyasaland* (Baltimore: Penguin, 1963), Frank Clements's *Rhodesia: A Study of the Deterioration of a White Society* (New York: Praeger, 1969), Judith Todd's *Rhodesia* (London: MacGibbon & Kee, 1966), and Kenneth Young's *Rhodesia and Independence: A Study in British Colonial Policy* (London: J. M. Dent, 1969). Keatley's superb study of the history of the Rhodesias and Nyasaland up to the breakup of the Federation in 1962–63 deserves particular mention; it provides, I believe, the best and most complete introduction to the history of Southern Rhodesia.

Robert C. Good's *U.D.I., The International Politics of the Rhodesian Rebellion* (London: Faber & Faber, 1973) and *A Principle in Torment: The*

United Nations and Southern Rhodesia (New York: Office of Public Information of the United Nations, 1969), provide the reader with excellent histories of the international response to the developing Rhodesian problem in the early 1960s. Good's book also includes analyses of relations between Southern Rhodesia and the rest of the world that should be required reading for anyone interested in the Rhodesian problem.

An article by Davis M'Gabe, "The Rhodesian African Majority," in *Africa Report*, February, 1967, provides another useful source on the history of African nationalism in the territory. Beyond newspaper reports in British and American newspapers, one of the best sources on the ANC is a pamphlet published in London by Eshmael Mlambo, the ANC European representative, entitled *No Future Without Us: The Story of the African National Council in Zimbabwe (Southern Rhodesia)*.

2. DILEMMAS AND COMPROMISES

Much the best works yet published on the international response to UDI are Good's *UDI* and Richard Hall's *The High Price of Principles: Kaunda and The White South* (New York: Africana Publishing Corporation, 1969). The latter is especially useful on British-Zambian relations. The descriptions of the factors underlying British policy in this period drew heavily on these books, as well as on newspaper accounts and interviews in London with British officials who were involved. (I would like to record here my particular thanks to the *Financial Times* for allowing me the use of their clipping files in London.) Accounts of United Nations actions with regard to Southern Rhodesia were drawn from *A Principle in Torment* and from United Nations documents. The library of the Carnegie Endowment for International Peace in New York was very helpful and efficient in providing these materials.

All of these sources (especially Good and Hall, together with an article by Guy Arnold, "Rhodesia: A Plan for Action," *Africa*, November, 1972) were useful in describing the Rhodesian policies of the African nations. The same applies to descriptions of the policies of South Africa and Portugal; I also drew here on *Newsbrief Rhodesia* and my research for a doctoral dissertation at Princeton University on American policy toward South Africa.

3. American Policy 1965–68:
The Necessity for Compromise?

Waldemar Nielsen's *The Great Powers and Africa* (New York: Praeger, 1969), Keatley's *The Politics of Partnership,* articles in the *New York Times,* and my dissertation research provided most of the materials on American policy toward Africa and Southern Rhodesia before UDI. A small number of interviews with American and British officials involved in the making of that policy were also valuable.

The bulk of this chapter—the history of the American response to UDI—depended very heavily on extensive interviews with both American and British officials. Public statements by both governments and the records of debate at the United Nations were also used, together with Good's *UDI*. Articles in the *New York Times,* the *Financial Times,* and the *Washington Post* were also useful.

The descriptions of the activities of liberal and conservative pressure groups outside the government were drawn from interviews, my dissertation, and Professor Vernon McKay's interesting article, "The Domino Theory: The Rhodesian Lobby," *Africa Report,* June, 1967. The Congressional debate in 1966–1967 has been reviewed best in "Controversy Over Present U.S. Policy Toward Rhodesia," the *Congressional Digest,* March, 1967.

There have been a number of interesting works on both sides of the question of the legality of United Nations sanctions against Rhodesia. The best are the Acheson-Goldberg exchange cited in the text; Charles Burton Marshall's *Crisis Over Rhodesia: A Skeptical View* (Baltimore: Johns Hopkins University Press, 1967); George T. Yates, III, "The Rhodesian Chrome Statute: The Congressional Response to United Nations Economic Sanctions Against Southern Rhodesia," *Virginia Law Review,* Vol. 58, No. 3, 1972; Professor Thomas M. Franck, "Policy Paper on the Legality of Mandatory Sanctions by the United Nations Against Rhodesia," Center for International Studies, New York University; and "Southern Rhodesia and the United Nations: The U.S. Position," *Department of State Bulletin,* Washington, D.C., March 6, 1967.

4. Tar Baby: The Shift in Approach

The amplification of the description by Terence Smith of the southern Africa policy review is based on extensive confidential interviews with both former and current officials. Some of these interviews were carried out in the course of research for my dissertation.

Sources for the description of the consulate controversy include interviews in London and Washington and articles in the *Financial Times,* the *Daily Telegraph,* the *Times,* the *Guardian,* the *New York Times,* and the *Washington Post.* As noted, the British press coverage of the issue, including the split between the State Department and the White House, was far more complete than the coverage by American newspapers.

The story of the double vetoes was also based on press stories and interviews, as well as the records of debate at United Nations and hearings held in March, May, June, September, October, November, and December 1970, before the House Subcommittee on Africa, entitled *Policy Toward Africa for the Seventies.*

Interviews in Washington provided almost all the information on the Union Carbide exception.

5. BUSINESS AS USUAL: ASSORTED ACTIVITIES
VIOLATING SANCTIONS

The description of the organization of the government's procedures in implementing sanctions is based on interviews with government officials and hearings held in 1972 by the Subcommittee on Africa of the Committee on Foreign Affairs, "Sanctions as an Instrumentality of the United Nations—Rhodesia as a Case Study." The account of the prosecutions of sanctions violators was based on a number of press reports, and a small number of interviews with knowledgeable government officials. The section on the Rhodesian Information Office drew heavily on hearings held by the House Subcommittee on Africa in May, 1973, entitled, "Implications for U.S. International Legal Obligations of the Presence of the Rhodesian Information Office in the United States." Interviews with supporters as well as critics of the Rhodesian Information Office supplemented the hearings. The remainder of this chapter—the review of activities by various American business concerns—was based almost totally on extensive interviews. It was issued as an interim report from the Carnegie Endowment for International Peace in late August, 1973. The version in this chapter was updated as of mid 1975.

6. The Byrd Amendment

This description of the legislative history of the Byrd Amendment is drawn primarily from the *Congressional Record;* extensive interviews with Congressmen, their staffs, lobbyists, and administration officials; Congressional hearings on the issue; and Senator Gale McGee's article on the Byrd Amendment, "The U.S. Congress and the Rhodesian Chrome Issue," *Issue,* Summer, 1972. Readers will also find of interest *Rhodesian Chrome,* a research report of the United Nations Association published in May, 1973, and reissued in June, 1974.

7. Irony in Chrome: The Consequences of the Byrd Amendment

Most of the statistics contained in this chapter are drawn from figures published either by the U.S. Bureau of Mines or the Department of State. Descriptions of debates in the Congress during 1971–72 are taken from hearings records as well as the *Congressional Record.* In addition, extensive interviews were carried out with industry and government officials. Much of the material in this chapter was issued as an interim report from the Carnegie Endowment for International Peace in early September, 1973. It has been updated, taking account of the hearings held by the Africa Subcommittee of the Senate Foreign Relations Committee on September 6, 1973, entitled "Importation of Rhodesian Chrome"; subsequent publications by the State Department; newspaper articles; and further interviews.

8. To Repeal a Policy

The description of the repeal effort of 1974 is based on interviews, occasional newspaper reports, and the *Congressional Record.*

Index